The "Goldhagen Effect"

Social History, Popular Culture, and Politics in Germany
Geoff Eley, Series Editor

(continued on last page)

The "Goldhagen Effect"

History, Memory, Nazism—
Facing the German Past

Edited by Geoff Eley

Ann Arbor

THE UNIVERSITY OF MICHIGAN PRESS

2003   2002   2001   2000   4   3   2   1

A CIP catalog record for this book is available from the British Library.

Library of Congress Cataloging-in-Publication Data

The Goldhagen effect : history, memory, Nazism—facing the German past
 / edited by Geoff Eley.
        p.   cm. — (Social history, popular culture, and politics in
 Germany
    Includes bibliographical references and index.
    ISBN 0-472-09752-0 (cloth : alk. paper) — ISBN 0-472-06752-4
 (pbk. : alk. paper)
    1. Goldhagen, Daniel Jonah. Hitler's willing executioners.
 2. Holocaust, Jewish (1939–1945)—Causes.   3. Antisemitism—Germany.
 4. War criminals—Germany—Psychology.   5. National socialism—Moral
 and ethical aspects.   I. Eley, Geoff, 1949–   II. Series.
 D804.3.G6483 G64   2000
 940.53'18—dc21   00-009689

Contents

Acknowledgments

Our aim in this volume is to conduct a critical and informative discussion of the public reception of Daniel Goldhagen's book *Hitler's Willing Executioners: Ordinary Germans and the Holocaust* (New York: Knopf, 1996), concentrating on reactions in Germany, the United States, Austria, Israel, and elsewhere in Europe. We're less interested in adjudicating the scholarly controversies raging around the book, which have already been amply treated in academic journals readily accessible to specialists and the professionally interested audience. The public controversy in Germany during 1996–97 has been helpfully anthologized in Robert R. Shandley, ed., *Unwilling Germans? The Goldhagen Debate* (Minneapolis: University of Minnesota Press, 1998), while the scholarly critiques may be consulted via the extensive citations in the footnotes of the essays that follow.

Our volume originated in a symposium sponsored by the University of Michigan Center for European Studies on 7 November 1997. Its purpose was to step back from the immediate controversies accompanying Goldhagen's controversial book—the substantive contents, forms of argumentation, quality of methods and research—to explore aspects of the public reception. Three of the papers presented on that occasion, by Omer Bartov, Atina Grossmann, and Pieter Judson, have been substantially expanded and revised for publication, supplemented by Jane Caplan's essay, previously published in an earlier version in Johannes Heil and Rainer Erb, eds., *Geschichtswissenschaft und Öffentlichkeit: Der Streit um Daniel J. Goldhagen* (Frankfurt am Main: Fischer, 1998). My own contribution was specially written for this volume.

In addition to my coauthors, I would like to thank Laura Downs, who also presented a paper at the symposium; Alice Ritscherle, who helped prepare the final manuscript for publication; and Susan Whitlock at the University of Michigan Press, whose editorial guidance, as always, was invaluable. Lastly, Kathleen Canning deserves special acknowledgment. She conceived, organized, and intellectually shaped the original symposium but was prevented by other commitments from editing the volume. Her vision and intelligence lie behind the project. This is her book as well.

Ordinary Germans, Nazism, and Judeocide

Geoff Eley

The Nazi Past in the German Present

"Dealing with the Nazi past" has been a continual preoccupation of German public life since 1945, but especially since the late 1960s, when the framework of a certain safe and ritualized official memory in the Federal Republic was dramatically broken apart. The Nazi era repeatedly captures attention in the wider public sphere. As I compose these thoughts, the claims of Nazi-persecution victims against Swiss banks for proposed restitution of $1.25 billion are approaching their Fairness Hearing in the Eastern District Court of New York (29 November 1999). Similar suits are pending against various German companies and U.S. firms with German subsidiaries. The German government, German industrialists, and German and U.S. lawyers representing forced laborers exploited by the Nazi war economy are disputing the size of a proposed compensation settlement.[1] The press regularly reports Jewish and other claims for return of art and other property pillaged under Nazism, involving galleries, museums,

---

1. During 1998–99, commissions of historians from Switzerland, Israel, the United States, Britain, and Poland reported on Swiss gold transactions with Nazi Germany and Swiss treatment of Jewish refugees. In December 1999, a separate report by Swiss banks and U.S. Jewish groups, headed by Paul A. Volcker, former U.S. Federal Reserve Chairman, reported that 54,000 Swiss accounts might be linked to Holocaust victims. See reports by Elizabeth Olson, *New York Times,* 17 November and 11 December 1999. In fall 1999, talks over the compensation claims of Nazi-era forced laborers passed through several crises before reaching partial resolution. In conjunction with the German government, German companies eventually raised their offer from $1.7 billion to $5.1 billion between September and December 1999, against claims of over $20 billion. See Roger Cohen, "Talks on Paying Nazi-Era Slaves Turn Sour," *New York Times,* 18 November 1999; Edmund L. Andrews, "Germany Accepts $5.1 Billion Accord to End Claims of Nazi Slave Workers," *New York Times,* 18 December 1999; and John Hooper, "Germany Begs Forgiveness as Nazi Victims' Deal Unfolds," *Guardian,* 17 December 1999.

and private dealers. Pursuit of war criminals persists: John Demjanjuk, a Ukrainian-born retired autoworker from Cleveland, eventually cleared of charges of having been a guard at Treblinka in proceedings lasting from 1977 to 1993, is being retried, this time for crimes at Sobibor.[2] Sensationalized discoveries of new documents continue taking specialists by surprise. On the basis of Heinrich Himmler's appointments diary uncovered in the KGB archives in Moscow, Christian Gerlach has brought us closer to locating Hitler's explicit directive for the "Final Solution" (in a meeting on 12 December 1941).[3] In August 1999, rival extracts were published in Germany and Israel of the long-classified prison diary Adolf Eichmann kept during his trial.[4]

These events cross the barriers between professional historians and wider interested publics. During the surrounding controversies, academic historians find themselves called to unaccustomed public account, whether in the daily and periodical press, on radio and sometimes television, on public platforms, or as consultants. Political contention, public culture, and scholarly research become closely imbricated together. For example, beleaguered by publicly disastrous lawsuits, companies are now scrambling through their archives for evidence forfending against litigation, increasingly by hiring prominent historians—Harold James (Princeton) at the Deutsche Bank; Gerald D. Feldman (Berkeley) at the insurance giant Allianz; Peter Hayes (Northwestern) at Degussa AG, accused of smelting gold looted from Holocaust victims; and Henry A. Turner (Yale) at General Motors, for its German subsidiary Adam Opel. Bertelsmann, the publishing and media conglomerate, accused in the Swiss press of publishing pro-Nazi and antisemitic books during the Third Reich, has commissioned a study from the leading Israeli historian Saul Friedländer (Hebrew

---

2. David Johnston, "Nazi Death Camp Case Reopened by US," *New York Times,* 20 May 1999. Demjanjuk was originally accused of being "Ivan the Terrible," a notoriously sadistic guard at the extermination camp of Treblinka. In a denaturalization proceeding, the U.S. Justice Department charged him with lying about his wartime experiences when entering the United States (1952), eventually extraditing him for trial in Israel (1989). He was convicted and sentenced to be hanged on the testimony of Treblinka survivors. After fresh evidence emerged from the former Soviet Union, reasonable doubt over Demjanjuk's identity was declared, and he was returned to the United States. However, if he was not Ivan the Terrible (who seemed to have been an Ivan Marchenko, last seen in 1943), Demjanjuk had clearly worked for the SS in Sobibor and elsewhere and was recharged on that basis.

3. See Christian Gerlach, "Die Wannsee-Konferenz, das Schicksal der deutschen Juden und Hitlers politische Grundsatzentscheidung, alle Juden Europas zu ermorden," *Werkstattgeschichte* 18 (1997): 7–44. For the discovery of Himmler's desk diaries, see Ian Traynor, "Appointments with Death," *Guardian,* 5 May 1999.

4. See Allan Hall, "Eichmann Memoirs Published," *Guardian,* 12 August 1999.

University and UCLA).[5] Such developments were barely imaginable two decades ago, when most German companies aggressively protected their archives against historians.[6]

Thus, dealing with the legacies and meanings of the Third Reich—coming to terms with the past, or learning to master its effects, *Vergangenheitsbewältigung*—has both exercised a much larger lay audience than historians usually anticipate reaching and provided crucial impetus for the quantity and direction of scholarly research. For the Judeocide per se, this properly began with the public debates surrounding Hannah Arendt's *Eichmann in Jerusalem* (New York, 1963) and the West German Auschwitz Trial during the early 1960s. Conversely, from that time forth controversies among German historians regularly spilled into wider public realms. Sometimes these concerned Nazism and the Third Reich more immediately. At other times they focused on earlier periods, as in the Fischer Controversy over Germany's aims in the First World War, the so-called German *Sonderweg,* and broader questions of continuity between the Third Reich and earlier periods of the German past. Thenceforth, the connection between scholarly history and the public sphere remained extremely active. Public consciousness repeatedly returns to the traumas of Nazi rule, genocide, and the Second World War.[7]

There are many ways of writing this history. The essays in this volume use reactions to Daniel Jonah Goldhagen's *Hitler's Willing Executioners: Ordinary Germans and the Holocaust* (New York: Knopf, 1996) to explore the complicated place that dealing with Nazism still holds in the public cultures of Germany, Austria, the rest of Europe, Israel, and the United States. The publication of Goldhagen's book was a remarkable event. It drew enormous popular interest. The book was reviewed in weeklies and the daily press and attracted widespread media coverage, entering the currency of interviews and talk shows and dominating party and dinner conversations. It became the object of forums and symposiums, most prominently at the Holocaust Memorial Museum in Washington, D.C. (8 April 1996), where Goldhagen debated with a phalanx of senior historians from Germany, Israel, and the English-speaking world, broadcast over the

---

5. See Barry Meier, "Chroniclers of Collaboration: Historians Are in Demand to Study Corporate Ties to Nazis," *New York Times,* 18 February 1999.

6. See, for example, Bernard P. Bellon, *Mercedes in Peace and War: German Automobile Workers, 1903–1945* (New York, 1990), xiii–xiv.

7. For a general discussion of these connections, see Charles S. Maier, *The Unmasterable Past: History, Holocaust, and German National Identity* (Cambridge, Mass., 1988); and more recently Mary Fulbrook, *German National Identity after the Holocaust* (Cambridge, 1999).

cable television channel C-Span. Goldhagen's publisher aggressively promoted this and other events, and in March 1996 Goldhagen took the book on tour. Photogenically at the center of this triumphal marketing blitz, he became an instant celebrity, riding a wave of hyperbole about the originality of his work.

Thus, even before the translation appeared (August 1996), controversy was raging in Germany. The first printing of 40,000 copies was exhausted in five days. This German reception largely repeated the pattern established in the United States, where specialists condemned the book and the reading public gave it acclaim. Leading scholars immediately attacked Goldhagen's work (for example, Norbert Frei in the *Süddeutsche Zeitung* and Eberhard Jäckel, Hans-Ulrich Wehler, and Ulrich Herbert in *Die Zeit,* followed later by Hans Mommsen), with a chorus of dismissal from the profession at large. Yet, at the same time, the public flocked to the author's publicity tour promoting the translation, expressing sympathy, even enthusiasm, for the book's main claims. One's response to Goldhagen's ideas was impossible to separate from this surrounding extravaganza, as his main thesis was certainly the one instated at the center of the publicity, and the book's substantive contribution was so thin and overhyped. In fact the scale of the publicity worked in inverse proportion to the modesty of the scholarly contribution.

Goldhagen and German History

Hitler's Willing Executioners fell into two parts. The second and largest provided an intensive and graphically detailed narrative of "central aspects of the Holocaust" that Goldhagen claimed were neglected or ignored in earlier scholarly accounts. These were, firstly, the role of reserve police battalions (as opposed to the SS) in hunting down and murdering Jews in Nazi-occupied Poland; secondly, the exploitation of Jewish labor power during the war, in a cynical and destructive system subordinating economic rationality to genocidal priorities, amounting to "annihilation through labor"; and, finally, the death marches in the last phase of the war, when Jewish survivors were evacuated from the concentration camps and force-marched to other locations. In each case, Goldhagen emphasized the enthusiasm of the German perpetrators for these tasks. He argued that the atrocities and humiliations dealt to Jewish victims far exceeded the behaviors consistent with any alternative interpretation, like fear of reprisals, reluctant accession to Nazi policies, deference to authority, emotional brutalization, administrative dehumanizing of the victims, and so on. This suggested a commitment to the process, and even the pleasures, of killing per se. Even more, Goldhagen used this to infer the German people's generalized identification with the Nazis' genocidal project. He described repeatedly both the sadistic zeal of rank-and-file functionaries and the singling out of Jews for the worst treatment, sharply separated from the regime's many other categories of victims and systematically marked for death. The death marches were terrible evidence to this effect, in his view. For while the killing of Jews was formally suspended, the ordinary perpetrators on the ground continued to murder as before, taking every chance to make the Jews' remaining lives as miserable and degrading as possible.

Goldhagen grounded his thesis in the book's first part, an extended historical preface (101 pages) outlining the history of German antisemitism in the nineteenth and early twentieth centuries. His argument was stunningly simple: the Judeocide depended on the willing participation of hundreds of thousands, perhaps millions, of "ordinary Germans," as opposed to the fanaticism of the SS or the Nazi Party's ideological militants, in the enactment of a long-standing desire to rid Germany of its Jews. Goldhagen called this his "cultural cognitive model," which conceptualized antisemitism as a deep pattern of behavior and beliefs already established in the era of the French Revolution: "From the beginning of the nineteenth century, antisemitism was ubiquitous in Germany. It was its 'common sense.' "[8] Even more: the German variant of antisemitism was uniquely virulent and comprehensive, implicitly genocidal from the start, or what Goldhagen called "eliminationist" or "exterminationist." This was what explained the Judeocide's success. In the words of de Tocqueville inscribed as the motto of the book, eliminationist antisemitism was "the spirit of [the] age and country." For the German people, it provided "the general run of their hopes and desires," against whose overpowering logic it was impossible to fight.

Everything Goldhagen argued about German participation in the Judeocide proceeded from this deep-historical view: it explained the ease of implementation, the absence of opposition or attempts to save Jews, and the exceptional cruelty accompanying anti-Jewish measures, in which killing per se never seemed enough. Eliminationist antisemitism was reorganized around the concept of race in the last third of the nineteenth century, becoming the uncontested official ideology, endorsed (Goldhagen claimed) by a majority of parliamentary deputies by the 1890s and extending across classes and political divisions. Because this was a *cultural norm,* a majority of ordinary Germans had become willing to kill Jews. This argument failed to explain why so little legislative discrimination, let alone physical violence, occurred against Jews in Germany before 1914 (by con-

---

8. Goldhagen, *Hitler's Willing Executioners,* 77.

trast with some other countries of Europe), although Goldhagen also seemed ready to acknowledge that some specificity at least—the Nazis' political project—was necessary before the Judeocide as such could occur.[9]

Remarkably little evidence was presented for this extreme view. Goldhagen's generalizations about German society during 1871–1945 involved an extraordinary circularity of argument. Thus the universality of a distinctive antisemitism in German society was asserted; for this *not* to have been the case, evidence of opposition to antisemitism or positive sympathy for the Jews needed to be present; in the absence of such evidence (also merely asserted), the universality of antisemitism was thereby proved. Despite the hugeness of his claims, Goldhagen made only the most cursory references to historiography of the pre-1914 period, with literally no national or cross-cultural comparisons, and the baldest of essentializing generalizations about Germany itself. He dismissed the normal requirements of evidence. As simplistically, he insisted that with Nazism's defeat in 1945 the traces of eliminationism became erased, because the democratic Constitution of 1949 brought West Germany and its citizens into the political community of the West. If antisemitism's continuity saturated the course of German history before 1945, after 1945 it was gone.

How should we judge the significance of this book? Its defenders have praised the vivid and concrete descriptions of ground-level atrocities committed by guards and other personnel, arguing that this experiential history of anti-Jewish violence had never been presented in such necessary and explicit detail. This was a corrective to the sometimes anaesthetized discussions of genocidal policies in existing works, which tended to focus on the bureaucrats and functionaries of Nazi terror, the notorious desk-murderers (*Schreibtischtäter,* or writing-desk perpetrators) like Eichmann and others, for whom Arendt's "banality of evil" became such an axiomatic description. This well-established historiography of the "Final Solution" was never exactly "faceless," because it delivered powerful individual portraits and collective sociologies of the careers that made the large-scale implementation of the Third Reich's policies possible. But there was no doubt that a certain distancing from the graphic immediacy of the atrocities came with the approach, making it more assimilable to the "objective" and emotionally neutral conventions of academic history. By contrast with this foregrounding of bureaucratic process and its appropriate languages of presentation, Goldhagen's approach jarred with its lengthy accounts of horrendous suffering, physical pain, and sadistic

---

9. Ibid., 131ff.

excess. To this extent, *Hitler's Willing Executioners* made it harder to escape the upsetting reality of Holocaust violence. It brought the sober and meticulous institutional histories of policy-making down to the ground, showing what they meant in the actions of deliberate and willful individuals.

Yet, for historians spending any time with Holocaust literatures, let alone the casual reader of general accounts (by William L. Shirer and since),[10] descriptions of atrocities weren't exactly hard to find in 1996. Memoirs, oral testimony, and journalistic writings contain no shortage of such accounts, while the scholarly literature dealing with particular concentration camps, the histories of individual ghettos, the killings on the Eastern Front, and the system of forced labor, particularly in its local or company-specific forms, now provides ample and extensive access to the brutalities entailed by the persecution of the Jews at all stages and levels of the Nazi order. Goldhagen's claims to originality are puzzling in this light. His book entered a context already densely occupied by publications and research in progress, an accumulation continuing mainly uninterrupted by the Goldhagen controversy, despite the back-and-forth of refutations and counter-refutations.[11]

There are also genuine issues of taste, strategy, and ethical choice involved in choosing to present this in all its vivid awfulness, particularly given the pornographic discourse sometimes associated with the circulation of such images. Raising this question isn't to argue for censorship, and Goldhagen's option for a graphic detailing of atrocities is certainly legitimate. But it does signal the complexities involved, as against the absolutism and highly moralizing tones of Goldhagen's justification for choosing his own approach, which effaced the ethical seriousness of his predecessors and, not surprisingly, provoked their annoyance. Thus for Hans Mommsen, "the restrained portrayal of the crimes" preferred by ear-

---

10. William L. Shirer, *The Rise and Fall of the Third Reich: A History of Nazi Germany* (New York, 1960).

11. For examples of scholarly research already heading for publication when *Hitler's Willing Executioners* appeared, see Leni Yahil, *Die Shoah: Überlebenskampf und Vernichtung der europäischen Juden* (Munich, 1998); Ulrich Herbert, ed., *Nationalsozialistische Vernichtungspolitik, 1939–1945: neue Forschungen und Kontroversen* (Frankfurt am Main, 1998); Dieter Pohl, *Nationalsozialistische Judenverfolgung in Ostgalizien, 1941–1944: Organisation und Durchführung eines staatlichen Massenverbrechens* (Munich, 1996); Thomas Sandkühler, *"Endlösung in Galizien": Der Judenmord in Ostpolen und die Rettungsinitiativen von Berthold Beitz, 1941–1944* (Bonn, 1996); Frank Bajohr, *"Arisierung" in Hamburg: Die Verdrängung der jüdischen Unternehmer, 1933–45* (Hamburg, 1997); Lutz Hachmeister, *Der Gegnerforscher: Die Karriere des SS-Führers Franz Alfred Six* (Munich, 1998); and Jules Schelvis, *Vernichtungslager Sobibor: Dokumente—Texte—Materialien* (Berlin, 1998).

lier Holocaust researchers "deliberately avoided" the possible "voyeuristic moment" released by "Goldhagen's portrayal of sadistic and gruesome violence."[12] Y. Michal Bodemann put it more strongly: "This is pornography," perpetrator's history, a "voyeuristic narration," because it dwelt on the "pleasure derived from murder and torture."[13]

Sometimes Goldhagen delivered new material. His detailed description of the death marches was one example. His treatment of the two Jewish work camps in Lublin, at Lipowa and the so-called *Flughafenlager,* was also an original contribution. However, his account of "Jewish 'Work'" scarcely did justice to the ramified complexities of forced labor in the Nazi war economy. Here Goldhagen's citation of existing scholarship was cursory, and readers might be forgiven for concluding that German historians had nothing to say about this subject, whereas for ten years an impressive amount of research and publication had developed. Ulrich Herbert, in particular, pioneered the intensive study of foreign labor of all kinds in the war economy, in which the slave labor of the concentration camps had its place.[14] Most recently, Hans Mommsen and Manfred Grieger's massive history of the Volkswagenwerk during the war offered a vital case study. The Volkswagen plant, conceived during 1934–37, was only completed by cooperating with the SS, which gave access to its reservoir of extraordinarily cheap labor power, including civilian deportees, prisoners of war, concentration camp inmates, and finally Hungarian Jews deported from Auschwitz. By 1945, foreign labor composed 85.3 percent of the workers at the Volkswagen main plant.[15]

By neglecting contexts like these, Goldhagen's arguments fell short of the best work in the field. Concentration camp laborers in the Volkswagen plant certainly suffered from the appalling atrocities Goldhagen detailed for the work camps in Lublin, and in many ways the racialized distinctions between Jews and other categories of forced labor (for example, Poles and

---

12. Hans Mommsen, "The Thin Patina of Civilization: Antisemitism Was a Necessary, but by No Means a Sufficient, Condition for the Holocaust," in Robert R. Shandley, ed., *Unwilling Germans? The Goldhagen Debate* (Minneapolis, 1998), 194. Originally published in *Die Zeit,* 31 August 1996.

13. Quoted in Josef Joffe, "'The Killers Were Ordinary Germans, Ergo the Ordinary Germans Were Killers': The Logic, the Language, and the Meaning of a Book That Conquered Germany," in Shandley, *Unwilling Germans?* 224. Originally published in *New York Review of Books,* 28 November 1996.

14. See Ulrich Herbert, *Hitler's Foreign Workers: Enforced Foreign Labour in Germany under the Third Reich* (Cambridge, 1998); Herbert, ed., *Europa und der "Reichseinsatz": Ausländische Zivilarbeiter, Kriegsgefangene und KZ-Häftlinge in Deutschland, 1938–1945* (Essen, 1991); and Herbert, "Labour and Extermination: Economic Interest and the Primacy of *Weltanschauung* in National Socialism," *Past and Present* 138 (February 1993): 144–95.

15. Hans Mommsen and Manfred Grieger, *Das Volkswagenwerk und seine Arbeiter im Dritten Reich* (Düsseldorf, 1996).

Soviet citizens, to name those lowest in the latter's hierarchy of exploitation) confirm Goldhagen's argument about the uniquely lethal and degrading treatment reserved for the Jews. But the primary antagonism of Germans for Jews doesn't exhaust the tasks of explanation. Atrocities at Volkswagen resulted not only from the racialized dehumanizing of the victims, but also from the power relations of the labor process, both managerially and on the shop floor, which were further radicalized by the ethnic enmities structured into the social experience of working in the war economy. Likewise, Ferdinand Porsche, the real architect of the Volkswagenwerk, was an archetype of the self-constructed apolitical specialist, driven ostensibly by the modernizing (and modernist) ethic of project-making and professional achievement. Yet he built the company by cultivating political relations with the SS and other parts of the Nazi regime, utilizing the machinery of racialized exploitation, and constructing an elaborate microcosm of the putative Nazi New Order. No less than the sadistic Johannes Pump and Anton Callesen—the SS heads of the Laagberg Concentration Camp servicing Volkswagen, who exactly personified Goldhagen's perpetrators—Porsche was a principal author of the brutalities the workers had to endure.

Goldhagen also took a narrow approach in his chapters on the reserve police battalions, which provided the main weight of his research. There, he covered the same ground pioneered by one of the leading historians of the "Final Solution," Christopher Browning, in his book *Ordinary Men.*[16] While Browning also acknowledged the importance of antisemitic ideology, he developed an incomparably more differentiated analysis to explain participation in the killing operations, stressing the situational logics of peer pressure, deference to authority, wartime brutalization, and dehumanizing of the victims too, thereby foregrounding the criminal propensities of "ordinary *men*" when placed under such circumstances, as opposed to the murderous antisemitic proclivities of "ordinary *Germans,*" as Goldhagen preferred. Browning's approach doesn't exhaust the possibilities for reading Battalion 101's behavior either, and much room remains for exploring the psychology, values, cultural formation, and political subjectivities of its members before their criminality becomes more intelligible. But Goldhagen's approach hardly advanced this goal. He avoided institutional analysis of the recruitment, training, and deployment of the police and selectively re-traversed Browning's archival trail, rather than offering a broader history of the auxiliary formations in occupied Eastern Europe. This raises big questions about the book's breadth

---

16. Christopher Browning, *Ordinary Men: Reserve Police Battalion 101 and the Final Solution in Poland* (New York, 1992).

and density of research, and in the absence of clear archival bases (the source listings were buried in the footnotes), we deserve some systematic historiographical accounting, given the hyperbole of the claims to originality.[17]

Ordinary Germans and Complicity in Nazism

Scholarship on the Third Reich has given sustained attention to popular collaboration with the Nazis and the forms of societal complicity, and Goldhagen's unwillingness to engage with these arguments and evidence made his work very vulnerable. Arguably, his deep-historical argumentation protected him against these existing historiographies. By insisting that antisemitic hostility descending from the early nineteenth century had become German culture's default condition (its "common sense"), translating into active desires for killing the Jews once the state's anti-Jewish offensive made this feasible, Goldhagen dispensed with any need to analyze the Third Reich's internal sociopolitical dynamics. But from the wider scholarship on Nazism, we know that popular acquiescence in the attacks on the Jews covered a wider range of responses. These certainly included the willing collaboration asserted by Goldhagen, and explicit conformity to official Nazi propaganda. But the full compulsions of the Third Reich's coercive political culture can't be ignored. Nor can pragmatic recognition of the prevailing requirements for personal and family survival—how livelihoods were to be defended, how careers were to be made, how jobs and incomes were to be secured. The issues of conformity and opposition, collaboration and resistance, accommodation and dissent—plus the grayness coalescing between these polarities—were never allowed to emerge in Goldhagen's account.

Mentioning these complications doesn't allay the ethical charges Goldhagen leveled against the Holocaust's ordinary perpetrators, whom he quite properly indicted for their elective participation in the killing. But they needed to be considered when judging the less direct complicity of other parts of the Third Reich's population—those with knowledge who

---

17. Goldhagen devoted much of his discussion of Battalion 101 to personal attacks on Browning and his use of evidence. He accused him of constantly reading his interpretations illegitimately into the material, and of constructing interpretations "out of thin air." See Goldhagen, *Hitler's Willing Executioners,* 551 n. 65; and Daniel Goldhagen, "The Evil of Banality," *The New Republic,* 13 July 1992, 49–52 (review of Browning's book). For Browning's rejoinder, see Christopher R. Browning, "Ordinary Men or Ordinary Germans?" in Shandley, *Unwilling Germans?* 55–73. For further discussion of the Browning-Goldhagen conflict, see Ruth Bettina Birn, "Revising the Holocaust," in Norman G. Finkelstein and Ruth Bettina Birn, *A Nation on Trial: The Goldhagen Thesis and Historical Truth* (New York, 1998), 107–14.

kept it to themselves, those who kept Nazi society working efficiently, those acquiescing in the anti-Jewish measures and the visible maltreatment and eventual disappearance of the Jews, those opting for "internal emigration," quite apart from the enforced silence of anti-Nazi opponents—because Goldhagen made the absence of active pro-Jewish sympathies into key evidence for antisemitism's universality. Goldhagen's approach flatly dismissed the obvious structural considerations, which profoundly limited the freedom of choice available to ordinary people. These included the violence and pervasiveness of the Third Reich's coercive apparatus and its draconian repression, society's recentering under the impact of the regime's relentless drive to co-opt all forms of collective associational activity, and the pressure of the necessity of self-protection in everyday life. Again, explicating these pressures on the free agency of "ordinary Germans" *doesn't* absolve the latter from ethical responsibility. But neither can the latter be shoehorned into a single, oversimplified notation. Within the frameworks mentioned above, recent historiography has explicitly and repeatedly accepted Germany's generalized societal responsibility for Nazism and the "Final Solution," and it's quite wrong to have insinuated the contrary.

In other words, one of the major gains of historical work on Nazi Germany has been to complicate the issues of popular complicity—the regime's ability to base itself on not just coercion but consent—and this is what Goldhagen's book occluded. Social and cultural historians have been exploring the Third Reich's ability to penetrate even the most private and "resistant" spaces of everydayness with its ideas. We've acquired a far better grasp of how its legitimacy could become grounded, whether in the workplace, the subcultures of youth, the sphere of recreation, or the family and the home. To have experienced the Third Reich from the inside, whether as one of its targeted enemies, as an ordinary person earning one's livelihood through paid employment, as a young person socialized into the mass organizations, as a woman fixed in the dominant discourses of maternalism and domesticity, or as a lower-rank civil servant or public employee, entailed complicated rules of comportment. In one's ordinary transactions, even the most mundane and trivial of daily decisions could be construed either as an ethical compromise with the regime and its values, or as a modest but existentially significant subversion.

This inevitably blurs the reassuring boundary between support and opposition, because even the most privatized and principled refusals of the regime's legitimacy were always already contaminated by its racialized languages and practices of public identification, just as the performance of conformity might also be subtly edged with dissent. Grasping these intolerable conditions—in which the possibility of a personal ethics, of living truthfully, became so unavoidably muddied—requires an enormous effort at historical empathy. Here, it's vital to add (given Goldhagen's ethical absolutizing of the distinction between "perpetrators" and "victims") that exactly the same efforts at imaginative understanding have guided recent work on Jewish experience under Nazism too.[18] The best such work ethically deconstructs the possible forms of response in situations where explicit opposition and public resistance were out of the question, making the pragmatics and exigencies of survival far more opaque than before. With his angry recentering of discussion around a generalized and undifferentiated thesis of cultural responsibility, Goldhagen abolished the need for such difficult and uncomfortable reflection. He removed those complexities of popular agency and motivation, individually and collectively, from the agenda. They simply disappeared into the black stain of the shared responsibility of all "ordinary Germans."

Perhaps Goldhagen's prime adversary in the public debates accompanying the German edition of his book was Hans Mommsen, whose standing has been second to none in the archivally founded historiography of the Third Reich, which properly began in the 1960s, not least with Mommsen's own study of the civil service.[19] Mommsen has been the tireless advocate of a profoundly important position in the debates of German historians over Nazism. He confronted the simplistic totalitarian model of Nazi rule with the inefficient, and commonly chaotic actualities of policy-making and administration under the Third Reich, replacing "intentionalist" assumptions (for example, that the Holocaust flowed directly from the long-planned intentions of Hitler and the other leaders) with the provocative view that Hitler was a "weak dictator," whose individual hands-on direction mattered less than the "cumulative radicalization" of Nazi practice. This had vital consequences for arguments about German responsibility, Mommsen argued, because the implementation of Nazi policies presupposed the compliance, endorsement, and apathy of broad social groups, especially civil servants, managers, businessmen, and the professions. As vitally, Mommsen has also vigorously argued this case whenever apologetics have threatened to defuse or diminish this upsetting recognition of broader societal complicity (as against the bounded responsibility of readily identifiable ideological fanatics). The resulting debates have

---

18. This began with pioneering social and institutional histories of ghettoization, such as Isaiah Trunk, *Judenrat: The Jewish Councils in Eastern Europe under Nazi Occupation* (New York, 1972); and Yisrael Gutman, *The Jews of Warsaw, 1929–1943: Ghetto, Underground, Revolt* (Brighton, 1982). For an early commentary on such work, see Michael R. Marrus, *The Holocaust in History* (New York, 1987), 108–55.

19. Hans Mommsen, *Beamtentum im Dritten Reich* (Stuttgart, 1966).

often spilled into the wider public sphere, in ways described at the start of this essay.

In transferring priority from the complex dynamics inside Nazi society to the old bugbear of the "German mind," Goldhagen dismissed the case patiently assembled by Mommsen and others for more complex understandings of what made the Third Reich tick. Here, it's important to be clear about what exactly historians like Mommsen had been arguing during the past thirty years, because Goldhagen created the impression they were diverting attention from the real enormities of antisemitic violence and its breadth of support. By stressing the "polycratic" basis of Nazi rule, rather than any monolithic dictatorship, and the pragmatic decision-making associated with Hitler's generally expressed demand for liquidating the Jews (rather than any long-planned blueprint for genocide), Mommsen has been accused of reducing the "Final Solution" to force of circumstances, placing it beyond any easily locatable responsibility, and even saying it was not something willed at all. For to see genocide resulting from a process of improvisation in chaotically evolving circumstances rather than from a specific order or decision, and from "cumulative radicalization" rather than the inexorable unfolding of a sovereign ideological drive, was to remove the "Final Solution" from agency, Mommsen's critics have argued, thereby freeing the Germans from their burden of responsibility.

These controversies became especially intense around the "Final Solution" itself, because the absence of any document detailing an order from Hitler himself opened the space for much legitimate disagreement, as well as for the more notorious forms of tendentious revisionism. On one side were those like Klaus Hildebrand and Andreas Hillgruber ("intentionalists"), who stressed the long-term ideological origins of the decision to exterminate the Jews in the uniqueness of Nazi racialism and Hitler's personal ideological outlook, so that the decisions of 1941–42 became the completely logical culmination of "the distinctive murderous will of the Nazi leadership." On the other side were "structuralists" like Hans Mommsen and Martin Broszat, who certainly agreed about the Nazi leadership's fundamental ideological disposition but saw antisemitism in a more complex relationship to the movement's makeup, treating the "Final Solution" as the unevenly evolving consequence of the opportunities and disorder created by the Third Reich's military victories in 1940–41. In this second view, historians needed to focus on the specific circumstances empowering the pursuit of *genocide* as such, as opposed to the other combinations of policies tried immediately after the occupation of Poland. These already expressed the regime's underlying racialist designs against the Jews. They also produced systematic forms of inhuman maltreatment, including mass deportations (possibly outside Europe, in the so-called Madagascar Plan), concentration of populations, and mass killings behind the military lines of the Eastern Front's "war of annihilation."[20] With the latter, we are close to the "Final Solution." But the industrialized killing machinery associated with Treblinka, Auschwitz, and the other extermination camps was devised only once the chaotic logic of the earlier policies was under way.

This second approach, heavily identified with Mommsen, was linked to larger arguments about German authoritarianism, in which the very possibility of "cumulative radicalization" was created by broader social structures and cultural dispositions, as well as by post-1933 policies of the Third Reich. Simply to become feasible, genocide presupposed widespread complicity of large sections of German society. This was secured via an openness to earlier policies, which ranged from violent destruction of the labor movement and other sources of anti-Nazi opposition, the policing of the public sphere, and the coercive machinery of state-centered conformity, to the bureaucratic victimizing of unwanted minorities. Beyond the period of the Third Reich itself, in this view, openness to Nazi policies was also linked to structurally rooted antidemocratic pathologies, which were in turn derived from deep peculiarities in Germany's illiberal political culture. This proneness of large parts of German society to forms of authoritarianism, which could be harnessed to Nazism's racialized New Order, was just as important to the shaping of the "Final Solution" as the continuities in Hitler's ideological hatred of the Jews since the publication of *Mein Kampf.* Within this framework, highly ramified arguments could still occur about the specific inception of the various stages of anti-Jewish measures between 1938 and 1941–42.[21]

Whereas "intentionalists" personalized the explanation of the "Final Solution" around Hitler's ideological outlook and dictatorial will, couching responsibility in terms of Nazi ideological fanaticism, "structuralists" moved attention away from Hitler and his demonic personality toward a much broader-based conception of German responsibility, stressing instead the social and institutional structures engendering the regime's

---

20. For an excellent introduction to these debates, see Ian Kershaw, *The Nazi Dictatorship: Problems and Perspectives of Interpretation,* 3d ed. (London, 1993), 80–107.

21. Browning is the doyen of such work, proceeding from exhaustive knowledge of the archives and meticulous analysis of the policy-making contexts at the center and on the ground. See Christopher R. Browning, *The Final Solution and the German Foreign Office: A Study of Referat D III of Abteilung Deutschland, 1940–1943* (New York, 1978); *Fateful Months: Essays on the Emergence of the Final Solution* (New York, 1985); and *The Path to Genocide: Essays on Launching the Final Solution* (Cambridge, 1992).

radical dynamism. In other words, structuralist approaches have related the antidemocratic, terroristic, racialist, and antisemitic aspects of Nazism to a more generalized notion of German societal complicity. By focusing on the broader social, political, and cultural dispositions of German society, they argued, as opposed to Hitler's personal role or the ideological cadres of his movement, we can understood much better how "ordinary Germans" were taught how to kill. We can understand how "normal" German society could be deformed into accepting the regime's racialist and antisemitic goals.

Such a concept of normality corresponds roughly to the idea of the "banality of evil" as it emerged from the controversies surrounding Arendt's *Eichmann in Jerusalem.* It helps us think about the ways Nazi dynamism presumed *not only* an animating will among the leaders, *but also* the compliance and collaboration of "non-Nazis" at all levels of German society after 1933, especially among the respectable strata in business, the professions, the armed services, and the civil apparatuses of the state. Without such larger reservoirs of acceptance and agreement, the functioning of the Third Reich's "racial state" was simply not thinkable. From this point of view, in making his arguments about "ordinary Germans," Goldhagen was running through a wide-open door, ironically one opened by Mommsen and others—precisely the critics arrayed against him in the 1996 public debates. It was thus Goldhagen's particular version of this argument that caused all the fuss. He reduced it to an especially extreme thesis about antisemitism, which banished from consideration all the surrounding analysis developed by Mommsen and his successors.

Broadening the Contexts of Nazi Racialism

The broadening of the contexts of Nazi antisemitism has taken two strong forms, one concerning the victims of Nazi racialism, the other concerning its perpetrators. On the one hand, research illuminated Nazism's other racialized enemies—not just the Sinti and Roma (Gypsies) and the other Eastern European subject nationalities (for example, as well as three million Jewish citizens of Poland, three million Catholic citizens were murdered too)—but also entire social categories, like Socialists and Communists, homosexuals, the mentally disabled, the infirm and incurably ill, the institutionalized elderly, and multiple groups of the socially incompetent or "asocials" (vagrants and the homeless, alcoholics, the long-term unemployed, habitual petty offenders, hard-core criminals, prostitutes, sexually active teenaged girls, unwed mothers), to be followed after 1939 by Polish intellectuals, Soviet prisoners of war, "political commissars," and so on. Stigmatizing these populations laid the ground for systematic extermination of the Jews in a double sense—both *discursively,* by labeling such groups as "unworthy of life" and thereby preparing the comprehensive assaults on the Jews; and *practically,* by the grisly process of experiment that began with the euthanasia program in October 1939 (Operation T-4), the persecution of Sinti and Roma, and the mass murder of two million Soviet POWs.[22]

On the other hand, to understand this broader context of maltreatment, we have to grasp the eugenicist and related ideologies of social engineering pervading the medical, health-care, criminological, and social-policy-making professions long *before* the Nazis came to power. As an impressive accumulation of still-emerging scholarship shows, processes of medicalization and racialization were well under way during the Weimar Republic, involving a variegated turn toward "biological politics"—in eugenics, population politics, welfare initiatives directed at women, family policies, criminology and penal reform, imagined projects of social engineering, and the deployment of science for social goals. From the early 1900s, antisemitic idioms figured in more elaborate repertoires of biological politics, where social, cultural, and political issues were systematically naturalized under the sign of race.

As Robert Proctor argued, "the ideological structure we associate with National Socialism was deeply embedded in the philosophy and institutional structure of German biomedical science." This broader discursive

---

22. Operation T-4 was named after its headquarters in a villa at Tiergartenstrasse 4 in Berlin. Beginning 9 October 1939, 70,273 people were killed under the first phase of the euthanasia program, which became disguised after 24 August 1941 in response to certain public pressure. After the killing resumed, total deaths by 1945 exceeded 200,000. The victims were psychiatric patients, asylum inmates, depressives, sick concentration camp inmates, young children of the latter, and nonconformists of various kinds. The scholarly accounts of T-4 are now especially rich: Ernst Klee, *"Euthanasia" im NS-Staat: Die Vernichtung "lebensunwerten Lebens"* (Frankfurt am Main, 1983); Hans-Walter Schmuhl, *Rassenhygiene, Nationalsozialismus, Euthanasia: Von der Verhütung zur Vernichtung "lebensunwerten Lebens,"* 1890–1945 (Göttingen, 1987); Götz Aly, "Medicine against the Useless," in Götz Aly, Peter Chroust, and Christian Pross, *Cleansing the Fatherland: Nazi Medicine and Racial Hygiene* (Baltimore, 1994), 22–98; Michael Burleigh, *Death and Deliverance: "Euthanasia" in Germany c. 1900–1945* (Cambridge, 1995); Henry Friedlander, *The Origins of Nazi Genocide: From Euthanasia to the Final Solution* (Chapel Hill, 1995). The wider citations have grown voluminous. See especially Michael Zimmermann, *Verfolgt, vertrieben, vernichtet: Die nationalsozialistische Vernichtungspolitik gegen Sinti und Roma* (Essen, 1989); Wolfgang Wippermann, *Wie die Zigeuner: Antisemitismus und Antiziganismus im Vergleich* (Berlin, 1997); Christian Streit, *Keine Kameraden: Die Wehrmacht und die sowjetischen Kriegsgefangenen, 1941–1945* (Stuttgart, 1978); W. Ayass, *"Asoziale" im Nationalsozialismus* (Stuttgart, 1995); and Robert N. Proctor, *Racial Hygiene: Medicine under the Nazis* (Cambridge, 1988). The best general survey of the relevant literatures, now already somewhat dated, is Michael Burleigh and Wolfgang Wippermann, *The Racial State: Germany, 1933–1945* (Cambridge, 1991).

field authorized Nazi racial programs via the longer traditions of racial hygiene, in "a larger attempt . . . to medicalize or biologize various forms of social, sexual, political, or racial deviance."[23] Far from corrupting "true" science by intruding inappropriate pressures from the outside, Nazism worked upon an established eugenicist paradigm by appealing to the available "imagery, results, and authority of science."[24] Accordingly, the ground for Nazi policies was discursively laid—not in a narrow or literal sense of "linguistic" preparation, but by systems of practice and elaborate institutional machineries of knowledge production, which over many years worked at demarcating deviant or "worthless" categories of people. Such ideas also passed into the common currency of public discussion, with manifold connections to everyday forms of belief. Popular assumptions became restructured, changing the parameters for what an acceptable social policy could be.

This direction of inquiry was encapsulated by the title of an emblematic essay by Detlev Peukert, called "The Genesis of the 'Final Solution' from the Spirit of Science."[25] Some of the most challenging work on Nazism follows the same logic, unsettling many older assumptions and breaking out of the increasingly sterile intentionalist-structuralist debates. Much of this research proceeds from classic "structuralist" ground (the broader social history and policy-making dynamics of the Nazi era), reperiodizing Nazism in a longer crisis of modernity dating from the early 1900s. In a similar vein, gender history has also been recasting the study of Nazism but typically played virtually no role in the Goldhagen debates, whether because of the familiar absence of feminist (or even women's) voices from the public forums, or because of the latter's lack of gendered perspectives.[26]

---

23. Proctor, *Racial Hygiene,* 6–7. See also Paul Weindling, *Health, Race, and German Politics between National Unification and Nazism, 1870–1945* (Cambridge, 1989).

24. Proctor, *Racial Hygiene,* 283.

25. Detlev J. K. Peukert, "The Genesis of the 'Final Solution' from the Spirit of Science," in Thomas Childers and Jane Caplan, eds., *Reevaluating the Third Reich* (New York, 1993), 234–52.

26. Of the thirty contributions collected by Shandley, *Unwilling Germans?* only one was by a woman historian, Ingrid Gilcher-Holtey, and a second was by the publisher Marion Gräfin Dönhoff. The baseline for gender history of the Third Reich was provided by Renate Bridenthal, Atina Grossmann, and Marion Kaplan, eds., *When Biology Became Destiny: Women in Weimar and Nazi Germany* (New York, 1984); Gisela Bock, *Zwangssterilisation in Nationalsozialismus: Studien zur Rassenpolitik und Frauenpolitik* (Opladen, 1986); and Claudia Koonz, *Mothers in the Fatherland: Women, the Family, and Nazi Politics* (New York, 1987). Among subsequent works, see especially Gabriele Czarnowski, *Das kontrollierte Paar: Ehe und Sexualpolitik im Nationalsozialismus* (Weinheim, 1989); Dagmar Reese, *Straff aber nicht stramm, herb aber nicht derb: Zur Vergesellschaftung von Mädchen durch den Bund deutscher Mädel im sozialkulturellen Vergleich zweier Milieus* (Weinheim, 1989); and Atina

A related area concerns histories of social policy and the welfare state.[27]

Nazism aspired to change Germany's public culture by attacking the social order's operative assumptions. It sought to reconstitute popular mores in the social circumstances of everyday life. Other historians have investigated the workplace, youth subcultures, and popular culture from this point of view.[28] The massive reliance of the Nazi war economy on the deployment of foreign labor, mostly enslaved or coerced, and defined by the racialized languages of the Nazi New Order, has been addressed too, particularly in its implications for patterns of working-class formation.[29] Finally, historians at the Hamburg Institute for Social Research (a non-university academic institution) and the Association for Research on National Socialist Health and Social Policies, of whom the most prominent is Götz Aly, have produced a dense series of studies and documentations of the Third Reich's racialized social policies, the grandiose population planning behind the New Order, and the Holocaust's economic logic.[30]

Grossmann, *Reforming Sex: The German Movement for Birth Control and Abortion Reform* (New York, 1995). For critical surveys linking this work directly to the Holocaust, see Adelheid von Saldern, "Victims or Perpetrators? Controversies about the Role of Women in the Nazi State," in David Crew, ed., *Nazism and German Society, 1933–1945* (London, 1994), 141–65; Atina Grossmann, "Feminist Debates about Women and National Socialism," *Gender and History* 3 (1991): 350–58; and Ann Taylor Allen, "The Holocaust and the Modernization of Gender: A Historiographical Essay," *Central European History* 30 (1997): 349–64.

27. See especially Young-Sun Hong, *Welfare, Modernity, and the Weimar State, 1919–1933* (Princeton, 1998); and David F. Crew, *Germans on Welfare: From Weimar to Hitler* (New York, 1998).

28. For the workplace, see Alf Lüdtke, "The Appeal of Exterminating 'Others': German Workers and the Limits of Resistance," in Michael Geyer and John W. Boyer, eds., *Resistance against the Third Reich, 1933–1990* (Chicago, 1994), 53–74; and Lüdtke, "What Happened to the 'Fiery Red Glow'? Workers' Experiences and German Fascism," in Lüdtke, ed., *The History of Everyday Life: Reconstructing Historical Experiences and Ways of Life* (Princeton, 1995), 198–251. For youth subcultures, see Detlev Peukert, "Die 'Halbstarken': Protestverhalten von Arbeiterjugendlichen zwischen Wilhelminischen Reich und Ära Adenauer," *Zeitschrift für Pädagogik* 30 (1984): 533–48; and Peukert, "Edelweisspiraten, Meuten, Swing: Jugendsubkulturen im Dritten Reich," in Gerhard Huck, ed., *Sozialgeschichte der Freizeit: Untersuchungen zum Wandel der Alltagskultur in Deutschland* (Wuppertal, 1980), 307–27. Detlev Peukert, *Inside Nazi Germany: Conformity, Opposition, and Racism in Everyday Life* (New Haven, 1987), mapped out this general terrain.

29. See the references to Herbert's work in n. 14 above.

30. See especially Götz Aly and Karl Heinz Roth, *Die restlose Erfassung: Volkszählen, Identifizieren, Aussondern im Nationalsozialismus* (Berlin, 1984); Götz Aly and Susanne Heim, *Vordenker der Vernichtung: Auschwitz und die deutsche Pläne für eine neue europäische Ordnung* (Hamburg, 1991); Götz Aly, *Macht, Geist, Wahn: Kontinuitäten deutschen Denkens* (Berlin, 1997); Aly, Chroust, and Pross, *Cleansing the Fatherland;* and Christian Gerlach, *Krieg, Ernährung, Völkermord: Forschungen zur deutschen Vernichtungspolitik im Zweiten Weltkrieg* (Hamburg, 1998). The best introduction is now through Götz Aly, *"Final Solu-*

Goldhagen acknowledged none of these literatures. Because they focus on the complex structures of the specifically German "ordinariness" that conduced to the Nazi project, his silence was remarkable. Instead of thoroughly reviewing these actual historiographies, he offered only his own over-synthesized claims about the essential character of German culture in the nineteenth century (his "cultural cognitive model"). These presumed at best a sub-Geertzian postulate of cultural coherence and at worst skated recklessly on the surface of enormously complicated histories. But even if the deep-historical argument about the cultural rootedness of "eliminationism" were more persuasive, ignoring the generative conditions of the Nazi era per se would still make no sense. This matters all the more given the tendentiousness of some of Goldhagen's other main claims, like the uniquely sadistic and murderous Jew-hatred ascribed to the German Holocaust perpetrators (as against those of other nationalities), or the uniquely horrific maltreatment reserved for Jews as against all other categories of the Third Reich's victims. These fallacious shortcomings of *Hitler's Willing Executioners* have been amply detailed by specialists familiar with the same archives and empirical ground.[31] Claims about the motivations and practices of antisemitic violence, whether in Goldhagen's chosen contexts (Battalion 101, the Lublin work camps, and the death marches) or others, required far denser grounding in the social and institutional histories of the Third Reich than he provided.

For example, Dieter Pohl's and Thomas Sandkühler's studies of Jewish persecution in Galicia combine the concreteness of Goldhagen's case studies with constructive awareness of existing historiography, building on existing work rather than asserting spurious claims to originality.[32] Moreover, it's unclear what purpose is served by insisting on the uniquely evil qualities of the maltreatment reserved for Jews. The horrors experienced

---

tion": *Nazi Population Policy and the Murder of the European Jews* (London, 1999). For a critical survey of the broader research context, see Ulrich Herbert, ed., *Nationalsozialistische Vernichtungspolitik, 1939–1945: neue Forschungen und Kontroversen* (Frankfurt am Main, 1998). See also the earlier symposium, Wolfgang Schneider, ed., *"Vernichtungspolitik": Eine Debatte über den Zusammenhang von Sozialpolitik und Genozid im nationalsozialistischen Deutschland* (Hamburg, 1991).

31. In particular, Birn, "Revising the Holocaust." See also Dieter Pohl, "Die Holocaust-Forschung und Goldhagens Thesen," *Vierteljahreshefte für Zeitgeschichte* 45 (1997): 1–48; and Browning, "Ordinary Men or Ordinary Germans?"

32. See especially Pohl, *Nationalsozialistische Judenverfolgung in Ostgalizien;* and Sandkühler, *"Endlösung in Galizien";* also Martin C. Dean, "The German *Gendarmerie,* the Ukrainian *Schutzmannschaft,* and the 'Second Wave' of Jewish Killings in Occupied Ukraine: German Policing at the Local Level in the Zhitomir Region, 1941–1944," *German History* 14 (1996): 168–92; and John-Paul Himka, "Ukrainian Collaboration in the Extermination of the Jews during the Second World War: Sorting Out the Long-Term and Conjunctural Factors," *Studies in Contemporary Jewry: An Annual* 13 (1997): 170–89.

by other categories of victims were in countless situations indistinguishable. Claiming otherwise becomes a demeaning wrangle, diminishing rather than enhancing scholarly and ethical debate. Furthermore, as the wider research on the "racial state" continues to show, violence wasn't confined to the nationality frontier of Eastern Europe and the killing fields behind the Eastern Front, but was endemic to the Third Reich's carceral system, including the latter's welfare and social policy complex.

The Third Reich's dehumanizing practices attacked an ever-expanding aggregation of "community aliens." Under Otto-Georg Thierack (appointed Minister of Justice, August 1942), for example, over 20,000 state prisoners were transferred into the camps for "annihilation through labor," some two-thirds of whom perished. They included "racial" categories (Jews, Poles, Sinti, and Roma), but also "asocials" convicted of criminal offenses and considered "unreformable." This system's operation bursts the explanatory bounds of Goldhagen's model of an "eliminationist" antisemitism descending from the nineteenth century. Once in the camp system, these "asocials" were subject to all the inhumanities wreaked on the Jews.[33] It's also clear that wide sections of officialdom and the professions ("non-Nazi" as well as "Nazi") were responsible for this policy, with complex situational, bureaucratic, and ideological motivations, much as historians like Mommsen have maintained. Why must Goldhagen bracket these questions?

Historical Scholarship and Public Culture

Given all these problems and the book's peculiar relationship to existing scholarship, *Hitler's Willing Executioners* may turn out to be merely a temporary, if noisy, explosion on the historiographical scene. Its importance comes less from its substantive contents, in fact, than from their *effects* in the public sphere. "No publicity is bad publicity," one might quip. But the enormous success of Goldhagen's book benefits not just its author's newfound celebrity status, but also German historical studies and

---

33. See Nikolaus Wachsmann, "'Annihilation through Labor': The Killing of State Prisoners in the Third Reich," *Journal of Modern History* 71 (September 1999): 624–59. Wachsmann tracked the treatment experienced by former state prisoners under the notorious labor regime of the quarry in Mauthausen (651): "This brutal treatment, senseless labor, and murder of the former state prisoners in Mauthausen, all of whom were non-Jews and predominantly German, contradicts recent claims that 'the Germans . . . gave senseless work almost exclusively to Jews'. Just like Jewish inmates, these 'asocial' state prisoners were also seen in Nazi propaganda as 'work-shy' and thus tortured with largely useless work. Forcing them to perform 'Sisyphean tasks' had no economic benefit; its goal was to make them suffer by demonstrating the complete uselessness of their physically destructive labor." The internal quotation is from Goldhagen, *Hitler's Willing Executioners,* 313.

German political culture in some important ways. There are three points to be made in conclusion, therefore, which set the scene for the essays in this volume. Two are concerned with aspects of the historiography of the Holocaust and the Third Reich, in ways that connect with the arguments already developed above. Here, Goldhagen's book responds to problems arising from existing historical studies, although in the end it functions more as symptom than cure. The third point concerns *Hitler's Willing Executioners* as a public event, where its lasting positive value may be found.

Most obviously, Goldhagen reinstated the Holocaust's enormous violence at the center of the German historical agenda—as a system of terror and atrocities, perpetrated on individuals as well as a general population, by individual killers with bloody hands, as well as by impersonal bureaucrats and the notorious *Schreibtischtäter*. He also placed the antisemitism at the center. Neither of these things were exactly "new" or "forgotten." But some recent logics of inquiry have encouraged fears that they might become subtly effaced. For all the incontrovertible importance of contextualizing the Judeocide in the encompassing plans for a racialized New Order in Eastern Europe, based on massive resettlement and rationalization of populations (the main focus of Götz Aly and his colleagues), for example, the centrality of the specifically antisemitic driving force sometimes threatened to be obscured or downplayed. Something similar might be said of Peukert's tracing of "the genesis of the 'Final Solution'" to generalized aspects of a crisis of modernity connected to "the spirit of science." The larger contexts of racialization of policy and thought, of population planning, of medicalization, and of biological politics have profoundly revised our understanding of how the enormity of the Holocaust could occur. But, measured against older approaches, which saw Nazi policies as flatly "the war against the Jews" (to cite the title of Lucy Dawidowicz's influential 1975 study), such discussions sometimes seem to be marginalizing the central event, rewriting the history of the Jewish fate as the history of something else, even the history of the Holocaust with the centrality of the Jews left out.

In fact, Aly's more recent formulations disallow that interpretation, specifically foregrounding "the antisemitic doctrine of the [Nazi] state," while explicating its systemic links to other regions of policy. His meticulous account of policy-making in 1939–41 then feeds into the abiding debates over the Judeocide's exact inception, arguing that "the most important prerequisites to the Holocaust did not emerge until the war began."[34] Whatever the ulterior purposes of Aly's research agenda, its

34. Aly, *"Final Solution,"* 1, 245. See also Götz Aly and Susanne Heim, "Forced Emigration, War, Deportation, and Holocaust," *Studies in Contemporary Jewry: An Annual* 13

findings compel discussion. In principle, insisting on the specific dynamics of the years 1939–41 in this way to explain the actual form of the genocide's implementation doesn't diminish the constancy or strength of Nazi antisemitism per se. Nor does establishing the interlinks between policies toward the Jews and the broader realms of Nazi population planning, whether these came through the systematic racialized imperialism envisaged for the East, the forced resettlement programs, the regime's social policies, or the deeper contexts of medicalization and eugenics. Likewise, analyzing Nazi anti-Bolshevism needn't obscure the importance of Nazi Jew-hatred, but on the contrary enhances our understanding of its appeal.[35] Goldhagen gives none of these historiographies and the associated debates their due, aggressively blazing his lone path. Nonetheless, his book's very monofocal relentlessness restored antisemitism's primacy to National Socialism and recalled historians' attentiveness to this central ground. The impact of *Hitler's Willing Executioners* has redirected discussion. There's no reason to abandon the expanded meanings of the "racial state" emerging from recent historiography. But Goldhagen's book makes it much harder for these to efface the specific fate of the Jews.

Secondly, Goldhagen also does a useful service in stressing the role of ideology as such in preparing the way for the "Final Solution." Here, social history's emphasis on "social context" has tended to obscure Nazism's success in transforming social values from below. Mommsen in particular privileges the "political and bureaucratic mechanisms that permitted the idea of mass extermination to be realized," counterposing these dichotomously to "ideological factors—[as] the effects of antisemitic propaganda and the authoritarian element in traditional German political culture." In so doing, he downgrades the insidiousness of Nazism's discur-

(1997): 56–73. These two texts finally provide access to the work of Aly and Heim in English, for otherwise it's been hard to find extensive and judicious descriptions. See, for instance, Michael Burleigh, "A 'Political Economy of the Final Solution'? Reflections on Modernity, Historians, and the Holocaust," in Burleigh, *Ethics and Extermination: Reflections on Nazi Genocide* (Cambridge, 1997), 169–82, which frames its critical explication as a more generalized polemic against critiques of modernity. Whereas the relentless materialist analytic of Aly's and Heim's initial works in the 1980s tended to reduce the Holocaust to its economic logic, their more recent texts are more nuanced. The problematic nature of so exclusive an emphasis on the resettlement complex of policies and practices in 1939–41 (substantively and methodologically) should not detract from the profound significance of the argument and findings. See also Aly's response to *Hitler's Willing Executioners,* "The Universe of Death and Torment," in Shandley, *Unwilling Germans?* 167–74, which is a moving and careful positioning of the various approaches.

35. The most important study organized around the relationship between Nazi antisemitism and anti-Bolshevism remains Arno J. Mayer, *Why Did the Heavens Not Darken? The "Final Solution" in History* (New York, 1988).

sive power.[36] For it's all very well to express skepticism about "Nazi ideology" in the narrower, formalistic sense of that term, and to doubt the penetration into everyday life of Nazism's programmatic propaganda. But as soon as we focus on the issue of complicity at all levels of German society after 1933, we immediately need an *extended* understanding of ideology, as being embedded in cultural practices, institutional sites, and social relations—in what people do and the structured contexts where they do it, rather than just the ideas they consciously think. Simply to remember the other targets of the Nazis' racialist aggressions is to remind ourselves of the radical extent of their ambitions to reorder social values in Germany. Reconstituting society as the *Volksgemeinschaft* was an ineluctably ideological process.

Götz Aly's and Susanne Heim's work on "pioneers" of the "Final Solution" is one way of pursuing this question of ideology, deriving the possibilities of wartime genocide from the earlier diffusion of a racialized paradigm of public policy and social administration.[37] As an ideological project in this sense (just to reiterate one of this essay's main arguments), the Judeocide required not just the senior Nazi leadership, but an elaborate machinery of governmentality and an extensive reservoir of active social support. In the words of one recent summary, "whilst real political decisions were taken within the secret inner spheres of the regime, both much of the initiative and the criteria for action came from key lobbying groups within the professional middle classes," involving "a wide measure of consensus among physicians, lawyers and bureaucrats."[38] One of the most devastating studies of this milieu is Ulrich Herbert's biography of Werner Best (1903–89), the highly educated lawyer who rose through the SS, helped build the Gestapo, assisted Reinhard Heydrich in the SS central administration until 1940, and became Reich Plenipotentiary in Denmark. A master of obfuscation after 1945, Best was entirely formed in the universe of radical-nationalist and antisemitic politics and completely embedded in the project-oriented policy-making apparatus described by Aly, a perfect embodiment of the frightening mixture of intellectual sophistication, racialist philosophy, and technocratic reason so crucial to Nazism's

---

36. See Hans Mommsen, "The Realization of the Unthinkable: The 'Final Solution of the Jewish Question' in the Third Reich," in Mommsen, *From Weimar to Auschwitz* (Princeton, 1991), 252.

37. Aly and Heim, *Vordenker der Vernichtung.*

38. Nicholas Stargardt, "The Holocaust," in Mary Fulbrook, ed., *German History since 1800* (London, 1997), 351. This is a judicious and perceptive summary of the main approaches and research.

appeal among the professions.[39] Goldhagen himself was uninterested in *these* areas of ideology, subsuming his explanation entirely in the eliminationist antisemitism he attributed to the nineteenth century. But his insistence on ideology per se allows it to be brought back into the discussion.

In these ways, the book's beneficial effects occur almost in spite of itself, and the same is true of the wider public reception. For *Hitler's Willing Executioners* tells a section of the general public (in Germany, the United States, to a lesser extent elsewhere) what it wants to hear—that Nazism and the Holocaust were the result of "the Germans" or "German History" in some undifferentiated sense, and that carefully situated explanations proceeding from the immediate dynamics of the Third Reich and other periods are unnecessary and, even worse, morally evasive. After all the patient work of contextualizing the history of the Third Reich and the Holocaust during the past three decades, not for the purposes of diminishing the scale of the catastrophe, but to make it more available for understanding, Goldhagen removed the Holocaust once again from history, making it the consequence of a totally exceptional set of developments, with no traces beyond 1945, and no bases for comparison. In so doing, as I've argued, he also misrepresented the character of current scholarship on the Judeocide and the Third Reich. Such work has illuminated the difficulties of studying the complexities of the Holocaust in ways Goldhagen systematically obscured. Moreover, *Hitler's Willing Executioners* reinstated a deeper argument about the peculiarities of the German past—the so-called *Sonderweg* thesis, which marks the pathology of Germany's historical development by comparison with the West—without ever engaging the contents of that important controversy.[40]

The "Goldhagen Effect"

To understand the nature of this public impact—the "Goldhagen effect," as this volume calls it—we need to shift focus from "history" (scholarly research on the Third Reich) to "memory" (historical representations in

---

39. Ulrich Herbert, *Best: Biographische Studien über Radikalismus, Weltanschauung und Vernunft, 1903–1989* (Bonn, 1996). See also the important work of Michael Thad Allen, "The Banality of Evil Reconsidered: SS Mid-Level Managers of Extermination through Work," *Central European History* 30 (1997): 253–94; and "The Puzzle of Nazi Modernism, Modern Technology, and Ideological Consensus in an SS Factory at Auschwitz," *Technology and Culture* 37 (1996): 527–71. See also Christopher R. Browning, "Bureaucracy and Mass Murder: The German Administrator's Comprehension of the Final Solution," in Browning, *Path to Genocide,* 125–44.

40. For the *Sonderweg* controversy, see David Blackbourn and Geoff Eley, *The Peculiarities of German History: Bourgeois Society and Politics in Nineteenth-Century Germany* (Oxford, 1984).

the wider public domain). For two decades now, public memory-work in Germany has been experiencing a huge and sustained boom. This has taken various forms, from official commemorations and public memorializing in speeches, ceremonies, exhibitions, museums, and monuments, through elaborate and small-scale pedagogies in the schools, mass media, and universities, to campaigning of all kinds, nationally and locally, as well as a forest of commercial, personal, and localized publications. The creation of new historical museums was an issue of public contention throughout the 1980s and 1990s, culminating now in the rebuilding of Berlin, with a public architecture commensurate both with its status as the German Republic's new capital and with its enduring connections to the events of the Third Reich.[41] The popular appeal of first-person testimony likewise sustains an extraordinary flow of memoirs and oral histories, including many stories reexcavated from obscurity, occasionally of dubious reliability.[42] This public discourse has been diffused extremely widely through German popular culture, framed by the television miniseries *Holocaust* (1979) and the reception of *Schindler's List* (1994).[43]

---

41. The debates over public memorializing would require a huge bibliographical essay all their own, a task compounded by the density of localized activity, as well as the rapidly moving profusion of national controversies and debates. The best general accounts are inevitably superseded within a few years. For an earlier stocktaking, see Maier, *Unmasterable Past;* Geoff Eley, "Nazism, Politics, and the Image of the Past: Thoughts on the West German *Historikerstreit, 1986–1987," Past and Present* 121 (November 1988): 171–208; and Peter Baldwin, ed., *Reworking the Past: Hitler, the Holocaust, and the Historians' Debate* (Boston, 1990). For the deeper post-1945 context, see Jeffrey Herf, *Divided Memory: The Nazi Past in the Two Germanies* (Cambridge, Mass., 1997); and especially Alf Lüdtke, "'Coming to Terms with the Past': Illusions of Remembering, Ways of Forgetting Nazism in West Germany," *Journal of Modern History* 65 (1993): 542–72. For some recent reflections, see James E. Young, "Germany's Memorial Question: Memory, Counter-Memory, and the End of the Monument," in Martin Morris, ed., *German Dis/Continuities,* special issue of *South Atlantic Quarterly* 96 (1997): 853–80; Katharina von Ankum, "German Memorial Culture: The Berlin Holocaust Monument Debate," *Response: A Contemporary Jewish Review* 68 (fall 1997/winter 1998). 41–48, and Brian Ladd, *The Ghosts of Berlin: Confronting German History in the Urban Landscape* (Chicago, 1997).

42. For a recent, extraordinary case, see Elena Lappin, "The Man with Two Heads," *Granta* 66 (summer 1999): 7–65. The article concerns the identity of Binjamin Wilkomirski, author of *Fragments: Memories of a Childhood, 1939–1948* (New York, 1996), published originally in Germany (1995), which won the National Jewish Book Award in the autobiography category amidst huge acclaim. In 1998, the book was denounced by a Swiss Jewish author, Daniel Ganzfried, as a fiction. The resulting controversy became resolved in November 1999 by confirmation of Wilkomirski's true origins as a non-Jewish Swiss adoptee, an identity he continued to deny. For an earlier defense of Wilkomirski's claims, see Harvey Peskin, "Holocaust Denial: A Sequel: The case of Binjamin Wilkomirski's *Fragments," The Nation,* 19 April 1999, 34–38.

43. See Yosefa Loshitzky, ed., *Spielberg's Holocaust: Critical Perspectives on "Schindler's List"* (Bloomington, 1997).

However, while public culture continues to demonstrate a voracious demand for literary and visual memorials to the drama and suffering of the Nazi era, since the mid-1980s a conservative sector of German opinion has consistently called for an end to exactly this fascination. Instead of dwelling endlessly on the unedifying parts of the German past by centering school curricula and museum pedagogies on the crimes of the Third Reich, such voices have argued, public historians should turn to other periods (like the Bismarckian Empire between the 1860s and 1914) to build healthier images of Germany's national past. Germans should finally free themselves from their "guilt obsession" about the deeds of the Nazis and lay the ghosts of the Holocaust to rest. Critical intellectuals—left liberals, social democrats, and others further to the Left—then accused these voices of tendentious apologetics in response. The biggest of the resulting controversies, the *Historikerstreit* (Historians' Debate), powerfully influenced public life during 1986–87, including the election campaigning of early 1987.[44] The philosopher and social theorist Jürgen Habermas established himself as the conscience of the republic in this sense, insisting that explicitly acknowledging responsibility for Auschwitz remained the indispensable starting point for democratic political culture after 1945. Moreover, the existence of Auschwitz disqualified German nationalism as an acceptable political stance. In a famous and much cited statement, Habermas argued:

> The only patriotism that will not alienate us from the West is constitutional patriotism. Unfortunately, a commitment to universalist constitutional principles anchored in conviction has only been possible in German national culture since—and because of—Auschwitz. Anyone who wishes to expunge the shame of this fact with facile talk of "guilt obsession," anyone who wants to recall the Germans to a more conventional form of national identity, destroys the only reliable basis of our tie to the West.[45]

Thus the political stakes for historical work on the Nazi era have remained very high. "Coming to terms with the past"—explicitly confronting the Third Reich's place in the longer course of German history—has been a condition of democratic political engagement on the Left since the 1960s. Conversely, suppressing such questions has always implied a right-wing politics in the present. It was the end of the Cold War that

---

44. See Eley, "Nazism, Politics, and the Image of the Past."

45. This is my translation from the original German. See Jürgen Habermas, "Apologetic Tendencies," in Habermas, *The New Conservatism: Cultural Criticism and the Historians' Debate* (Cambridge, Mass., 1989), 227. For Habermas's intervening political commentaries, see Jürgen Habermas, *A Berlin Republic: Writings on Germany* (Lincoln, 1997).

began changing the valency of these arguments. The collapse of the German Democratic Republic (GDR) in 1989 promised greater space for conservative nationalists who wanted to "normalize" German history by freeing its narratives from the destructive teleology of 1933–45, because reunification (1990) seemed to make German nationalism legitimate once again. Among intellectuals—historians, other academics, writers, artists, filmmakers, journalists—intensive debates over national identity and its accountability to the past ensued, with varying resonance and penetration in the public sphere. While the fiftieth anniversary of the end of the Second World War was a major flashpoint, as were the various proposals for monuments and memorials (notably the Berlin Holocaust memorial), controversial interventions also occurred without such immediate occasions.[46] Interestingly, despite the Left's patent demoralization after 1989–90, critical intellectuals largely managed to contain the right-wing challenge, not least because the xenophobic violence against foreigners in the early 1990s seemed to offer shocking evidence of what relaxing the moral-political vigilance would mean.

In fact, the main memorial events of the 1990s—each of which brought widespread activity of academic historians in Germany's national public sphere—compellingly confirmed the public's continuing desire for historical accountability. The extraordinary popular success of *Schindler's List,* the remarkable popularity of Victor Klemperer's diaries (published concurrently with the Goldhagen controversy), and then the massive sales and public adulation of Goldhagen's *Hitler's Willing Executioners* all suggested that Germany's reading, watching, and museum-going publics accepted the importance of continuing to expose the crimes of Nazism.[47] Far from being alienated by this latest reiteration of the "guilt obsession," Goldhagen's massed audiences during his promotional tour positively reveled in the lurid descriptions of the atrocities he argued the Third Reich's ordinary populace endorsed.

In this respect, the so-called Wehrmacht exhibition ("War of Extermination: Crimes of the Wehrmacht, 1941 to 1944"), which first opened in Hamburg in March 1995, has also drawn huge attendances. Sponsored by the non-university Hamburg Institute for Social Research, the exhibition

---

46. See, for instance, Gerd Gemünden, "Nostalgia for the Nation: Intellectuals and National Identity in United Germany," in Mieke Bal, Jonathan Crew, and Leo Spitzer, eds., *Acts of Memory: Cultural Recall in the Present* (Hanover, 1999), 120–33.

47. Klemperer was a professor of literature, whose diaries recorded the everyday experiences of a Jew living under the Third Reich. See Victor Klemperer, *Ich will Zeugnis ablegen bis zum letzten: Tagebücher, 1933–1945,* ed. Walter Nowojski, 2 vols. (Berlin, 1995). The diaries were translated as *I Will Bear Witness: A Diary of the Nazi Years, 1933–1941* (New York, 1999).

marked the intersection between the pioneering research of Aly and others and the wider public sphere.[48] It certainly drew bitter opposition. When Jutta Lumbach, President of the Federal Constitutional Court, opened the Karlsruhe showing of the exhibition (January 1997), she needed special police protection after the threats and defamations she received. But its graphic depiction of the Army's participation in the mass murder of the Jews and other Nazi atrocities in Serbia and the occupied Soviet Union bridged from the scholarly findings of historians to the wider public and broke through the taboo surrounding the innocence of the Army and its ordinary soldiers, perhaps the most obstinate of all the fictions blocking discussion of Germany's responsibility after 1945. During 1995–98, 550,000 visitors saw the exhibition in twenty-seven cities in Germany and Austria, making it "*the* contemporary history exhibition in the Federal Republic: the longest-lasting and the most visited."[49]

In principle, this memory boom is no different from the equivalent syndromes elsewhere, likewise predicated around the working through of complex political legacies, collective identifications, and generational tensions dating from the Second World War. Similar stories can certainly be told of other national historiographies. Growing controversy surrounds

---

48. The exhibition grew from the Hamburg Institute's project "Civilization and Barbarism," which aimed "to investigate the destructiveness of the twentieth century on the eve of the new millennium, and to explain the legacy it has bequeathed as we enter the next century." See Hannes Heer, "The Difficulty of Ending a War: Reactions to the Exhibition 'War of Extermination: Crimes of the Wehrmacht, 1941 to 1944,'" *History Workshop Journal* 46 (autumn 1998): 188; and Hamburg Institute for Social Research, ed., *The German Army and Genocide: Crimes against War Prisoners, Jews, and Other Civilians, 1939–1944* (New York, 1999). Separate but parallel sites of independent research include the series *Beiträge zur nationalsozialistischen Gesundheits- und Sozialpolitik* (whose primary authors include Aly, Heim, Angelika Ebbighaus, and Karl-Heinz Roth) and the journal *1999: Zeitschrift für Sozialgeschichte des 20. und 21. Jahrhunderts* (1986–).

49. Heer, "The Difficulty of Ending a War," 188. The exhibition was scheduled to open in New York City in December 1999, but after controversies in Germany surrounding the identification of a small number of photographs, it was postponed. See Roger Cohen, "New York Opening of Exhibition on Nazi Atrocities Is Delayed," *New York Times,* 5 November 1999; and Michael Z. Wise, "Bitterness Stalks Show on Role of Wehrmacht," *New York Times,* 6 November 1999. Scholarly research had been proceeding around these questions for over two decades, often amidst big controversy, especially surrounding the official history of the Second World War courageously pursued by Wilhelm Deist, Manfred Messerschmidt, and other historians in the Military History Research Office in Freiburg: Wilhelm Deist et al., eds., *Das Deutsche Reich und der Zweite Weltkrieg,* 10 vols. (Stuttgart, 1979–), published in translation by Oxford University Press. See also Omer Bartov's two pioneering books, *The Eastern Front, 1941–45: German Troops and the Barbarisation of Warfare* (London, 1985) and *Hitler's Army: Soldiers, Nazis, and War in the Third Reich* (New York, 1991); and Theo Schulte, *The German Army and Nazi Policies in Occupied Russia* (Oxford, 1989).

the memorializing and public memory of the Holocaust in the post-Zionist moment of Israeli intellectual life, in a highly complex relationship to Israeli public culture going back again to the trial of Eichmann. An extremely interesting analysis might also be conducted on the specifically U.S. scene of such debates, whence much of the nonscholarly impetus for rethinking these questions has clearly come.[50] There are also cognate fields of controversy in other European countries mobilizing the simultaneous concerns of scholars and wider publics around the Second World War, sometimes focusing on the fate of the Jews specifically, in the usual field of questions regarding perpetrators, bystanders, and victims, sometimes more broadly focused on matters of resistance and collaboration. At all events, they involve the longer-term legacies of the Second World War for the public culture in the intervening period. The continuing debates in Italian public life regarding legacies of fascism and antifascism would be one example of this varying transnational effect; coming to terms with the "Vichy Syndrome" in France would be another. In Britain, the reconfiguring of the legacies of the Second World War, in a complex process extending now over two decades, allows similar fields of comparison to be found. And so on.[51]

Ultimately, *this* is the primary context for understanding *Hitler's Willing Executioners,* namely, a public discourse of national remembrance and its relationship to political culture and the allowable forms of national identification. In March 1997, *Blätter für deutsche und Internationale Politik* awarded Goldhagen its Democracy Prize. This was conferred in Bonn before an audience of 2,000, addressed by Jan Philipp Reemtsma (leading left philanthropist and head of the Hamburg Institute for Social Research) and Jürgen Habermas. In his commendation, Habermas quoted the Prize Trustees, who declared that through the "urgency, the forcefulness, and the moral strength of his presentation," Goldhagen had "provided a powerful stimulus to the public conscience of the Federal Republic," sharpening "our sensibility for what constitutes the background and the limit of a

---

50. See Peter Novick, *The Holocaust in American Life* (New York, 1999).

51. Again, detailed bibliographical accounting would exceed the bounds of this essay. For examples, see Tom Segev, *The Seventh Million: The Israelis and the Holocaust* (New York, 1993); Yael Zerubavel, *Recovered Roots: Collective Memory and the Making of Israeli National Tradition* (Chicago, 1995); Laurence J. Silberstein, *The Postzionism Debates: Knowledge and Power in Israeli Culture* (New York, 1999); Tony Kushner, *The Holocaust and the Liberal Imagination: A Social and Cultural History* (Oxford, 1994); Henry Rousso, *The Vichy Syndrome: History and Memory in France since 1944* (Cambridge, Mass., 1991); Nancy Wood, *Vectors of Memory* (Oxford, 1999); and Martin Evans and Ken Lunn, eds., *War and Memory in the Twentieth Century* (Oxford, 1997).

German 'normalization.' "[52] In this way, the impact of Goldhagen's book was co-opted into the political pedagogy Habermas, Reemtsma, and other left intellectuals had been practicing in their various ways since earlier in the 1980s. This aimed at heading off the initiatives for building a conventional German patriotism, by insisting on the indissoluble ethical unity between Germany's democratic vitality and continuing to take responsibility for the crimes of the Third Reich. Accordingly, public debate came full circle to the earlier controversies of the Bitburg fiasco (1985) and the *Historikerstreit* (1986–87), which properly began this running battle of ideas.

In making his forthright statement of support, Habermas explicitly celebrated the *effects* of the book, simultaneously distancing himself from the detailed debates about its substance, which he urged could be left to the professional historians. In affirming the importance of Goldhagen's general thesis, he also disavowed much of its monocausal simplicity and upheld the scholarly achievements of its critics (naming Mommsen, Jäckel, Herbert, Pohl, and Sandkühler). Reemtsma also took this line, discussing the success of the book divorced from its detailed scholarly contribution. The point again was its pedagogy. Reemtsma argued that by choosing to focus on the actions of perpetrators, in all their horrendous inhumanity, in which cruelty and murder became the freely chosen behavior of morally responsible individuals, Goldhagen allowed the vital importance of the ethical grounding of democratic values to be reaffirmed.[53] The other big events of popular memorializing in the 1990s also allowed the political ethics of individual responsibility to be faced. *Schindler's List,* the Klemperer diaries, the Wehrmacht exhibition—all these come to mind.

This was the "Goldhagen effect." The book's reception and the remarkable enthusiasm around its publication and the author's public appearances weren't "about" the substantive historical and historiographical arguments at all. They were the latest installment in a long-running public struggle to ground the ethics of democratic citizenship in a country where fascism seemed to have successfully claimed—and disqualified—the national past as a source of inspiration. Goldhagen's book regalvanized public attentions for a self-critical perspective precisely as the countervail-

---

52. Jürgen Habermas, "Goldhagen and the Public Use of History: Why a Democracy Prize for Daniel Goldhagen?" in Shandley, *Unwilling Germans?* 263.

53. Jan Philipp Reemtsma, "Turning Away from Denial: *Hitler's Willing Executioners* as a Counterforce to 'Historical Explanation,'" in Shandley, *Unwilling Germans?* 255–62. For the full proceedings of the award ceremony, see Karl D. Bredthauer and Arthur Heinrich, eds., *Aus der Geschichte lernen—How to Learn from History: Verleihung des "Blätter"-Demokratiepreises 1997 an Daniel Jonah Goldhagen: Eine Dokumentation* (Bonn, 1997).

ing pressures mounted for bringing Germany's struggle with its Nazi past to some final and reassuring closure. It struck a chord. In this sense, *Hitler's Willing Executioners* will remain an event in the history of Germany's late-twentieth-century public culture long after the noise surrounding its scholarly credentials has faded away.[54]

---

54. For some areas of continuing controversy, see Jürgen Elsässer and Andrei S. Markovits, eds., *"Die Fratze der eigenen Geschichte": Von der Goldhagen-Debatte zur Jugoslawien-Krieg* (Berlin, 1997); and Matthias Küntzel and Klaus Thörner et al., eds., *Goldhagen und die deutsche Linke, Oder: Die Gegenwart des Holocausts* (Berlin, 1997).

Reception and Perception: Goldhagen's Holocaust and the World

Omer Bartov

Whether it generated enthusiasm or wrath, *Schadenfreude* or indifference, the "Goldhagen phenomenon" provides us with an opportunity to investigate the impact of Nazism and the Holocaust on the redefinition of national and group identities at the end of the millennium. My goal in this chapter is thus not to reevaluate the merits and limitations of Daniel Jonah Goldhagen's *Hitler's Willing Executioners: Ordinary Germans and the Holocaust,* but rather to view its reception as a kind of measuring rod for the changing and differing perceptions of the Holocaust in several national contexts.[1] While a number of previous commercially successful representations of Jewish persecution under the Third Reich have similarly both reflected and molded public attitudes, the crucial distinction here is that Goldhagen's book was the first scholarly study of the Shoah to have gained the status of an international bestseller.[2] Hence, this chapter will be also concerned with the gap (more obvious in some countries than in others) between the book's critical reception by the scholarly community and its unprecedented popularity among otherwise very different reading publics. These different reactions to the book arguably reveal a

---

1. Daniel Jonah Goldhagen, *Hitler's Willing Executioners: Ordinary Germans and the Holocaust* (New York, 1996). For my own criticism of the book, see Omer Bartov, "Ordinary Monsters," *New Republic,* 29 April 1996, 32–38. For a collection of reviews of the book, see Julius H. Schoeps, ed., *Ein Volk von Mördern? Die Dokumentation zur Goldhagen-Kontroverse um die Rolle der Deutschen im Holocaust* (Hamburg, 1996). The most recent relevant publication is Norman G. Finkelstein and Ruth Bettina Birn, *A Nation on Trial: The Goldhagen Thesis and Historical Truth* (New York, 1998).

2. For views on the most recent of such popular representations of the Holocaust, and on its reception in the United States, Germany, Israel, and France, see Yosefa Loshitzky, ed., *Spielberg's Holocaust: Critical Perspectives on "Schindler's List"* (Bloomington, 1997).

lack of communication between self-enclosed academic discourses and popular opinions on an issue that remains central to individual, group, and national self-definition throughout much of the Western Hemisphere.

In the following pages I thus discuss American, German, French, and Israeli reactions to Goldhagen's book. What interests me in each case is the extent to which the controversy over the book was integrated into, changed the terms of, or remained peripheral to other major public, intellectual and academic debates. Depending on the specific national context, such debates concern the relationship between history and memory, tensions between group and national identity, distinctions between complicity and resistance, generational conflicts, and, not least, the links between past and present atrocity. Clearly, this controversy touches on a question that should concern all scholars: To what extent can we mold public opinion without compromising our professional principles and reputation? And conversely, can we remain entirely aloof from the influence of our environment, its politics, prejudices, and seductions? In order to illustrate the complexities of this issue, I demonstrate, by way of conclusion, that Stanley Milgram's behaviorist theories, frequently cited during the Goldhagen debate as an example of an ideologically neutral explanation of human conduct in extreme situations, were in fact strongly influenced by his own class, gender, and ethnic prejudices.[3] This only reinforces my conviction that even the most careful and balanced scholarly interpretations of human conduct are invariably implicated in the conventions of their time.

Holocaust Identity: Multiculturalism and the Politics of Victimhood

Even before it became available in bookstores, Goldhagen's book began drawing massive media attention in the United States, most of it ranging from positive to wildly enthusiastic.[4] Indeed, one is hard put to think of

---

3. Stanley Milgram, *Obedience to Authority: An Experimental View* (New York, 1974).

4. Among early reviews of the book, see, for example, *Kirkus Reviews,* 1 February 1996; *Publishers Weekly* 243, no. 6 (5 February 1996): 72; Jacob Heilbrunn, "Jolting, Flawed Account of Germany and the Holocaust," *Washington Times,* 17 March 1996; Paul Johnson, "An Epidemic of Hatred," *Washington Post,* 24 March 1996; Louis Begley, "Just Plain Volk," *Los Angeles Times,* 24 March 1996, 4; Jack Schwartz, "The Face of Evil," *Newsday,* 24 March 1996; David Pryce-Jones, "The University of Evil," *Wall Street Journal,* 26 March 1996; Richard Bernstein, "Was Slaughter of the Jews Embraced by Germans?" *New York Times,* 27 March 1996; Ellen K. Coughlin, "'Willing Executioners,'" *Chronicle of Higher Education,* 29 March 1996; Ken Swart, "Accomplices to Genocide," *Fort Lauderdale Sun-Sentinel,* 31 March 1996; Dinitia Smith, "Challenging a View of the Holocaust," *New York Times,* 1 April 1996, C11, C18; John Elson, "What Did They Know?" *Time,* 1 April

another scholarly book, even of smaller dimensions and less heavily burdened by academic jargon, that has met with such a barrage of reviews, commentary, and interviews in the print and electronic media. The unprecedented excitement surrounding the book has been attributed by some to a cleverly managed public relations campaign by the publisher, combined with the media savvy of the author and, not least, Goldhagen's assertion that he had come up with a definitive answer to one of the century's most troubling questions, namely, why did the Holocaust happen? But while these explanations cannot be wholly dismissed, I would argue that from the perspective of the present they do not sufficiently clarify the larger context of this phenomenon.

The most striking aspect of the book's reception in the United States was the difference between the media's all-out enthusiasm and the far more cautious and often highly critical reaction of the scholarly community.[5] In the meantime, of course, thanks to the media's short attention

---

1996, 73; Richard Cohen, "In a Day's Work," *Washington Post,* 2 April 1996; A. M. Rosenthal, "Some Ordinary Germans," *New York Times,* 2 April 1996; Richard Grenier, "Most Evil of Them All?" *Washington Times,* 5 April 1996; Jonathan R. Cohen, "The Holocaust Grew from Germany's National Character," *Baltimore Sun,* 7 April 1996; Kenneth F. Ledford, "Hitler's Willing Workers," *Plain Dealer,* 7 April 1996; Michael Kenney, "The Germans' New Accuser," *Boston Globe,* 9 April 1996; Carol Rosenberg, "New Study Sets Off Raging Debate over Holocaust," *Times-Picayune,* 11 April 1996; George F. Will, "Ordinary Germans?" *Washington Post,* 14 April 1996, C7; Francis L. Loewenheim, "Holocaust Study Fails to Persuade," *Houston Chronicle,* 14 April 1996; Martin Merzer, "Author Goes Step Beyond on Holocaust," *Miami Herald,* 14 April 1996; Volker R. Berghahn, "The Road to Extermination," *New York Times Book Review,* 14 April 1996; Gordon A. Craig, "How Hell Worked," *New York Review of Books,* 18 April 1996, 4–8; Clive James, "Blaming the Germans," *New Yorker,* 22 April 1996, 44–50; R. C. Longworth, "Germans' Role in the Holocaust Unique?" *Chicago Tribune,* 21 April 1996, C4; Robert Andersen, "Extraordinary Evil," *Chicago Tribune,* 21 April 1996, C3; Marc Fisher, "The German Question," *Washington Post,* 25 April 1996, C1–C2; John Nichols, "Goldhagen's Holocaust History: Blunt, Unblinking," *Madison (Wis.) Capital Times,* 26 April 1996, 15A; Michael Bezdek, "Ordinary Germans Indicted for the Holocaust," *Los Angeles Times,* 28 April 1996, A10; Jerry Adler, "History Lesson," *Newsweek,* 29 April 1996; Stanley Hoffmann, "Recent Books on International Relations," *Foreign Affairs,* May/June 1996, 144; and Robert S. Wistrich, "Helping Hitler," *Commentary* 102/1 (July 1996): 27–31. To be sure, not all the reviews cited here were positive, and some were quite critical. But the mass attention of the media, and the fact that reactions around the world were readily available through the Internet, made it appear that this was a very important phenomenon. Some of the main American and British reviews are available (in German translation) in part 1 of Schoeps, *Ein Volk von Mördern?*

5. For some later reactions to the book, see, for example, Christopher R. Browning, "Human Nature, Culture, and the Holocaust," *Chronicle of Higher Education,* 18 October 1996, A 72; Browning, "Daniel Goldhagen's Willing Executioners," *History and Memory* 8 (spring/summer 1996): 88–108; Lothar Nettenacker, review in *German Historical Institute Bulletin* 18 (November 1996): 70–74; Fritz Stern, "The Goldhagen Controversy: One Nation, One People, One Theory?" *Foreign Affairs* 75, no. 6 (1996): 128–38; Steven E. Aschheim,

span, the book has been relegated to the status of "history," on those rare occasions that it is still referred to at all. As for specialists, Goldhagen's study has become a kind of "unmentionable presence," alluded to in numerous academic lectures, conference papers, articles, and book reviews, but rarely discussed in detail. While many American scholars are now inclined to see it as an example of "bad scholarship," not a few would concede that it has some inherent merits, and would even more readily accept that it has had an impact (whether positive or negative) both on future scholarship and on the lay public.[6]

Thus we find that from a condition of extreme divergence between media enthusiasm and scholarly rejection, Goldhagen's book is now

---

"Archetypes and the German-Jewish Dialogue: Reflections Occasioned by the Goldhagen Affair," *German History* 15 (1997): 240–50; Adam Shatz, "Browning's Version," *Lingua Franca,* February 1997, 48–57; Robert Gellately, "Review of Daniel J. Goldhagen, *Hitler's Willing Executioners,*" *Journal of Modern History* 69 (1997): 187–91; David North, *Anti-semitism, Fascism, and the Holocaust: A Critical Review of Daniel Goldhagen's "Hitler's Willing Executioners"* (Oak Park, Mich., 1997); F. H. Littell, ed., *Hyping the Holocaust: Scholars Answer Goldhagen* (East Rockaway, N.Y., 1997); Lawrence Douglas, "The Goldhagen Riddle," *Commonweal,* 9 May 1997, 18–21; and István Deák, "Holocaust Views: The Goldhagen Controversy in Retrospect," *Central European History* 30 (1997): 295–307. For Goldhagen's response to his American critics, see his "Motives, Causes, and Alibis," *The New Republic,* 23 December 1996, 37–45. For a later exchange among Goldhagen, Browning, and myself, see *New Republic,* 10 February 1997, 4–5.

6. For some examples of both negative and positive reactions in the British media, most of which were readily available to Americans via the Internet, as well as in some scholarly journals, see Michael Pye, "Germany Accused," *Scotsman,* 24 February 1996, 17; Robert Harris, "The Awful Truth," *Sunday Times,* 24 March 1996; Gitta Sereny, "The Complexities of Complicity," *Times,* 28 March 1996; Hella Pick, "Your Neighbour the Murderer," *Guardian,* 29 March 1996, T15; Elie Wiesel, "Little Hitlers," *Observer,* 31 March 1996, 14; Jan Morris, "The Hate of the Common People," *Independent,* 30 March 1996, 10; Robert Mclaughlan, "Killers of the Holocaust Who Refused to Say 'No,'" *Herald* (Glasgow), 1 April 1996, 13; "If All Were Guilty, None Were," *Economist,* 27 April 1996, 91–92; Jeremy D. Noakes, "No Ordinary People," *Times Literary Supplement,* 7 June 1996; Mark Mazower, "Fighting Demonization with Demonization," *Patterns of Prejudice* 30, no. 2 (1996): 73–75; Peter Pulzer, "Psychopaths and Conformists, Adventurers and Moral Cowards," *London Review of Books,* 23 January 1997, 20–21; Ruth Bettina Birn, "The Whodunit and the Holocaust," *Sunday Times,* 23 March 1997, and the longer version, Birn (in collaboration with Volker Riess), "Revising the Holocaust," *Historical Journal* 40, no. 1 (1997): 195–215, and the author's response, in an American journal, to this scathing analysis, Daniel Jonah Goldhagen, "The Fictions of Ruth Bettina Birn," *German Politics and Society* 15 (fall 1997): 119–65; Birn's revised version appears in Finkelstein and Birn, *A Nation on Trial,* 101–48. For a rather disturbing piece of anti-American antisemitic diatribe in what is considered a respectable paper, see Taki, "Book Burning Lights Up in the Big Bagel," *Sunday Times,* 7 April 1996; and, in the same context, also Kevin Myers, "An Irishman's Diary," *Irish Times,* 13 April 1996, 11. Both reviews protest the decision by St. Martin's Press not to publish David Irving's biography of Joseph Goebbels, allegedly due to Jewish American media pressures, and compare this with Goldhagen's success in the same media outlets.

treated with relative media indifference and somewhat greater scholarly interest or even partial recognition of its potentially positive achievements. What, then, can this process tell us about the book's role in American perceptions of the Holocaust, and how did preconceived notions about the genocide of the Jews influence the reception of the book? What have we learned about the gap between scholarly and public opinion? Finally, what is the relationship between the book's reception and the American politics of identity, discourse on victimhood, and quest for identifiable enemies?

There is little doubt that in the past couple of decades the Holocaust has moved from a marginal place in American political conversation and scholarly activity to a highly prominent position.[7] While no single cause can account for this "Americanization" of the Holocaust, it can only be understood as part of the emergence of multiculturalism, namely, the shift from the politics of the "melting pot" to a growing emphasis on the distinct cultural identities and historical roots of the many immigrant communities that make up the United States. And while each ethnic group will assert its own unique history, what has surfaced as a particularly potent symbol of identity has been a consciousness of (past, and often also present) victimhood among those groups that still feel threatened or are still burdened by the memories of past suffering, either in the United States or in their countries of origin (or both).[8] To be sure, this focus on victimhood is often also linked to a sense of pride and self-esteem, related to the ability of such groups to survive persecution and maintain or even further

7. See on this, for instance, Michael Marrus, "The Use and Misuse of the Holocaust," in Peter Hayes, ed., *Lessons and Legacies: The Meaning of the Holocaust in a Changing World* (Evanston, Ill., 1991), 106–19; and Peter Novick, "Holocaust Memory in America," in James E. Young, ed., *The Art of Memory: Holocaust Memorials in History* (Munich, 1994), 159–65. For American Jewry's reactions to the Holocaust during the event, see Henry L. Feingold, *Bearing Witness: How America and Its Jews Responded to the Holocaust* (Syracuse, N.Y., 1995); and Gulie Ne'eman Arad, "American Jewish Leadership and the Nazi Menace" (Ph.D. dissertation, Tel Aviv University, 1994). On American exposure to the Holocaust in the media, see Jeffrey Shandler, *While America Watches: Televising the Holocaust* (New York, 1999).

8. I refuse to use the term *race,* often employed in this context, since I believe that it attempts to categorize a group by means of a biological definition that cannot be proved and that has served in the past, and continues to serve today, the cause of violence, persecution, and genocide. I have always thought that the single greatest sin of affirmative action in the United States was its attempt to fight racism by applying categories of race. Just as one cannot fight antisemitism by calling for equality between "racially" distinct "Aryans" and "Semites," so too American anti-Black racism cannot be defeated by speaking of African Americans as a distinct race (and after all, the term "race relations" in the United States refers primarily to relations between "Caucasians" and Blacks). Racism can be contained only by first of all denying the racial differences between ethnic groups in the human species. For an interesting analysis of definitions of race, see Uli Linke, *German Bodies: Race and Representation after Hitler* (New York, 1999).

develop their distinct culture. But precisely for this reason, even the assertion of accomplishment derives much of its force from the narrative (historical or mythical) and memory (personal or collective) of prior victimization and persecution.

The rise of "Holocaust consciousness" (a rather unsavory term) must thus be understood in the context of American identity politics, even while it is obviously also related to the impact, most especially, of the Eichmann trial and the 1967 Six Day War, both on American Jewry and, albeit to a lesser extent, on the rest of the American public. Conversely, once the Holocaust moved to the fore of Jewish consciousness, it gradually acquired the status of the ultimate paradigm of victimhood (and evil) in the United States and subsequently in much of Europe. Consequently, assertions of identity by other minorities are often accompanied by claims of having experienced a Holocaust of their own. There is something grotesque about this process, of course, since the Holocaust was all about annihilating the physical identity and erasing the memory of a whole people. Yet having come to be seen as a historical episode that galvanized Jewish identity through a consciousness of common victimhood, it (or its near equivalents) became a much sought-after commodity for other minorities seeking to establish and fortify their own common fate and unique characteristics. Moreover, the Holocaust has great appeal for the media, since it contains precisely those "powerful" visual and emotional components that draw audiences and increase ratings, and because it can easily be simplified into a tale of good and evil, innocence and monstrosity, which culminated in a triumphal happy end whereby the (American) values of liberty and democracy defeated the forces of (German) darkness.[9]

This is where the very different trends in scholarship got in the way. Just as the lay public began to think of the Holocaust as one of the core events of the century, caused primarily by German antisemitism, increasing numbers of scholars shifted the emphasis to other factors in German and European society. In the United States, this was most clearly demonstrated by the growing attention paid to Raul Hilberg's work of 1961, reissued in a much expanded and revised edition in 1985, as well as to studies by such scholars as Karl Schleunes and Christopher Browning.[10] Unlike the case of Germany, this *did not* mean that antisemitism was ever totally dismissed as an important motivating factor, as illustrated, for instance,

---

9. See, in more detail, Omer Bartov, *Murder in Our Midst: The Holocaust, Industrial Killing, and Representation* (New York, 1996), esp. chapters 3, 5, and 8.

10. Raul Hilberg, *The Destruction of the European Jews,* rev. ed., 3 vols. (New York, 1985); Karl A. Schleunes, *The Twisted Road to Auschwitz: Nazi Policy toward German Jews, 1933–1939,* 2d ed. (Urbana, 1990); Christopher R. Browning, *Fateful Months: Essays on the Emergence of the Final Solution* (New York, 1985); Browning, *The Path to Genocide: Essays on Launching the Final Solution* (Cambridge, 1992).

by the respect in which the work of Saul Friedländer has always been held.[11] It did mean, however, that monocausal interpretations of the kind favored by the general public and the media were no longer considered sufficient by the majority of scholars. Moreover, even the growing preoccupation of scholars with questions of identity and the impact of cultural studies by no means led to a revival of teleological historical interpretations of the kind popularized by A. J. P. Taylor in the immediate aftermath of World War II.[12] Earlier studies on the precursors of Nazism by American scholars of European origin such as Fritz Stern, George Mosse, and Walter Laqueur were complemented by works that investigated both the complex roots of German antisemitism and the numerous attempts to create a German-Jewish symbiosis throughout the latter part of the nineteenth century and the early decades of the twentieth century.[13]

Consequently, while the historical literature on Nazism and the Holocaust rapidly expanded, its interpretation of that period increasingly differed from the popular—in part media-generated—consensus on the genocide of the Jews. The triumphal note that accompanied many early works was replaced by an awareness of the troubling similarities between Germany and other modern societies. Although a few scholars had pointed in that direction many decades before,[14] it was only in the 1980s

11. See, for instance, Saul Friedländer, *Nazi Germany and the Jews,* vol. 1, *The Years of Persecution, 1933–1939* (New York, 1997); Friedländer, *Memory, History, and the Extermination of the Jews of Europe* (Bloomington, 1993); Friedländer, "From Antisemitism to Extermination: A Historiographical Study of Nazi Policies toward the Jews and an Essay in Interpretation," in François Furet, ed., *Unanswered Question: Nazi Germany and the Genocide of the Jews* (New York, 1989), 3–31; and Friedländer, introduction to Gerald Fleming, *Hitler and the Final Solution* (Berkeley, 1984), vii–xxxvi.

12. A. J. P. Taylor, *The Course of German History* (London, 1945). See more on this in Ian Kershaw, *The Nazi Dictatorship: Problems and Perspectives of Interpretation,* 3d ed. (London, 1993), 1–16, esp. 6–7.

13. Fritz Stern, *The Politics of Cultural Despair: A Study in the Rise of the Germanic Ideology* (Berkeley, 1961); George L. Mosse, *The Crisis of German Ideology: Intellectual Origins of the Third Reich* (New York, 1964); Walter Laqueur, *Young Germany: A History of the German Youth Movement,* 2d ed. (New Brunswick, 1984; originally published in 1962). For some recent works, see, for example, John Weiss, *The Ideology of Death: Why the Holocaust Happened in Germany* (Chicago, 1996); Jehuda Reinharz and Walter Schatzberg, eds., *The Jewish Response to German Culture: From the Enlightenment to the Second World War* (Hanover, 1985); Steven E. Aschheim, *Culture and Catastrophe: German and Jewish Confrontations with National Socialism and Other Crises* (New York, 1996); Anson Rabinbach, *In the Shadow of Catastrophe: German Intellectuals between Apocalypse and Enlightenment* (Berkeley, 1997); and Marion A. Kaplan, *Between Dignity and Despair: Jewish Life in Nazi Germany* (New York, 1998).

14. See, for example, Franz Neumann, *Behemoth: The Structure and Practice of National Socialism* (London, 1942); and Ernst Fraenkel, *The Dual State* (New York, 1941). For other titles, see Abbot Gleason, *Totalitarianism: The Inner History of the Cold War* (New York, 1995), 227 n. 53. See also Hannah Arendt, *The Origins of Totalitarianism* (New York, 1951); and Jacob L. Talmon, *The Origins of Totalitarian Democracy* (London, 1952).

that the role of the bureaucracy, the professions (especially physicians and lawyers), and, more generally, the European nation-state's crisis of modernity took center stage in the scholarly debate.[15] The progressively complex, at times rather jargon-ridden scholarly literature appeared all the more inaccessible to the person "on the street." If the politics of identity demanded clearly etched victims and perpetrators, academic discourse seemed to prefer moral relativism, radical skepticism, and convoluted, self-centered argumentation.[16]

It was at this point that Goldhagen's book exploded on the scene. Here was a scholarly text that proposed finally to clear the air of all academic obfuscation and ambivalence and provide a clear and definitive answer to a question that had, over the previous couple of decades, become of major concern to large sectors of the public, had moved to the fore of the political debate, and was consequently also of great commercial interest to the media. Goldhagen did not "merely" propose to tell the public why the Holocaust had happened and who was guilty of it; he also led a frontal attack against all those scholars who had apparently become wholly incapable of seeing what the general public had intuitively known all along, that it was "the Germans" who had done it, that they had always wanted to do it, that they did it because they hated Jews, and that once called upon to do it, they did it with great enthusiasm and much pleasure. This kind of argumentation played both on the anti-German sentiments of large sectors in the American public and on the growing frustration with academic discourse. It also came along with an important safety valve, since it not only steadfastly ignored all other antisemitic traditions, but also insisted on the absence of this sentiment in postwar Germany, America's loyal ally.

Presented by a young scholar endowed with the credentials of a Harvard degree and the moral authority of being the son of a survivor, Goldhagen's thesis had the strength of being so obvious that one just had to wonder how nobody had thought of it before. Indeed, here was an answer that had all the qualities of an Agatha Christie murder mystery—the smoking gun was right there for all to see, yet precisely because it was so

---

15. See, for example, Michael Kater, *Doctors under Hitler* (Chapel Hill, 1989); Ingo Müller, *Hitler's Justice: The Courts of the Third Reich,* trans. Deborah Lucas Schneider (Cambridge, Mass., 1991); Jeffrey Herf, *Reactionary Modernism: Technology, Culture, and Politics in Weimar and the Third Reich* (Cambridge, 1984); Detlev J. K. Peukert, *The Weimar Republic: The Crisis of Classical Modernity,* trans. Richard Devenson (New York, 1992); and Zygmunt Bauman, *Modernity and the Holocaust* (Ithaca, N.Y., 1989).

16. For an attempt to apply, among other things, literary theory and psychological models to interpretations of the Holocaust, see Saul Friedländer, ed., *Probing the Limits of Representation: Nazism and the "Final Solution"* (Cambridge, Mass., 1992), especially the essays by Hayden White and Dominick LaCapra.

obviously placed, everyone had missed it. (For the more literary-minded, this book's exercise in unveiling the obvious might be reminiscent of Edgar Allan Poe's *The Purloined Letter,* which Jacques Lacan and Jacques Derrida have made into a major trope in psychoanalysis and literary criticism.)[17] Criticism by seasoned scholars of the young rebel's thesis only enhanced his reputation in the public domain, confirming his status as a lone fighter against an established and self-satisfied academic elite. Goldhagen's appearances in the media, his constant repetition of the "simple truth" that any layperson could grasp, were far more convincing than the seemingly convoluted assertions and qualifications made by his "rivals." Conversely, his own jargon-ridden text, the hundreds of footnotes, the sheer size of the book, all seemed to prove that this was indeed a most serious scholarly undertaking.

Media hypes have a notoriously short life expectancy. The long-term consequences of the American debate are more difficult to predict. To some extent, the situation was confused by the fact that while Goldhagen directed his initial attacks against American scholars, they were much more to the point regarding the German historiography of the Holocaust. As noted above, in the United States the issue of antisemitism never entirely disappeared from the scholarly debate as one of the important factors leading to the Nazi genocide of the Jews. Moreover, the very size and diversity of American academe has allowed for the existence of widely differing opinions and has hindered the hegemony—at least for more than a brief period—of any convention of interpretation or the dominance of any group of scholarly gurus. Nevertheless, it would appear that even in the United States Goldhagen contributed to an increased preoccupation with antisemitism and Jewish-German relations. To be sure, Goldhagen's book itself was the product of a certain *Zeitgeist,* but it doubtlessly further legitimized this renewed interest. Initial worries that the reorientation of scholarship toward a greater emphasis on ideological motivation and traditional prejudice, for which some historians, including myself, had been calling since the mid-1980s, would be undermined by Goldhagen's sweeping generalizations and inflated rhetoric appear to have been greatly exaggerated.[18]

---

17. See *The Great Tales and Poems of Edgar Allan Poe* (New York, 1951); Jacques Lacan, *Écrits* (Paris, 1966), which includes his *Seminar on "The Purloined Letter,"* partially translated in *Yale French Studies* 48, *French Freud* (1973); Jacques Derrida, "Le Facteur de la Vérité," *Poétique* 21 (1975), and *Yale French Studies* 52, *Graphesis* (1975). See also Barbara Johnson, "The Frame of Reference: Poe, Lacan, Derrida," in Shoshana Felman, ed., *Literature and Psychoanalysis: The Question of Reading: Otherwise* (Baltimore, 1982), 457–505.

18. See, for example, Omer Bartov, "The Barbarisation of Warfare: German Officers and Men on the Eastern Front, 1941–1945," *Jahrbuch des Instituts für Deutsche Geschichte* 13

Since public debates tend to present polarized views, the argument over the book was constructed as a confrontation between Goldhagen's insistence on the primacy of German antisemitism and Christopher Browning's emphasis on the dynamics of peer pressure.[19] In retrospect, however, we can say that neither of these explanatory models can be fully accepted at the cost of entirely dismissing the other. Rather, only a more nuanced analysis of the social-cultural environment, and of the relationship between ideological and circumstantial factors, can bring us closer to an understanding of the perpetrators' motivation and conduct. As a recently published study of another police battalion has convincingly demonstrated, for instance, the members of this unit were neither "ordinary men" nor "ordinary Germans," thanks to a selection and indoctrination process that set them apart from the German population as a whole.[20] In this case, at least, it appears that one needs to take into account the Third Reich's educational and political climate, the specific ideological training of the men in question, and the brutalizing effects of the fighting in the East, in order to gain a full picture of how these policemen were transformed into murderers.

To sum up, while Goldhagen's book both reflected and enhanced the American public's interest in, if not fascination with, the Holocaust, its long-term impact on the scholarship of the period has not been particularly significant. As the smoke of the dispute clears, we find the camps more or less where they had been before. Goldhagen increasingly speaks about his book to public audiences, mostly nonacademic Jewish groups, who are glad to hear him confirm what they had always believed; meanwhile, scholars continue to pursue the central questions raised by the Holocaust: the balance between ideology and circumstances, age-old prejudices and the impact of mass politics and modern science, state-organized genocide and individual complicity, resistance and collaboration, historical uniqueness and comparability. In the public sphere, by focusing on pre-1945 German antisemitism, the Goldhagen debate has unfortunately obscured those aspects of Nazi genocidal policies that should be of concern to all citizens of modern, bureaucratic, technological states. This may

---

(1984): 305–39; Bartov, *The Eastern Front, 1941–45: German Troops and the Barbarisation of Warfare* (London, 1985); Bartov, "Indoctrination and Motivation in the Wehrmacht: The Importance of the Unquantifiable," *Journal of Strategic Studies* 9 (March 1986): 16–34; Bartov, "Daily Life and Motivation in War: The Wehrmacht in the Soviet Union," *Journal of Strategic Studies* 12 (June 1989): 200–214.

19. Christopher R. Browning, *Ordinary Men: Reserve Police Battalion 101 and the Final Solution in Poland* (New York, 1992).

20. Edward B. Westermann, "'Ordinary Men' or 'Ideological Soldiers'? Police Battalion 310 in Russia, 1942," *German Studies Review* 21 (February 1998): 41–68.

be heartening to some and disturbing to others. But the argument that after the fall of Nazism the Germans became "just like us," and that therefore they are as unlikely to perpetrate genocide again as "we" are, can produce an excessive sense of complacency not merely about postwar Germany but about the rest of "us." The danger is that instead of perceiving the Holocaust as an event that should warn us about the potentials of our civilization, we would relegate it to a no longer relevant past. This may be one of the more comforting conclusions of Goldhagen's book and one reason for its commercial success, but it unfortunately does not reflect the reality of our world, whose last fifty years have witnessed the perpetuation of genocide and atrocity on a scale that belies the erroneous impression that following the Holocaust the worst is behind us.

Liberating Atrocities: Policemen, Soldiers, and Ordinary Germans

Even before the publication of the German translation, Goldhagen's book was met with a tremendous wave of media interest in Germany. Unlike reactions in the United States, however, initial German reactions tended to be either dismissive or hostile.[21] It should be noted that the German

---

21. For some American reports of early German reactions, see, for example, Rick Atkinson, "In Germany, a Collective 'Howl of Protest,'" *Washington Post,* 25 April 1996, C2; Alan Cowel, "Germans, Jews and Blame: New Book, New Pain," *New York Times,* 25 April 1996, A4; Jerry Adler with Stefan Theil in Berlin, Theresa Waldrop in Bonn, David Gordon in New York, and Daniel Pedersen in London, "Why Did They Do It? Angry Reaction to a New Book Asserting That When It Came to Jews, All Germans Were Fanatics," *Newsweek,* 29 April 1996, 42; Terrence Petty, "Germans Denounce Holocaust Theory," *Los Angeles Times,* 28 April 1996, A10; and Barbara Demick/Knight-Ridder News Service, "Germans Enraged over Book by American That Points Them Out as Willing Tools of Hitler," *San Jose Mercury News,* 30 April 1996, 11A. For early reactions in the German press, see, for example, Helmut Raether, "U.S. Scholar Says Germans Were 'Hitler's Willing Executioners,'" *Deutsche Presse-Agentur,* 3 April 1996; Mariam Niroumand, "Little Historians," *Die Tageszeitung* 13/14 (April 1996); Tom Henegahn, "German Critics Slam New U.S. Book on Holocaust," *Reuter,* 15 April 1996; Rudolf Augstein, "Der Soziologe als Scharfrichter," *Der Spiegel* 16 (15 April 1996): 29–30 (Augstein who, interestingly, speaks of "der einschlägige israelische [!] Fachhistoriker Raul Hilberg," responds to his own question—what can we learn from the book?—by asserting that "Das Ergebnis ist mager, man kann auch sagen, es ist gleich Null," and comments that "Es wäre aber irrig, die amerikanische Debatte einzig [!] den meist jüdischen Kolumnisten, Nichthistorikern also, zuzuschreiben"); Werner Birkenmaier, "Ein ganzes Volk auf der Anklagebank?" *Stuttgarter Zeitung,* 17 April 1996, 9; Peter De Thier, "Deutsche als Hitlers willige Henker? Experten zerpflücken das Buch eines US-Historikers über den Holocaust," *Berliner Zeitung,* 23 April 1996; Gertrud Koch, "Eine Welt aus Willen und Vorstellung," *Frankfurter Rundschau,* 30 April/1 May 1996; Fritjof Meyer, "Ein Volk von Dämonen?" "'Ich bin sehr stolz': Henryk M. Broder über Goldhagen, Vater und Sohn," "'Eine Art Paranoia': Wie die alliierten die deutsche Kollektivschuld

"middlebrow" and "highbrow" print and electronic media provide a much larger forum for scholarly opinion than their American equivalents. Hence we cannot speak of a clear-cut distinction between media and scholarly reactions in the German case. Indeed, some early scholarly views about the book could be encapsulated in the statement of one prominent historian, Eberhard Jäckel, who stated that Goldhagen's study was "simply a bad book."[22] Other contributions, however, tended to be far more cautious, reflecting, among other things, disagreements within the German scholarly community about the place of the Third Reich in the larger context of German history, and regarding the centrality of the Holocaust for the history of Nazism.[23]

Once the translation of the book was published in Germany, and especially following Goldhagen's lecture tour there, described by one commentator as a "triumphal campaign," media and scholarly opinion underwent a remarkable transformation, drawing far closer to the lay German public's unexpectedly enthusiastic reception of both the book and

---

begründeten," all in *Der Spiegel* 21 (20 May 1996): 48–77 (includes also an assessment of the American reaction by the magazine's reporters in the United States; the magazine's cover carries the title "Neuer Streit um Kollektivschuld: Die Deutschen: Hitlers willige Mordgesellen?" The editor's introduction to this issue [p. 3] is dedicated to the book. It includes the following interesting line: "Ein großer Bewunderer des Autors ist Erich Goldhagen—der Vater, von jüdischer Herkunft und aus der heutigen Ukraine, später [namely, after having survived the Holocaust] Dozent in Harvard. SPIEGEL-Redakteur Henryk M. Broder, von jüdischer Herkunft und aus Polen, besuchte ihn . . ."); and Mitchell G. Ash, "Die Debatte über Goldhagen im Internet," *Die Tageszeitung,* 16 July 1996, 12. Some of the main reviews of the book in the German press, by German as well as American and Israeli scholars and journalists, are now available in part 2 of Schoeps, *Ein Volk von Mördern?* These include important essays by Volker Ullrich, Norbert Frei, Christopher Browning, Josef Joffe, Gordon Craig, Gulie Ne'eman Arad, Eberhard Jäckel, Hans-Ulrich Wehler, Ulrich Herbert, and Andrei Markovits. Augstein's above-cited 15 April review was reprinted without any change or correction (Hilberg still appears as an Israeli historian). For Goldhagen's response to his German critics just before the publication of his book's German translation, see his "Das Versagen der Kritiker," *Die Zeit,* 2 August 1996, 9–14. See also a compilation of contributions to the German debate, Volker Ullrich, ed., *Die Goldhagen-Kontroverse* (*Die Zeit, Dokument* 1, 1996); and Matthias Heyl, "Die Goldhagen-Debatte im Spiegel der englisch- und deutschsprachigen Rezensionen von Februar bis Juli 1996: Ein Überblick," *Mittelweg* 36 (August/September 1996): 41–56.

22. Eberhard Jäckel, "Einfach ein schlechtes Buch," *Die Zeit* 21 (17 May 1996): 14, reprinted, with slight changes, in Schoeps, *Ein Volk von Mördern?* 187–92.

23. See especially Hans-Ulrich Wehler, "Wie ein Stachel im Fleisch," *Die Zeit* 22 (24 May 1996), a much longer version of which is reprinted in Schoeps, *Ein Volk von Mördern?* 193–209; and Ulrich Herbert, "Aus der Mitte der Gesellschaft," *Die Zeit* 25 (14 June 1996): 5–6, of which a longer version appears in Schoeps, *Ein Volk von Mördern?* 214–24, significantly retitled "Die richtige Frage."

its author.[24] This can be traced at least in part to the situation that repeated itself over and over again in the packed lecture halls, where older professors who attacked Goldhagen with some vehemence were in turn confronted by clear expressions of hostility from audiences of third-generation Germans who preferred to embrace the beleaguered young (Jewish) American scholar precisely because they felt that for once they were being told the "truth" that their teachers had always refused to admit.

There was clearly something troubling about early German reactions to the book. Anti-American and anti-Jewish sentiments were reflected in broad hints that the book's success in the United States was linked to the predominance of Jews in the media.[25] The quality of American universities was questioned, the underlying assumption being that Goldhagen's obviously flawed Ph.D. dissertation, which served as the basis for his book,

---

24. The German translation of the book, *Hitlers willige Vollstrecker: Ganz normale Deutsche und der Holocaust,* was published in August 1996. See Volker Ullrich, "Daniel J. Goldhagen in Deutschland: Die Buchtournee wurde zum Triumphzug" (and note subtitle: "Die Historiker kritisieren 'Hitlers willige Vollstrecker': Das Publikum empfindet das Buch als befreiend"), Die Zeit 38 (13 September 1996); Evelyn Roll, "Goldhagens Diskussionsreise: Der schwierige Streit um die Deutschen und den Holocaust" (note the revealing subtitle: "Eine These und drei gebrochene Tabus: Je mehr ihn seine Kritiker bedrängen, um so näher rückt der Wissenschaftler seinem Publikum—da ist einer, der die richtige Frage nach den Tätern stellt"), *Süddeutsche Zeitung,* 9 September 1996, 3; and Amos Elon, "The Antagonist as Liberator," *New York Times Magazine,* 26 January 1997, 40–44. See further, for instance, Hans-Joachim Thron, "Die Deutschen—ein Volk von Henkern? Der US-Wissenschaftler Daniel Goldhagen legt sich mit der Historikerzunft an—'Der Mann mauert,'" *Stuttgarter Zeitung* 180 (6 August 1996): 3; Wolfgang Sofsky, "Normale Massenmörder," *Neue Zürcher Zeitung* 10 (11 August 1996): 45; "Todbringende 'Humanisten': Rudolf Augstein zur Geschichte des Holocaust und zu den neuen Thesen," Fritjof Meyer, "'Riesige Mehrheit': Die deutsche Übersetzung glättet Goldhagens Thesen," "Was dachten die Mörder? Der US-Politologe Daniel Jonah Goldhagen über den Streit um sein Holocaust-Buch und das Bild der Täter" (interview with Augstein), all in *Der Spiegel* 33 (12 August 1996): 40–55 (issue title: "Hitler: Vollstrecker des Volkswillens?" Note the remarkable change in Augstein's tone from his previous comments on the book. He writes on p. 49: "Allein die Tatsache aber, daß die Holocaust-Geschichte noch einmal aufgerollt wird, kann nur gut sein, es wird in jedem Fall einiges bewegen. Wenn Goldhagen das erreicht, erreicht er viel"); Werner Birkenmaier, "Ein zorniges, moralisches Buch," *Stuttgarter Zeitung* 189 (16 August 1996): 5; Josef Joffe, "Goldhagen in Germany," *New York Review of Books,* 28 November 1996, 18–21; "Reckoning with Goldhagen," extracts from contributions to the Goldhagen debate edited by Theofilos Wawrosch-Klonaris, *German-American Cultural Review,* winter 1996, 4–5; Dieter Pohl, "Die Holocaust-Forschung und Goldhagens Thesen," *Vierteljahreshefte für Zeitgeschichte* 1 (1997): 1–48; and Mitchell Ash, "American and German Perspectives on the Goldhagen Debate: History, Identity, and the Media," *Holocaust and Genocide Studies* 11 (winter 1997): 396–411.

25. As in Augstein, "Soziologe als Scharfrichter," in Schoeps, *Ein Volk von Mördern?* 106.

would never have been accepted at a German university.[26] Conversely, one could detect a visible degree of defensiveness regarding the central claim of Goldhagen's study, namely, that all (or at least most) Germans in the Third Reich were willing executioners (whether they actually perpetrated murder or would have been happy to do so if asked). Goldhagen's self-presentation as the son of a survivor led some German critics to question his ability to write an objective historical account (while of course expressing sympathy with his own and his father's predicament).[27] This was an interesting moment, since while in the United States Goldhagen's family history was seen as a validation of his work, and as adding moral authority to his text, in Germany the curious assumption was made that Germans could somehow maintain greater "scientific" detachment from the

---

26. See, for example, Wehler, "Wie ein Stachel," in Schoeps, *Ein Volk von Mördern?* 206–7: "Diese Verhalten wirft die Frage nach der Beachtung elementaren akademischer Kontrollmechanismen auf." Citing other cases in which American universities failed to "control" the quality of academic work, he concludes: "Und jetzt der neue Tiefpunkt im Fall Daniel Goldhagen: Erheiternd ist das nicht, erneut das Versagen des akademischen Prüfungsfilters zu Beobachten." However, a similar complaint was made also by Yehuda Bauer, recently retired from the Hebrew University and now director of the Research Institute at Yad Vashem, in his lecture at the 8 April 1996 symposium organized by the Research Institute at the United States Holocaust Memorial Museum in Washington, D.C., on Goldhagen's book. See Maria Mitchell, H-German, <german@h-net.msu.edu>, 11 April 1996, who paraphrases Bauer as follows: "Goldhagen, he said, should not be held responsible for this shoddy work, in particular for its lack of a comparative focus. Instead, it is his advisor who must be blamed: How was this work awarded a Ph.D. at Harvard when it doesn't even cover the most basic issues?" There is also a video recording of the debate made by C-Span.

27. See, as one of many examples, Andreas Geldner, "Porträt der Woche: Daniel Goldhagen," *Stuttgarter Zeitung,* 10 August, 1996, 10. The caption under Goldhagen's picture reads "Der Ankläger." Geldner describes the author's father as "einer der wenigen Überlebenden aus dem jüdischen Ghetto in Czernowitz" and, without mentioning by whom the majority were in fact murdered, notes that "Erich Goldhagen war . . . mit deutscher Kultur und Sprache aufgewachsen. Noch heute ist sein Deutsch perfekt." He tells the endlessly repeated story that "Zwar wollte der Vater . . . nichts vom eigenen Weg durch die Hölle erzählen, aber 'innerhalb eines intellektuellen Rahmens,' wie Daniel Goldhagen es nennt, war die Geschichte des Holocaust in der Familie allgegenwärtig." Having prepared his readers, Geldner explains: "Ehrgeizig widmete sich Daniel Goldhagen . . . dem vom Vater vorgezeichneten Thema. Zweimal hielt er sich für längere Zeit in der Bundesrepublik auf, der er übrigens bescheinigt, den Antisemitismus weitgehend überwunden zu haben." Now that the readers have been convinced of Goldhagen's prejudices yet are "liberated" by him from any direct blame, Geldner can end his article by casting doubt on the author's ability for detached scholarly judgment while presenting it by way of his rejection of such accusations: "Daniel Goldhagen reagiert unwillig, wenn biographische Bezüge hergestellt werden, wenn schon nicht wissenschaftlich, sondern moralisch zu rechtfertigen. Vom 'Gespenst meiner Identität und Herkunft' spricht er dann, das letztlich dazu diene, allen Juden zu unterstellen, sie könnten nicht wissenschaftlich über den Holocaust schreiben." See also Frank Schirrmacher, "Hitler's Code: Holocaust aus faustischem Streben? Daniel John [*sic*] Goldhagens Remythisierung der Deutschen," *Frankfurter Allgemeine Zeitung,* 15 April 1996, 31.

horrors of the Holocaust than Jews, who, unlike their German counter-parts, would never be liberated from their "understandable" mystifying predilections and emotional involvement.

None of this should have come as much of a surprise to those who remembered similar arguments made during the *Historikerstreit* of the mid-1980s.[28] Much more striking was the realignment of attitudes not merely toward Goldhagen's book—criticism of which by no means entirely disappeared—but, much more significantly, regarding the need to recognize the centrality of, and to change the methodology of research on, the Holocaust. This trend did not begin, of course, with the publication of the book, but the debate surrounding it seems to have provided those involved in a reorientation of German scholarship on the Third Reich with an opportunity to air and promote their views. It had been assumed in some quarters that following reunification, the Nazi period would finally recede into the historical past and no longer feature as prominently as it had previously done in public debates. Reactions to Goldhagen's book, however, along with several other cases mentioned below, demonstrated that Nazism has remained a crucial issue in German political, intellectual, and scholarly discourse.[29]

We can thus conclude at this juncture that German reactions to Goldhagen's book shifted quite quickly from outright media rejection to a more balanced, and in some cases even very positive, evaluation. Academic opinion, initially either very cautious or wholly negative, has by

---

28. See, for example, the following statement by Martin Broszat: "German historians and students of history . . . have the obligation to understand that victims of Nazi persecu-tion and their bereaved relatives can even regard it as a forfeiture of the right to their form of memory if historical research on contemporary history, operating only in scientific terms, makes claims in its academic arrogance to a monopoly when it comes to questions and con-cepts pertaining to the Nazi period. Respect for the victims of Nazi crimes demands that this mythical memory be granted a place. . . . Among the problems faced by a younger generation of German historians more focused on rational understanding is certainly also the fact that they must deal with just such a contrary form of memory among those who were persecuted and harmed by the Nazi regime, and among their descendants—a form of memory which functions to coarsen historical recollection." Martin Broszat and Saul Friedländer, "A Con-troversy about the Historicization of National Socialism," in Peter Baldwin, ed., *Reworking the Past: Hitler, the Holocaust, and the Historians' Debate* (Boston, 1990), 106. See also *For-ever in the Shadow of Hitler? Original Documents of the Historikerstreit, the Controversy con-cerning the Singularity of the Holocaust,* trans. James Knowlton and Truett Cates (Atlantic Highlands, N.J., 1993).

29. See, for example, Gernot Facius and Adelbert Reif, "Der Judenmord war das Kernereignis des Jahrhunderts," interview with Ulrich Herbert, *Die Welt,* 16 March 1998, 9. Herbert notes that in surveying all major works on the Nazi period published before 1990, he found that on average 85 percent of the text was devoted to the period before 1939, meaning that only 15 percent of the text dealt with the war, and only 5 percent with the Holocaust.

now similarly evolved to a more positive stance, despite the usual scholarly qualifications. Moreover, since history books have a longer shelf life in Germany than in the United States, and because scholars are more closely involved in the media, the debate has not yet been wholly relegated to the status of "history." This of course has to do also with the greater central-ity of the Nazi past to questions of German identity and politics. Indeed, the somewhat more positive evaluation of the book by German scholars today—as compared with their American colleagues—concerns their appreciation of its political impact rather than its inherent qualities, a point clearly made by the sociologist Jürgen Habermas in his speech on the occasion of giving Goldhagen the Democracy Prize for his book (a some-what controversial decision as far as German historians were con-cerned).[30] Generally, then, it would appear that by now a degree of con-sensus has been reached among German scholars regarding the book's political contribution and potential long-term effects on the changing focus of German research on, and perceptions of, Nazism and the Holo-caust, all of this despite a commonly held view regarding the untenable nature of Goldhagen's thesis as a whole.

It has been noted that among Goldhagen's most enthusiastic German audiences were numerous members of the third generation, namely, young people whose own parents were either born after the war or were still chil-dren during the waning years of the Third Reich. For these men and women, most of whom were apparently middle-class university students, the book was said to have produced a "liberating experience."[31] How are we to understand this seemingly curious formulation, whereby a study asserting that the vast majority of Germans during the Third Reich were either actual or potential murderers was somehow perceived by Germans born in the 1970s as liberating? It should first be realized that as far as these young crowds were concerned, the Holocaust was an event that occurred when their grandparents were about their own age. Unlike their parents, whose complex relationship with the "perpetrator generation" was often expressed in long silences, outbursts of rage, and occasional use of distorted Holocaust imagery for their own political agendas, the third

---

30. Jürgen Habermas, "Über den öffentlichen Gebrauch der Historie: Warum ein 'Demokratiepreis' für Daniel J. Goldhagen? Eine Laudatio," *Die Zeit* 12 (14 March 1997): 13–14; Jan Philipp Reemtsma, "Abkehr vom Wunsch nach Verleugnung: Über 'Hitlers willige Vollstrecker' als Gegenstück zur 'historischen Erklärung,'" *Blätter für Deutsche und Internationale Politik,* April 1997, 417–23; Ulrich Raulff, "Der lange Schrecken: Goldhagen, Habermas, Reemtsma: Ein Preis, drei Reden," *Frankfurter Allgemeine Zeitung,* 12 May 1997.

31. See, for example, Ullrich, "Die Buchtournee"; and Joffe, "Goldhagen in Ger-many."

generation has a more detached view of the Nazi past.[32] Interestingly, some have noted that members of the third generation communicate more easily with their grandparents (not an uncommon phenomenon in generational relations) and have more sympathy for their predicament under Nazism.[33] Conversely, or perhaps precisely for this very reason, they can also afford to take up a more accusatory stance vis-à-vis that generation as a whole, since whatever they might say about it has little direct bearing either on their own life experience and self-perception or on that of their grandparents.

Second, but also related to generational relations, young German students seem to be increasingly impatient with the complex and often highly theoretical and detached (not to say bloodless) interpretations of Nazism offered by their professors.[34] As has been pointed out by some younger scholars,[35] academics of the older generation were rarely capable of confronting the reality of mass murder head-on and preferred to integrate it into a larger, somewhat abstract theoretical framework, in which conceptualizations of totalitarianism, bureaucratic rule, and a fragmented decision-making process largely left out both the blood and gore of genocide

---

32. See, most recently, Dagmar Herzog, "'Pleasure, Sex, and Politics Belong Together': Post-Holocaust Memory and the Sexual Revolution in West Germany," *Critical Inquiry* 24 (winter 1998): 393–444. See also Uli Linke, "Murderous Fantasies: Violence, Memory, and Selfhood in Germany," *New German Critique* 64 (winter 1995): 37–59.

33. Such an observation was made to me a few years before the Goldhagen debate by several German scholars belonging both to the second and to the so-called Hitler Youth generation (those who just missed service in the Wehrmacht when the war ended). It might be noted that in Israel, too, there is reportedly better communication and empathy between survivors and their grandchildren, for whose benefit, incidentally, many Holocaust memoirs have ostensibly been written since the 1980s. See, for instance, Alan Cowel, "After 50 Years, Europe Revisits Its War Stories: History Has Become New as a Younger Generation Casts Aside Its Parents' Comforting National Myths," *New York Times,* 6 July 1997, 10; and Rafael Moses, ed., *Persistent Shadows of the Holocaust: The Meaning to Those Not Directly Affected* (Madison, Conn., 1993).

34. Ulrich Herbert, ed., *Nationalsozialistische Vernichtungspolitik, 1939–1945: Neue Forschungen und Kontroversen* (Frankfurt am Main, 1998). Among the most important recently published German monographs on the Holocaust, see Dieter Pohl, *Nationalsozialistische Judenverfolgung in Ostgalizien, 1941–1944: Organisation und Durchführung eines staatlichen Massenverbrechens* (Munich, 1996); Thomas Sandkühler, *"Endlösung" in Galizien: Der Judenmord in Ostpolen und die Rettungsinitiativen von Berthold Beitz, 1941–1944* (Bonn, 1996); and Walter Manoschek, *"Serbien ist judenfrei": Militärische Besatzungspolitik und Judenvernichtung in Serbien, 1941/42* (Munich, 1995).

35. See especially Ulrich Herbert, "Vernichtungspolitik: Neue Antworten und Fragen zur Geschichte des 'Holocaust,'" in Herbert, *Nationalsozialistische Vernichtungspolitik,* 9–66; and Herbert, "Eine 'Führerentscheidung' zur 'Endlösung'? Neue Ansätze in einer alten Diskussion," *Neue Zürcher Zeitung,* 14/15 (March 1998): 69–70.

and the still troubling question of guilt and responsibility. Goldhagen's rhetoric during his visit to Germany managed both to reintroduce such issues to the debate and, at the same time, to distance the younger generation from the event and its ostensible primary cause, by emphasizing—much more than he had done in his book—that postwar Germany had gone through a complete metamorphosis and was therefore no longer plagued by that unique brand of antisemitism that had previously made it essentially different from "us." In this manner, the twenty-year-olds who applauded his lectures and booed his critics were liberated both from the seemingly obfuscating interpretations of their often authoritarian professors and from any sense of collective guilt or otherness, all by a young (Jewish) American maverick who dared to challenge the conventional interpretation and confront the old establishment on its own territory.

This does not mean, of course, that young German students of Nazism accepted Goldhagen's arguments at face value; on the contrary, the impression is that they share much of their older colleagues' criticism of his simplistic thesis. But they do seem to have felt liberated also in the sense that they could think about the period in moral terms viewed previously as irrelevant or even detrimental to scholarly work. They could also now turn their attention to individual brutality and ideological conviction without needing to justify themselves to their scholarly mentors against accusations of being diverted to marginal issues of little explanatory value. The fact is that while Goldhagen's attack on his American colleagues was hardly justified, there was much to criticize about the German historiography of the Third Reich and especially its marginalization of the Holocaust. From this perspective, we can say that Goldhagen's book had a beneficial effect in Germany, since it helped legitimize a new focus on the role of antisemitism in the Holocaust, asserted the centrality of the Holocaust for the history of Nazi Germany—previously denied by a number of prominent older scholars—and focused interest on recently published or forthcoming works by younger scholars heading in precisely that direction. Indeed, until recently very little serious research on the actual perpetration of genocide had been undertaken by German historians, not so much for lack of documentation (although recently opened archives in former communist countries have significantly expanded the source base), but due to the insistence of older historians, in what is still a very hierarchical "guild," on "functionalist" theories that largely ignored empirical research and desisted from historical reconstructions of the realities of mass murder.

Approaches to the study of Nazism have always been related to politics and self-perception. As initial interpretations of Hitler's dictatorship as either a takeover by a criminal clique or the culmination of a militaristic tradition led by a traditional elite unrepresentative of the mass of the population were finally rejected in the 1960s, they were replaced by a complex mechanistic explanatory model that portrayed an elaborate process of "cumulative radicalization" within the context of a "polycratic" regime as the main engine of genocide.[36] Not only was ideology seen as largely irrelevant, human agency and motivation was also described as marginal. To be sure, there was no denying that the killing itself might have been carried out in part by sadists or even antisemites, but this was not perceived as the fundamental facet of the phenomenon, but at most as its symptom and ultimate consequence. And since the functioning of the cogs did not explain the machine as a whole, once the bureaucratic and decision-making apparatus was analyzed, there seemed little need to examine its low-level operators.[37] Historical explanations could thus be constructed that left the majority of the perpetrators, as well as their relationship to the mass of German society, out of the picture. Conversely, Goldhagen's book dramatized precisely the opposite end of the process and thereby underlined the necessity of returning to the face-to-face killing and providing a satisfactory explanation for the manner in which it was perpetrated. Even if one rejected the book's argument regarding the psychology and motivation of the killers, and the extent to which they represented their society, it certainly demonstrated that avoiding this question altogether was no longer possible.

The extent to which German society has found it difficult to come to terms with the individual, human aspects of the Holocaust, concerning both the perpetrators' motivation and conduct and the victims' identity and fate, is illustrated by the fact that the public was compelled to confront the realities of mass murder mainly as a result of outside interventions. This process began with the Allies' insistence that residents of communities next to concentration camps view the horrors perpetrated in close proximity to their homes; it continued with the screening of documentaries to Germans under military occupation and the holding of the Nuremberg trials; and it has continued with the periodic arrival in Germany of Holocaust representations written or produced elsewhere, ranging from Anne Frank's diary to the television mini-series *Holocaust* to Steven Spielberg's *Schindler's List*. It may be recalled that the *Historikerstreit* of the 1980s, in

---

36. See, for example, Friedrich Meinecke, *Die deutsche Katastrophe* (Wiesbaden, 1946); Gerhard Ritter, *Europa und die deutsche Frage* (Munich, 1948); Martin Broszat, "Hitler and the Genesis of the 'Final Solution': An Assessment of David Irving's Theses," in H. W. Kock, ed., *Aspects of the Third Reich* (London, 1985), 390–429; Hans Mommsen, "The Realization of the Unthinkable: The 'Final Solution of the Jewish Question' in the Third Reich," in Mommsen, *From Weimar to Auschwitz* (Princeton, 1991), 224–53.

37. Having examined one bureaucrat of the "Final Solution," Hannah Arendt reached a similar conclusion. See her *Eichmann in Jerusalem: A Report on the Banality of Evil* (New York, 1963).

which one group of scholars came out against another for allegedly trivializing the crimes of the Third Reich, in fact did not bring with it any new work on the realities of genocide but was focused on questions of German national identity and its relationship to the past.[38] It was rather the impact of imported products, even when their inherent quality was at times rather questionable, that enhanced the public's sensitivity to the past, unleashed public debates over the role of the Holocaust in the German present, and, despite initial criticism of their political, historical, and aesthetic merits by the intelligentsia and the academic community, eventually influenced trends in German writing and research, representation and rhetoric. Goldhagen's book can be seen as yet another link in this chain of foreign interventions that have compelled, or allowed, a shift from an often mute and ignorant "Betroffenheit" to an integration of genocide as an inseparable part of German self-perception.[39]

In this context it is also interesting to note the different reactions to Browning's study *Ordinary Men* in the United States and Germany. Although it did not achieve the status of an international bestseller, Browning's book did reach a relatively wide readership for an academic work and was revisited during the Goldhagen debate. American scholars were often convinced by Browning's emphasis on peer pressure, and his application and extension of Stanley Milgram's theory on obedience to authority, as playing a cardinal role in instigating atrocity. This thesis, moreover, seemed to confirm previous interpretations, which relegated ideological motivation to a secondary place, such as Raul Hilberg's and Hannah Arendt's studies. It was also related to early sociological theories, such as the concept of "primary groups" propounded by Morris Janowitz and Edward Shils.[40] Browning's work, however, did not have a comparable effect on the American media and lay public, not least, perhaps, because there was nothing particularly sensational about it, peer pressure being a rather familiar and generally accepted notion within American educational, sports, and military institutions. Conversely, as far as American, and especially Jewish American, perceptions of Germany were con-

---

38. See, for example, Hans-Ulrich Wehler, *Entsorgung der deutschen Vergangenheit? Ein polemischer Essay zum "Historikerstreit"* (Munich, 1988); Charles S. Maier, *The Unmasterable Past: History, Holocaust, and German National Identity* (Cambridge, Mass., 1988); and Richard J. Evans, *In Hitler's Shadow: West German Historians and the Attempt to Escape from the Nazi Past* (New York, 1989).

39. For a comparison between two modes of coming to terms with the past, see Ian Buruma, *The Wages of Guilt: Memories of War in Germany and Japan* (New York, 1994).

40. See Edward A. Shils and Morris Janowitz, "Cohesion and Disintegration in the Wehrmacht in World War II," *Public Opinion Quarterly* 12 (1948): 280–315; and my analysis, in Omer Bartov, *Hitler's Army: Soldiers, Nazis, and War in the Third Reich* (New York, 1991), 29–58.

cerned, it appears that the popular notion that Germans and Nazis were synonymous during the war was not about to be abandoned merely because a historical study had demonstrated the role of peer pressure in motivating a group of perpetrators.

German reactions to Browning's book reflected very different sensibilities and conventions. While his close-up view of a small group of perpetrators heralded Goldhagen's better-publicized study, Browning's directly opposite conclusions tended to confirm the consensus in German scholarship and public opinion that discipline, authority, and peer group pressure had played a much greater role than antisemitism and ideological motivation. To be sure, this view had been under attack at least since the mid-1980s, when research on the Wehrmacht had shown the impact of indoctrination on the conduct of regular soldiers in the field.[41] But Browning's well-argued test case, and his use of a seemingly dispassionate (if, as I will argue below, problematic) behaviorist theory taken from another discipline, was especially welcomed by those German students of the period who could now say that "even" a well-known American Holocaust scholar had dismissed the role of prejudice and ideology. For this very reason, *Ordinary Men* gained public prominence in Germany only after the publication of *Hitler's Willing Executioners,* since it could be cited as a seemingly foolproof refutation of Goldhagen's thesis.[42]

Moreover, while Goldhagen's study was ultimately received with a good deal of approval by significant sectors in academe and the media, other arguments regarding the impact of antisemitism on pro-Nazi sentiments in the Third Reich and the involvement of "ordinary Germans" in criminal policies elicited strongly negative reactions from some of the public and the political establishment and were met with a fair amount of scholarly skepticism. This was especially the case with the exhibition "War of Extermination: The Crimes of the Wehrmacht, 1941–44," which has been roaming Germany and Austria for the last three years.[43] The reception of this exhibition, produced by German rather than foreign scholars—who are, however, not members of the historical "guild" but rather of the Institute for Social Research in Hamburg—sheds some more light

---

41. See n. 18 above.

42. See, for example, "Böse Menschen, böse Taten, und die normale Holocaust-Forschung: Der Historiker Christopher Browning über Goldhagen und Genozid," an interview with Thomas Sandkühler, *Frankfurter Allgemeine Zeitung,* 6 February 1997, 42.

43. See especially Klaus Naumann, "Wenn ein Tabu bricht: Die Wehrmachtsausstellung in der Bundesrepublik," and Walter Manoscheck, "Die Wehrmachtsausstellung in Österreich: Ein Bericht," both in *Mittelweg* 36 (February/March 1996): 11–32. See also Hannes Heer and Klaus Naumann, eds., *Vernichtungskrieg: Verbrechen der Wehrmacht, 1941 bis 1944* (Hamburg, 1995).

on the manner in which Goldhagen's book was read and understood by the German public. For what most analyses of Goldhagen's reception in Germany seem to have missed is that for all its insistence on the lack of distinction between Germans and Nazis, his book focuses primarily on the conduct of policemen, who cannot, by any stretch of the imagination, be said to represent German society. German policemen were about as representative of their society as police forces anywhere else in the world, and probably even less so, given the emphasis on ideological instruction and the ideological selection procedures in these units. But even those unaware of the specific differences between the recruitment and training of policemen and regular soldiers could not think of the former as "ordinary Germans." People anywhere may feel proud about their fathers' or grandfathers' wartime service, but even Germans are unlikely to boast of the glorious deeds of ancestors who wore police uniforms. Goldhagen might claim that the members of the police battalions he investigated were "regular folk," but the vast majority of Germans remembered their own or their relatives' experiences as soldiers. Hence the much greater discomfort with the Wehrmacht exhibition, since, being a mass conscript army, the Wehrmacht did indeed represent German society; saying that it perpetrated mass crimes was tantamount to a collective charge against German society (or at least its adult male population). The Holocaust may not have been a "national project," as Goldhagen has asserted, but the war definitely was. The assertion that the war was a criminal undertaking that also facilitated the genocide of the Jews meant that the twenty million soldiers who had served in the ranks of the Wehrmacht could not escape blame for the Holocaust. Such a statement was obviously seen by conservative circles as an attempt to besmirch the army's "shield of honor" and slander a whole generation of young men who had returned from the battlefield to rebuild both Germanys. It also threatened to reverse the process of rehabilitating the Wehrmacht and normalizing the past begun during President Ronald Reagan's notorious visit to the Bitburg military cemetery in 1985.[44] No wonder that, to cite just one example, the organization of former Wehrmacht soldiers in the Austrian city of Salzburg, whose membership consists by now mostly of the veterans' sons and daughters, warned their fellow citizens to protect their children from the Wehrmacht exhibition lest it poison their minds and undermine their love for family and (the German) fatherland.[45]

---

44. See especially Geoffrey Hartman, ed., *Bitburg in Moral and Political Perspective* (Bloomington, 1986).

45. See, for example, "Eltern, schützt Eure Kinder! Landesschulrat: Keine Empfehlung zum Besuch der Reemtsma-Ausstellung," *Kameradschaft Aktiv* ½ (January/February 1998): 8; "'Wehrmachtsausstellung': Fälschung empört Salzburg," "Ein Sturm der Entrüstung gegen die unselige 'Wehrmachtsausstellung' in Salzburg: 'Mein Vater war kein Mörder!'"

One final point on the German case. Goldhagen's book is explicitly about the perpetrators and as such is similar to the bulk of German scholarship on the Holocaust, in which the victims appear only as the final product of the process to be reconstructed and explained. What distinguishes this book, however, is that the author's empathy is given exclusively to the victims rather than the perpetrators. In demonizing the perpetrators, Goldhagen makes no attempt to understand them; his focus is on portraying them as sadistic murderers who enjoy their "work" of torturing and killing Jews. The bulk of German scholarship, as well as, for that matter, Browning's book, is devoted to understanding what made these men behave as they did. Goldhagen, for his part, calls forth sympathy, pity, and compassion for the victims, and anger and frustration vis-à-vis the killers. This is a new perspective in German scholarship, although some such examples do exist in English-language works.[46] This is not to say that German scholars have ever shown any sympathy for the killers, but rather that they concentrate on figuring out how their minds worked, not on how their actions were experienced by those they murdered.[47] Indeed, empathy with the victims has always appeared impossible for German scholars; even new research being written and published in Germany now has yet to overcome this obstacle.[48] This may have to do both with the

---

and other articles, all in *Salzburger Krone* 13, 573 (24 February 1998). The veterans' association organized a counter-exhibition, "Kriegsgefangenschaft in Russland, 1945–1953," with the support of the mayor of Salzburg, Dr. Josef Dechant. Some of these reactions had to do with my own lecture on the Wehrmacht in Salzburg. However, for very different reactions to my lecture on this theme in Dresden, just before the opening of the exhibit there, see, for example, Jörg Marschner, "Die saubere Wehrmacht ist eine Legende," *Sächsische Zeitung,* 17/18 January 1998, 3; and Heidrun Hannusch, "Vortrag von amerikanischen Historiker in Vorbereitung der Wehrmachtsausstellung stieß auf enormes Interesse: Prof. Bartov: 'Einen offen liegenden Nerv getroffen,' " *Dresdner Neueste Nachrichten,* 9 January 1998. The exhibition itself was the occasion of a confrontation between neo-Nazi and left-wing demonstrators in Dresden. See also Wolfram Wette, "Bilder der Wehrmacht in der Bundeswehr," *Blätter zur Deutsche und Internationale Politik,* February 1998, 186–96.

46. See, on this issue, István Deák, "Memories of Hell," *New York Review of Books,* 26 June 1997, 38–43. See also Ulrich Herbert, "Hitlers Wut und das Weggucken der Deutschen: Saul Friedländers großartiges Buch über die ersten Jahre der Judenverfolgung im Dritten Reich," *Süddeutsche Zeitung,* 24 March 1998, L14, who compliments Friedländer for providing the perspectives of the perpetrators, the victims, and German society as a whole.

47. Wolfgang Sofsky, *The Order of Terror: The Concentration Camp,* trans. William Templer (Princeton, 1997), seems to attempt to deal with the victims but is devoted primarily to political inmates. See my review essay on this book, "The Penultimate Horror," *The New Republic,* 13 October 1997, 48–53.

48. See, for instance, the statement in Pohl, *Nationalsozialistische Judenverfolgung,* 15: "Auf der Basis des umfangreichen, teilweise jetzt erst zugänglich gewordenen Quellenmaterials widmet sich die vorliegende Arbeit, und dies möchte ich besonders hervorheben, fast ausschließlich dem *Verfolgungsprozeß,* d.h. der Besatzungspolitik und den Tätern der nationalsozialistischen Judenverfolgung. . . . Zur Erforschung der jüdischen Geschichte unter

perceived "otherness" of the victims and with the psychological burden such an approach would entail for scholars who still believe in the need for detachment. Hence too, I would argue, one reason for the commercial success and widespread impact of Victor Klemperer's recently published diaries, which finally made it possible for the German public to read an account of German society under Nazism from the perspective of one who was both a complete insider, a patriot who saw the Nazis as "un-German," and yet was made into a total outsider, increasingly shunned by his environment, while remaining throughout Hitler's twelve-year rule in the midst of German society.[49] One would hope that in the future German scholars will find it possible to write a history of Germany's victims, rather than of its perpetrators. Perhaps one merit of Goldhagen's book in Germany is that by launching a debate over the practice of face-to-face murder, it will in the long run motivate German scholars to study these same situations also from the perspective of the victimized.

Diversionary Tactics: Camps, Genocides, and France's Shoah Syndrome

Both in France and Israel, Goldhagen's book met with less commercial success and aroused only limited intellectual interest, mostly generated by its reception in the United States and Germany rather than by local concerns. The main cause of this cooler reaction is that debates over Nazism and the Holocaust in both countries at the time of the book's publication were focused on issues that had little to do with the main thrust of Goldhagen's thesis. Hence, despite a fair amount of publicity, the book cannot be said to have had a major effect on public opinion or scholarly debate in France and Israel. A closer examination of the book's reception, however, indicates that the relative indifference observed in these two countries can be traced back to almost diametrically opposed reasons. In France, after a few reviews in the daily print media, some more positive than others, the book was vehemently

---

deutscher Besatzung in Ostgalizien wären jiddische und hebräische Sprachkenntnisse erforderlich, über die ich nicht verfüge. Diese Einschränkung ist schmerzlich, aber unumgänglich."

49. Victor Klemperer, *Ich will Zeugnis ablegen bis zum letzten: Tagebücher, 1933–1945,* ed. Walter Nowojski with Hadwig Klemperer, 2 vols. (Berlin, 1995). The warm welcome that Saul Friedländer's book received in Germany may also be related to this complex, whereby German scholars still unable to write about the Jewish victims are pleased to see such works by (often Jewish) foreign scholars appear in German. See Herbert, "Hitlers Wut."

attacked by several scholars and intellectuals writing in a couple of special issues of academic journals devoted to the debate.[50] One young French scholar used the opportunity to publish a small book that provided the background and outlined the main arguments of the debate in the United States and especially in Germany for the benefit of French readers who had little knowledge of these developments.[51] Following this, "le phénomène Goldhagen" quickly blew over, and there is little likelihood that it will be resurrected in the future.

French scholarship on the Holocaust is anything but impressive, and apart from a few major works, even translations of foreign studies are hard to come by.[52] This is not to say that French scholars and intellectuals, as well as the media, are not concerned with questions related to World War II. But in France the main focus is not on the genocide of the Jews, but rather on collaboration and resistance during the German occupation, on the one hand, and on the general question of totalitarianism and political repression, including the phenomenon of concentration

---

50. See, for example, Daniel Vernet, "Les Allemands et la culpabilité collective de la Shoah: Le livre du politologue américain Daniel Goldhagen relance aux États-Unis et outre-Rhin la question de la complicité du peuple allemand dans l'entreprise génocidaire menée par les nazis," *Le Monde,* 26 April 1996; François Schlosser, "Une nation d'assassins?" *Le Nouvel Observateur,* 28 November–4 December 1996, 136–38; Nicolas Weill, "Le meurtre antisémite, une maladie d'Allemagne? Objet de polémiques, l'essai de Daniel Goldhagen fait resurgir la figure de l'antisémitisme allemand," and N. W. (full name not given), "Succès populaire, réserve des historiens: De la thèse de doctorat au bestseller, l'essai de Daniel Gold-hagen, est devenue en quelques mois l'objet d'une virulente controverse," both in *Le Monde des Livres,* January 1997; Édouard Husson, "Le phénomène Goldhagen," and Philippe Burrin, "Il n'y a pas de peuple assassin!" both in "Débat: Génocide: Les Allemands tous coupables?" *L'Histoire* 206 (January 1997): 80–85; *Le Débat* 93 (January–February 1997): 122–88, translations of articles on Goldhagen's book by Josef Joffe, Fritz Stern, Robert Wistrich, and myself, and a response by Goldhagen; *Les Temps Modernes* 52 (February–March 1997): 1–61, articles on Goldhagen's book by Raul Hilberg, Claude Lanzmann, Pierre Bouretz, Liliane Kandel, and Pierre Yves Gaudard; and Delphine Bechtel, "Un Livre en débat," *Vingtième Siècle* 54 (April–June 1997): 138–40 (much of this issue is devoted to articles on concentration camps in the twentieth century, by Annette Wieviorka, David Cesarani, Anne Grynberg, Nicolas Werth, Michel Fabréguet, Barbie Zelinger, and Juliane Wetzel, as well as an essay by Georges Petit, "Témoignage d'un ancien déporté"). The French translation of the book, *Les Bourreaux volontaires de Hitler: Les Allemands ordinaires et l'Holocauste,* was published in January 1997.

51. Édouard Husson, *Une culpabilité ordinaire? Hitler, les Allemands et la Shoah: Les enjeux de la Controverse Goldhagen* (Paris, 1997).

52. For example, Raul Hilberg's *The Destruction of the European Jews* appeared in French only in 1988, twenty-seven years after its original publication in English. The important annual publication *Les Cahiers de la Shoah* began appearing only in 1994.

camps, on the other.[53] Both the Francocentric perspective and the political-theoretical discussion do, of course, take the Holocaust into account, but rarely as a topic in its own right. In fact, whenever the Holocaust is mentioned, one often detects a tendency to relativize, marginalize, or generalize it. Moreover, in the last few years France has become greatly preoccupied, and, as some would have it, even obsessed, with a reexamination of the Occupation, collaboration with the Nazi regime, and what the historian Henry Rousso has called the "Vichy Syndrome," namely, the manner in which the Fourth and Fifth Republics had long refused to come to terms with those "somber years."[54] Yet for all that, scholarship on and knowledge about Nazism and the Holocaust remain remarkably sparse.

This is one major reason why Goldhagen's book has had very little bearing on contemporary French debates about the past. The argument that the Germans were mostly Nazi came as no surprise to the French and could not have conceivably been a cause for any sort of sensation. Compared with the various scandals surrounding the Klaus Barbie trial, the Bousquet, Touvier, and Papon affairs, and, not least, the revelations regarding former president Mitterrand's affiliation with the extreme Right in the 1930s and his service for the Pétain regime before he finally opted for the Resistance, Goldhagen's book appeared to be merely stating the obvious.[55] The book's ponderous style, repetitive arguments, moralistic tone, and obsession with the perpetrators' brutality were certainly not the right ingredients to provoke an intellectual debate in France. Moreover, Goldhagen's focus on the genocide of the Jews and his lack of interest in the murder of any other categories of people either by the Nazi regime and its collaborators or by other regimes in the course of the century meant that his book could not fit into the debate over totalitarianism and genocide that was taking shape in France at precisely the same time.[56] Conversely, the book's insistence on the uniqueness of German antisemitism, and its

53. For a survey of recent literature on Vichy, see Omer Bartov, "The Proof of Ignominy: Vichy France's Past and Present," *Contemporary European History* 7 (1998): 107–31. For a survey of the debate on the camps and totalitarianism, see Enzo Traverso, *L'Histoire déchirée: Essai sur Auschwitz et les intellectuels* (Paris, 1997), 71–99.

54. Henry Rousso, *The Vichy Syndrome: History and Memory in France since 1944,* trans. Arthur Goldhammer (Cambridge, Mass., 1991). On the growing "obsession" with memory, see Éric Conan and Henry Rousso, *Vichy: An Ever-Present Past,* trans. Nathan Bracher (Hanover, 1998).

55. See, for example, Erna Paris, *Unhealed Wounds: France and the Klaus Barbie Affair* (New York, 1985); Alain Finkielkraut, *Remembering in Vain: The Klaus Barbie Trial and Crimes against Humanity,* trans. Roxanne Lapidus with Sima Godfrey (New York, 1992); Richard J. Golsan, ed., *Memory, the Holocaust, and French Justice: The Bousquet and Touvier Affairs* (Hanover, 1996); and Pierre Péan, *Une jeunesse française: François Mitterrand, 1934–1947* (Paris, 1994).

56. See François Furet, *Le Passé d'une illusion* (Paris, 1995), and the response by Ian Kershaw, "Nazisme et stalinisme: Limites d'une comparaison," *Le Débat* 89 (March–April

adamant refusal to compare it with either East or West European mani-
festations, could not but be quietly welcomed in a nation whose own antisemitic record, from Dreyfus to the 1930s, let alone under Vichy, had been
obscured for many years thanks in part to the far greater ferocity of the
Nazi regime.[57]

It is, of course, perfectly reasonable to argue that the links between
the two current debates in France, and the lacunae that characterize both
sets of arguments, could be identified with greater ease if more attention
were paid to the Holocaust. For what has remained most troubling about
France under the Germans has been the collaboration of the Vichy regime,
as well as much of the French administrative apparatus in the Occupied
Zone, in the genocide of the Jews.[58] And what distinguishes most clearly
between types of modern dictatorships, oppressive regimes, and totalitarian systems is the extent to which they resort to genocidal policies. Thus
the main difference between Stalinist Russia and Nazi Germany, much
debated in France, is that the former did not carry out genocide on the
basis of race, and the latter did. And yet these distinctions and observations are rarely made in contemporary French debates, and Goldhagen's
book has had remarkably little effect on them.[59]

The roots of both debates stretch back to the early postwar period; in
fact, the dispute over pacifism, fascism, and communism, ultimately presented as compelling a choice between Hitler or Stalin, goes back to the
1930s and must be seen as one of the causes for French conduct during the
Occupation.[60] And while French writers, filmmakers, and philosophers
made a lasting contribution to the portrayal of political prisoners' lives in

---

1996): 177–89. See also Krzysztof Pomian, "Totalitarisme," *Vingtième Siècle* 47 (July–September 1995): 4–23. Another useful analysis of the general context of Arendt's conceptual-
ization of this term and its reception is Steven E. Aschheim, "Nazism, Culture, and *The Origins of Totalitarianism:* Hannah Arendt and the Discourse of Evil," *New German Critique* 70
(winter 1997): 117–39.

57. See, most recently, Vicki Caron, "The Antisemitic Revival in France in the 1930s:
The Socioeconomic Dimension Reconsidered," *Journal of Modern History* 70 (March 1998):
24–73, which also offers an excellent review of the literature.

58. Philippe Burrin, *France under the Germans: Collaboration and Compromise,* trans.
Janet Lloyd (New York, 1996); Marc Olivier Baruch, *Servir l'État français: L'administration
en France de 1940 à 1944* (Paris, 1997). On the churches, see Étienne Fouilloux, *Les chrétiens
français entre crise et libération, 1937–1947* (Paris, 1997).

59. For some excellent recent work on the Soviet Union, see Peter Holquist, "State Vio-
lence as Technique: The Logic of Violence in Soviet Totalitarianism" (forthcoming); and
Amir Weiner, "Nurture, Nature, and Memory in a Socialist Utopia: Delineating the Soviet
Socio-Ethnic Body in the Age of Socialism" (forthcoming). For a focus on Germany, see
Omer Bartov, "Defining Enemies, Making Victims: Germans, Jews, and the Holocaust,"
American Historical Review 103 (June 1998): 771–816.

60. Christian Jelen, *Hitler ou Staline: Le prix de la paix* (Paris, 1988); Norman Ingram,
The Politics of Dissent: Pacifism in France, 1919–1939 (Oxford, 1991); Eugen Weber, *The*

the Nazi "concentrationary universe," the ambiguities of complicity and resistance, and the role of antisemitism in European civilization,[61] France also served as an early staging ground for a "negationist" literature determined to deny the genocide of the Jews or at least to diminish its scope and significance.[62] Nor was this an ephemeral phenomenon that could be relegated to a fanatic, pro-fascist fringe. "Negationist" arguments have been produced by both the Right and the Left and have been made by people with university degrees and often-impressive intellectual credentials. By now this seems to have become an established trend, whereby the more vociferous deniers of the genocide of the Jews seem to be only the extreme manifestation of a much more pervasive, albeit more moderate, relativizing assertion that rejects the distinction between Himmler's death camps and the Soviet gulags, usually accompanied by the moralizing claim that the overemphasis on Jewish victimhood has led to the repression of the memory of other victims and to indifference to current atrocities. This acute discomfort with the centrality of the Holocaust for the European experience has been most powerfully expressed recently by Alain Brossat, professor of philosophy at the Sorbonne, whose latest book avers that the Jewish insistence on "their" Holocaust actually facilitated the continuation of genocide after 1945, as illustrated, to his mind, by the direct link between the "Final Solution" and the Palestinian refugee camps.[63]

Hollow Years: France in the 1930s (New York, 1994); Philippe Burrin, *La Dérive fasciste: Doriot, Déat, Bergery, 1933–1945* (Paris, 1986); Omer Bartov, "Martyrs' Vengeance: Memory, Trauma, and Fear of War in France, 1918–1940," in Joel Blatt, ed., *The French Defeat of 1940: Reassessments* (Providence, 1998), 54–84. On fascism in the 1930s, see Robert Soucy, *French Fascism: The Second Wave, 1933–1939* (New Haven, 1995); and Zeev Sternhell, *Ni droite ni gauche: L'idéologie fasciste en France* (Paris, 1983).

61. See, for example, David Rousset, *L'Univers concentrationnaire* (Paris, 1946); Robert Antelme, *L'Espèce Humaine* (Paris, 1947); Charlotte Delbo, *Auschwitz and After,* trans. Rosette C. Lamont (New Haven, 1995) (Delbo completed parts of this trilogy soon after her liberation but began publishing it in France only as of 1965); Jean-Paul Sartre, *Réflexions sur la question juive* (Paris, 1946); Albert Camus, *Between Hell and Reason: Essays from the Resistance Newspaper "Combat,"* trans. Alexandre de Gramont (Hanover, 1991); and Léon Poliakov, *Histoire de l'antisémitisme* (Paris, 1956). For a very critical look at postwar France, see Tony Judt, *Past Imperfect: French Intellectuals, 1944–1956* (Berkeley, 1992). The most important filmmakers that come to mind in this context are Alain Resnais, Marcel Ophuls, René Clément, and Louis Malle.

62. The best survey of this phenomenon is in Pierre Vidal-Naquet, *Assassins of Memory: Essays on the Denial of the Holocaust,* trans. Jeffrey Mehlman (New York, 1992). See also Deborah Lipstadt, *Denying the Holocaust: The Growing Assault on Truth and Memory* (New York, 1993).

63. Alain Brossat, *L'épreuve du désastre: Le xxe siècle et les camps* (Paris, 1996), 20, 23: "Le naturalisme qui prévaut aujourd'hui dans l'approche de l'Extrême et des catastrophes résolument *passéifiés* a pour effet que celui qui, dans son approche compréhensive de l'extermination des Juifs par les nazis, place exclusivement l'accent sur la singularité de cette action

In this atmosphere, it is interesting to note that even Henry Rousso, whose book on the "Vichy Syndrome" heralded the French reexamination of the past, has become increasingly uneasy with the tendency of some Jewish French intellectuals to focus attention on the fate of the Jews under German occupation, at the expense of the previous concentration on the Resistance.[64] It should be noted that in French representations of the Occupation in the early postwar decades, the victims of Nazism—or at least those victims who mattered and deserved commemoration—seemed to have been almost exclusively members of the Resistance.[65] It is only relatively recently, and not least due to the trials of French collaborators and the political scandals they generated, that much of the public has come to view French Jewry and Jews who had taken refuge in France but were denied citizenship or stripped of it by the late Third Republic and Vichy as the main victims of both the German occupiers and the French authorities. This process of coming to terms with the victimization of French men and women by their own compatriots—all under the mantle of foreign occupation—has been long in the making and has produced a great deal of recrimination and denial. It can be traced back to Marcel Ophuls's remarkable 1969 film *The Sorrow and the Pity,* which announced the crumbling of de Gaulle's "myth of the Resistance." But it is still possible that one reason for the success of Claude Lanzmann's no less extraordinary 1985 film *Shoah* (whose title has subsequently become the name commonly used in France for the Holocaust) was that it avoided any mention of French collaboration and instead concentrated on Polish brutality and indifference. Indeed, despite claims of overemphasis on the Holocaust in recent public debates, the lack of systematic knowledge of its realities and the obvious reluctance of educational institutions to include it on their

---

objectivée sous le nom de Shoah et considère comme rigoureusement en dehors du sujet cette 'suite de l'histoire' dans laquelle les camps palestiniens vont inexorablement s'enchaîner au désastre Juif, n'a pas la moindre conscience de la condition de *discours* de son analyse ou son récit. . . . Tant que la spoliation et l'oppression des Palestiniens feront figure de compensation pour le crime d'Auschwitz; tant que l'unicinté' des crimes nazis sera *aussi* l'alibi de la distraction voire du révisionisme décomplexé face aux extermination soviétique et aux massacres coloniaux—la vie sans fin de la catastrophe continuera de s'enfoncer dans la chair de l'ordre démocratique en voie de mondialisation."

64. Conan and Rousso, *Vichy,* open their book with the sentence "Our nation's conscience is obsessed with memories of the Occupation." They see this as "a warning signal for the future of French identity and the strength of its universalist values." They end their introduction by stating that they "felt it was urgent to get away from the sanctification of the memory of World War II that we have been seeing recently: in our opinion, it is the biggest favor we could do for it" (1, 15).

65. On this issue, see the seminal work by Annette Wieviorka, *Déportation et génocide: Entre la mémoire et l'oublie* (Paris, 1992).

curricula are indicated by the fact that only one seminar in the whole of France is devoted entirely to the study of the genocide of the Jews.[66]

It is the discussion of totalitarianism that seems to satisfy the French need for a more comprehensive view of inhumanity and to cast *la grande nation* in the role of an intellectual center for universalist values rather than corner it into an apologetic or negationist stance. Hence also the current fascination with camps and genocides, consciously evoked in the plural form so as to stress their universal implications.[67] To be sure, the term *totalitarianism* has always retained an ambivalent quality, burdened as it was with political and ideological implications for both those who proudly applied it to their own regimes and those who attributed it as a derogatory term to others or merely sought to analyze it.[68] Similarly, by speaking of camps in the plural, one is always in danger of confusing or making false connotations between, for instance, concentration and extermination camps on the one hand, and camps for prisoners of war, refugees, or displaced persons on the other. There is little doubt that the camp phenomenon, just like totalitarianism, is inherent to our century (at least since the Boer War), but precisely for this reason one must resist its political misrepresentation and abuse. Finally, and perhaps most perniciously, while the term *genocide* has served to describe a whole range of forms of annihilation, from physical extermination to cultural repression, using its plural form only further enhances the confusion and ultimately renders it wholly useless as a description of a prevalent and yet very specific type of event. The excessive use and loose application of this terminology may of course create an awareness of the breadth and depth of inhumanity in the world and motivate people into action against repressive regimes, criminal organizations, and unjust wars. Conversely, however, this may also have the effect of making for such an open-ended definition of evil that one would no longer be able to distinguish between types and degrees of violence, victimhood, and resistance, indeed, between humanity and inhumanity, to the extent of producing a fatal combination of self-righteousness and moral paralysis. In other words, since action against evil often entails violence, that is, choosing the lesser evil rather than waiting for utopia, radical relativism and absolute morality may end up by legitimizing a total abdication of responsibility and accommodation

66. This is the "Seminaire sur l'histoire de la Shoah" at Université de Paris I (Sorbonne); there is also a research seminar on this topic at the École des hautes études en sciences sociales.

67. See, for instance, "Camps et génocides: L'homme, la langue, les camps," Colloque international à l'Université de la Sorbonne, responsables: Catherine Coquio, Irving Wohlfarth, 29–31 May 1997.

68. See Gleason, *Totalitarianism.*

with the powers that be; it is this latter stance, after all, that characterized the majority of the French during the Occupation.

In a recent debate conducted on the pages of the French daily *Le Monde,* the writer Henri Raczymow protested the assertion by the historian Stéphane Courtois, in his preface to the *Black Book of Communism,* that "the death from hunger of a child of a Ukrainian Kulak intentionally driven to starvation by the Stalinist regime 'has the same value' (*vaut*) as the death from hunger of a Jewish child driven to starvation by the Nazi regime."[69] Raczymow argued that this statement represented an "ever more prevalent trend of thinking, an historical, literary, and moral trend, which considers that any crime has the same value (*vaut*) as another, any victim the same value as another." For Raczymow, "this current is not made up of negationists (those who negate the reality of the gas chambers), but much more, it appears, of people who are exacerbated by the claim—made by Jews—of the absolute uniqueness of the Shoah, its incommensurability, its incomparability." This argument was answered in turn by Catherine Coquio, professor of comparative literature at the Sorbonne, who accused Raczymow of failing to understand the implications of his own assertion: "He says that the life of a child in one place is not worth [*vaut*] the same as [the life of a child] in another." Thereby, she writes, he does not see that "all life is incomparable, and its value is incalculable." For Coquio, "that a writer would, at this point, become unaware of the meaning of his own words, that is to say of the value of words and phrases, just like the value of every human face, is an overwhelming defeat for all of us who employ words and phrases."[70] Another response, this time by the Bulgarian-born French critic Tzvetan Todorov, whose book *The Abuses of Memory* was also attacked by Raczymow, rejected the notion of uniqueness. Citing the original *Black Book* on the Nazi crimes in the Soviet Union, he noted that Vassili Grossman, coeditor of the book with Ilya Ehrenburg, had written the following lines: "The Germans say: The Jews are not human beings. That's what Lenin and Stalin say: The Kulaks are not human beings." For Todorov, "every human being has the same price"; hence one can never say that one crime is "worth" more than another. What he finds identical in all genocides is not the historical details, but that on the "moral plane" they are "'worth' . . . absolute condemnation." Pursuing this logic, Todorov goes on to express admiration

---

69. Henri Raczymow, "D'un 'détail' qui masque le tableau," *Le Monde,* 21 January 1998. He refers to Stéphane Courtois, ed., *Le Livre noir du communisme* (Paris, 1997), 19. Raczymow is the author of numerous novels, of which *Un Cri sans voix* (Paris, 1985) had been published in English as *Writing the Book of Esther* (New York, 1995).

70. Catherine Coquio, "'Valeur' des vies, 'valeurs' des mots," *Le Monde,* 27 January 1998.

for all those who fought against the Nazis or the Soviets, against torture in Algeria or massacres in the former Yugoslavia, and claims that the debate is neither about comparison nor about uniqueness, but about the use and abuse of memory and its capacity either to facilitate atrocity or to motivate people to resist it.[71]

None of those who took part in the debate were historians of the Holocaust, including the writers of the books criticized by Raczymow, among whom is also the Belgian sociologist Jean-Michel Chaumont, author of *The Competition of Victims*.[72] Indeed, this debate was not at all about the Holocaust, but rather about the meaning, memory, and political use of crimes against humanity. Raczymow's insistence on the uniqueness of the Holocaust, of course, had nothing to do with a lack of awareness on his part of the suffering endured by millions of people in numerous other mass crimes. His was an argument about the reluctance of French intellectuals to focus on the Holocaust as an event in its own right, especially since France itself—including many of its intellectuals at the time—had played a much greater role in that very specific event than they wish to concede. And the arguments leveled against him merely proved his point. The rhetorical question about the suffering of children was precisely the kind of abuse of memory against which Todorov himself had rightly warned. For the individual suffering of innocents under any regime and in any historical context does not tell us enough about the nature of the regime and the meaning of the event; but it can serve as a device to relativize or normalize the past, as the example of the German *Historikerstreit* in the mid-1980s had already shown. Suffering is never relative, but its assertion does not suffice to distinguish one historical event from another, does not make one "better" or "worse." Todorov, whose earlier book *Facing the Extreme* valiantly tries to recover the existence of what he calls "moral life in the concentration camps," makes no effort to distinguish between Hitler's and Stalin's camps.[73] This is anything but a coincidence in the French context. Only a couple of years ago, the late French historian François Furet, a former left-winger turned conservative, published a book on totalitarianism in which he resurrected the claim made in the 1950s that communism and Nazism were inherently the

---

71. Tzvetan Todorov, "Je conspire, Hannah Arendt conspirait, Raymond Aron aussi . . ." *Le Monde,* 21 January 1998; the book in question is his *Les Abus de mémoires* (Paris, 1995). The original *Black Book* appeared in a definitive French edition as Ilya Ehrenbourg and Vassili Grossman, *Le Livre noir: Textes et témoignages* (Paris, 1995).

72. Jean-Michel Chaumont, *La Concurrence des victimes* (Paris, 1997).

73. Tzvetan Todorov, *Facing the Extreme: Moral Life in the Concentration Camps,* trans. Arthur Denner and Abigail Pollak (New York, 1996). For more detailed comments, see Omer Bartov, "The Lessons of the Holocaust," *Dimensions* 12, no. 1 (1998): 13–20.

same.[74] It is indeed as part of this trend that France has now become pre-occupied with the newly published *Black Book of Communism,* whose very title seeks to remind one of the original book on the genocide of the Jews, and whose underlying assertion is that there was no difference between Nazi and Soviet crimes (incidentally erasing the fact that it was communist Russia, not the French intelligentsia, that destroyed Nazism).[75]

Thus France remains torn between trying to come to terms with its own ignominious legacy and asserting its status as the center of European civilization and the conscience of humanity. In the process, the Holocaust is either shoved aside and ignored, or is presented as an obstacle to humanizing contemporary politics. It should be pointed out that while the "syndrome of Vichy" was identified by a Frenchman (of Jewish origin), the history of Vichy as a willing collaborationist regime was uncovered by an American historian, Robert Paxton, and the extent of French accommodation with the German occupation was recently examined in depth by the Swiss historian Philippe Burrin.[76] It is thus difficult to see how Goldhagen's book could have had any impact on these debates; at the most, it served to divert attention once more from France's active involvement in the genocide of the Jews. For, if we are to believe Goldhagen, it was only the Boches who had done it.

In their recent book *Vichy: An Ever-Present Past,* Éric Conan and Henry Rousso argue that it would be an error to accuse the French of failing to come to terms with the past.[77] Robert Paxton, in his foreword to the English translation of the book, wholeheartedly embraces this assertion.[78] Indeed, over the past fifteen years, France has experienced a series of scandals, revelations, trials, confessions, and recriminations, all concerned with the "somber years" of 1940–44; one could say that Rousso's "Vichy Syndrome" has come to haunt the nation with a vengeance. Conan and Rousso believe that the effects of this preoccupation with the past, especially because of the manner in which this French version of *Vergangenheitsbewältigung* has been practiced, have by now become largely counterproductive. The slogan about the "duty to remember," they claim, has made it impossible for the nation to face up to the future; rather than facilitating action against contemporary problems and injustices, the obsession

---

74. Furet, *Le Passé d'une illusion.*

75. In this context see also the study in comparative genocide, Yves Ternon, *L'État criminel: Les Génocides au xxe siècle* (Paris, 1995).

76. Robert O. Paxton, *Vichy France* (New York, 1972); Burrin, *France under the Germans.*

77. Conan and Rousso, *Vichy.*

78. Robert O. Paxton, foreword to Conan and Rousso, *Vichy,* ix–xiii.

with the past merely obstructs one's view of the present. Moreover, as Conan and Rousso rightly argue, remembering is not the same as knowing; references to the past are all too often made by people who are quite ignorant of its realities. Hence memory must be replaced, or at least enhanced, by historical knowledge, whose production is the task of the historian. This "duty to know" must be accompanied, the authors claim, by the "right to forget," so as to be able to get on with life in the present.

The problem is, of course, that one cannot forget what one does not remember, and that knowledge about the past, which is indeed still scarce in France precisely because the process of coming to terms with it began so late, is fragmented, biased, and selective. This is not only a French problem. Even in Germany, where important scholarly work on Nazism has been carried on for years, some crucial aspects of that past were left untouched, couched in clichés and expressions of grief rather than studied and analyzed. Both in Germany and in France, what has been lacking is an understanding of how a nation turns against a part of its own population, and this hiatus in historical knowledge, this national amnesia camouflaged by euphemisms of distance and strangeness, is also at the root of current German and French xenophobia and definitions of national identity. That past refuses to go away because it is still happening in the present, and it happens in the present because its past roots had never been sufficiently uncovered. It is also the case that in both nations there has been a tremendous amount of resistance to facing up to the fact that the genocide of the Jews, more than anything else, made those "dark years" unique in their own national history, and that therefore this specific episode must, indeed, be studied in much greater depth and not merely be confined to forgetting through mechanisms of remembrance and commemoration. But precisely because France's past is more ambivalent than Germany's, because France initiated antisemitic policies but not the murder itself, and because its actions were mostly carried out under German occupation, resistance to this realization has been all the greater. This was the cause for the remarkable success of de Gaulle's "myth of the Resistance," and this is why "negationism" and "revisionism" have taken root among respectable intellectual and academic circles. For the Holocaust is stuck in the throat of all those who wish to present France as still charged with a "civilizing mission" and as the cradle of humanism. That the Jewish fate is the obstacle to reasserting French national identity, and that its history and memory are now reflected in new waves of anti-foreign sentiments, cannot but make for deep, perhaps often unconscious resentment. Hence the bizarre contemporary argument that the genocide of the Jews diverts attention from "human" suffering and victimhood, which has replaced the previous focus on the fate of the "truly" French victims, the political resisters, at the expense of the allegedly passive, partly foreign Jewish victims.

To be sure, an obsessive preoccupation with remembering can obscure both the realities of the past and the problems of the present. It seems, however, that France still has a long way to go before it will internalize a knowledge of its role in genocide, not through scandals and television shows, but by much more research, study, and teaching. The past never goes away before it becomes known; as long as it remains a dark secret, it will keep haunting the present. The assertion of the German "revisionists" in the 1980s that the burden of the past made it impossible for Germany to forge a new national identity was ultimately answered by an increased effort to learn about that past rather than to put it aside. So too in France, only an enhanced learning process will enable it to forge for itself a national identity rooted in knowledge and understanding, and not in empty rhetoric and recriminations.

Overexposure: Holocaust Fatigue and Israel's Banality of Horror

The publication of the Hebrew translation of Goldhagen's book was originally planned as a joint undertaking by Yad Vashem, the Holocaust Memorial and Research Institute in Jerusalem, and the publishing house of *Yediot Ahronot,* a mass circulation daily. But growing scholarly criticism of the book seems to have convinced Yad Vashem, which has published numerous important studies of the Holocaust over the past four decades, to pull out of the project. Moreover, despite a media blitz by the remaining commercial publisher, Israeli reactions to the book, both in the media and by the scholarly community, were largely unenthusiastic, and in several cases downright dismissive. The book did make the nonfiction bestseller list for a few weeks, but since in Israel even the most popular among such works rarely reach a wide audience, it seems unlikely that its sales figures were particularly impressive. To be sure, a relatively positive review by Yisrael Gutman, a respected Holocaust expert and former director of Yad Vashem's Research Institute, was published in an Israeli daily even before the book appeared in Hebrew.[79] It was this review that Gold-

---

79. Yisrael Gutman, "Daniel Goldhagen and the Inconceivable Cruelty of the Germans," *Ha'aretz,* 12 July 1996 (in Hebrew). Unless otherwise indicated, all Hebrew titles and cited texts have been translated by me. A very different view is offered by Oded Heilbrunner, "How Antisemitic Were the Nazis?" *Ha'aretz,* 26 July 1996 (in Hebrew). The subtitle reads: "It was not deep-seated antisemitism that led Germany to annihilate the Jews, as is being argued today in the worldwide controversy. Germany was not more antisemitic than other European lands in the 1930s, perhaps even less. A combination of events caused an historical accident." See also, in this context, a review essay on Victor Klemperer's diaries (n. 49

hagen cited in his response to criticism by German scholars, just as in his preface to the paperback American edition he cited the positive reception of the German translation as confirming the importance of his book and the unfairness of American criticism. But Gutman's review was hardly representative of the Israeli reception.[80] Moreover, if one takes the trouble to read Gutman's essay in full, it becomes clear that it was mainly focused on the specific Israeli context and thus had much more to do with what some local scholars perceive as the distortion of the Holocaust by the so-called new historians, on the one hand, and with perceptions of contemporary Germany, on the other, than with the inherent merits of the study itself. Indicatively, when Yad Vashem organized a symposium with Goldhagen during his visit to Israel, the organizers insisted on its being a closed

---

above), which is written in a similar spirit: Anat Feinberg, "I Am a European German, and the Nazis Are Not Germans," *Sefarim* 173 (19 June 1996): 4 (in Hebrew). For other reviews of the book before its publication in Hebrew, see Gulie Ne'eman Arad, "The Unbearable Simplification of Interpretation," *Sefarim* 167 (8 May 1996): 4, 13 (in Hebrew), who argues that "for many of the book's readers it will be 'easy' to connect to this 'radical' thesis, as it is called by the author. Within the Jewish-American community, for instance, the conception that the danger of a Holocaust for the Jewish people has not passed serves as a central component of consciousness in the struggle for the continuation of a particular Jewish identity. No wonder that many see the Holocaust as a kind of new 'secular religion' there. Here [in Israel] too the 'danger' of a Holocaust has served a political purpose by being transferred to the security-existential sphere"; and Moshe Zimmermann, "Germany and the Goldhagen Festival," *Ha'aretz,* 18 October 1996 (in Hebrew), whose subtitle is "The German historians' public attack on Daniel Goldhagen and his book *Hitler's Willing Executioners* revealed more than anything else their envy of this Jewish-American's success. More than they came out to defend German historiography from someone whom they consider a charlatan, they strove to protect the German historical guild, which, despite its thorough scholarly work, had failed to compete with this new and popular book as far as public attention is concerned." Zimmermann, a professor of German history at the Hebrew University, took part in some of the discussions in Germany. He further reports that two weeks after Goldhagen's "triumphal campaign" in Germany, the German historians' annual convention in Munich failed to include a single panel on Goldhagen's thesis. A counter-meeting was improvised by some publishers and participants that drew about a fifth of those who had originally arrived for the official convention, although the University of Munich refused to give them a lecture hall; but here too the media and the public were blamed for not paying enough attention to the work of serious scholars. Interestingly, out of more than 200 lectures at the convention, only ten were devoted to issues of the Third Reich and World War II, of which none seems to have dealt with the Holocaust. Zimmermann argues that this reveals the gap between German scholars and the public, whose interest in the Nazi era was indicated by the commercial success of Goldhagen's book and Klemperer's diaries. He also rightly predicts that in Israel, "Goldhagen's book will not cause a storm, since the public will not find anything new in it."

80. For reviews following the book's publication in Hebrew, see, for example, Anita Shapira, "A Sermon on Ordinary Germans," *Sefarim* 258 (4 February 1998): 1, 12, 14 (in Hebrew); and Yehuda Bauer and Yisrael Gutman, "The Crucial Point Is Ideology," *Ha'aretz,* 16 April 1998 (in Hebrew).

forum to which only a select group of scholars was invited. Apparently, researchers and administrators at Yad Vashem were beset by a certain sense of embarrassment and discomfort about a book that, at least from their perspective, had been the occasion for a commercialization of the Holocaust wholly foreign to their own approach and predilections.[81]

While Israeli reviews of the book were by and large negative, some observers pointed out its potential utility for others, and especially for Germans, since it was felt that even though Goldhagen had not discovered anything that was unknown to the Israeli public, such knowledge was lacking in Germany.[82] By now, on those infrequent occasions that the book is mentioned in the media, it is normally described as a "typical" product of American commercialism whose success was derived from a combination of simplistic arguments with sophisticated sales and publicity techniques. Apart from revealing a degree of anti-American sentiment,

---

81. Ron Meiberg, "Goldhagen Is Worth Gold," *Ma'ariv,* 21 November 1997, 5 (in Hebrew), writes: "The 'Yad Vashem' Institute was supposed to participate in the Hebrew publication of the book but pulled out of the production. The feeling at the Institute was that it would not be proper to 'weigh in' on the popular aspect of the book and its author with all the authoritative weight of the Institute. Which is a polite way of saying that they wanted no part of it. Another version is that Goldhagen prefers working with large publishers who have a proven record of promotion, rather than with small academic publishers." Meiberg asked Professor Yehuda Bauer, director of the Research Institute at Yad Vashem, why the decision was made in a closed forum: "So that the 40 participants in this permanent forum will be able to express themselves freely and with intellectual integrity. Without the media," was Bauer's answer. Meiberg asked: "If you were a publisher and the manuscript of this book were submitted to you, would you have published it?" Bauer: "I would not have been willing to publish the book, but I am not a publisher and this was not my decision. Since the book is a fait accompli and is making waves, our duty is to confront it." Meiberg, who calls Goldhagen "the Schwarzenegger of the Holocaust," is representative of Israeli journalists who were far less polite and cautious about the book and the author than their European and American colleagues. The book was published in Hebrew translation in November 1997.

82. See, for example, Shulamit Volkov, "The Germans Were Shaken," *Ma'ariv,* 22 January 1998 (in Hebrew). Volkov writes: "As might have been expected, Daniel Goldhagen's book, in its new Hebrew dress, did not cause a public storm in Israel. A year and a half ago, shortly after it was published in English and even before its appearance in German, I spent a few weeks at the Institute for Advanced Studies in Berlin, where there was only one topic of conversation: Goldhagen's book. . . . No wonder that the Germans were so horrified by this book, and no wonder that Israelis were indifferent to it. Actually, it merely confirms what so many Israelis always 'knew.'" See also Moshe Zimmermann, "Goldhagen or Kornfein," *Ha'aretz,* 16 April 1998 (in Hebrew), who reports that according to a poll commissioned by the Institute for German History at the Hebrew University in March 1998, no less than 83.3 percent of those asked about their opinion on Goldhagen's book replied that they had never heard of it; 11.3 percent responded that they had heard of the book but had no opinion. Only 5.4 percent had an opinion, of whom 3.5 percent agreed with Goldhagen and 1.9 did not. Kornfein is the goalkeeper of a local soccer team, and Zimmermann estimated (tongue in cheek) that he would have received higher ratings.

especially among Israeli academics and intellectuals, it should also be noted that Goldhagen's personal style failed to appeal to the lay public, which seems to prefer older, more traditional scholars and is wary of young, well-groomed foreigners who come to tell Israelis what they believe they know best.

Indeed, precisely Goldhagen's claim that he offered a "final" and definitive interpretation of the Holocaust—an assertion that made for much of his book's appeal in the United States and Germany—seems to have repelled numerous Israeli critics and readers. Israelis have been exposed for many years to a veritable flood of information, imagery, and demagogy on the Holocaust: newspaper articles and scholarly publications; educational and political rhetoric; cinematic, theatrical, artistic, and musical representation; commemorative sites and gatherings; and, not least, a highly intimate contact with the realities and memories of the Holocaust through personal accounts in the family circle or among close friends. In this context, a book with such far-reaching claims as Goldhagen's could not but be viewed with a skeptical, even resentful eye. The tone, the rhetoric, and the self-righteous indignation rather than specific findings of the study were rejected. Hence the question, "What can he tell us about the Holocaust—as a whole, rather than the actions of this or that murder squad—that we don't know already?" Moreover, since the book's main thesis was so familiar to Israelis, it could not but appear banal; people simply could not understand what was innovative about an argument that presented the Germans as antisemitic murderers of Jews. This was what they learned in school, read in books, heard on the radio, watched on television, and heard from relatives. Israelis might be curious about German reactions to this statement; but as for the person on the street, this was simply obvious. Hence, the public showed interest mainly in the book's impact abroad, that is, in the phenomenon rather than the text.[83]

One might indeed say that Goldhagen's book appeared in Israel at a time when overexposure to documentation, representation, and rhetoric had produced what I would call "Holocaust fatigue." Since people now "know" what it was all about, and since they all too often expect the Holocaust to be used for contemporary political purposes, they tend to seek shelter from this barrage of information and misinformation. Some simply refuse to hear any more about the Shoah. Thus, for instance, while in Germany public lectures on the Holocaust are very well attended by young people, in Israel audiences consist mainly of scholars and the elderly. A second, more sophisticated technique of "sheltering" from conventional

---

83. For more on Israeli perceptions of the Holocaust, see, for example, Tom Segev, *The Seventh Million: The Israelis and the Holocaust,* trans. Haim Watzman (New York, 1993).

Holocaust rhetoric is to turn it on its head. This obviously does not remove the Holocaust from the public agenda, since it stimulates new and often highly acrimonious debates. Yet what is at stake in these controversies is not German complicity, but rather the role of the Holocaust in the creation and consolidation of Israeli national identity. This is not an issue to which Goldhagen's book has much to contribute. But because his book appeared on the Israeli scene just as the local debate over the Holocaust was intensifying, elements of Goldhagen's arguments were mobilized by both sides in the controversy. For some, he served as a tool against the "new historians" who were attempting to rewrite the conventional Zionist narrative of the Holocaust. For others, Goldhagen provided proof for the brutalizing effects of a dehumanizing ideology and military occupation. At the same time, however, it was argued that, in the Israeli context, it was precisely the kind of rhetoric of Jewish victimization offered by Goldhagen, the insistence on remembering what had not been experienced and could not be reversed, and the inability to take revenge against the real perpetrators, that was having a pernicious effect on young Israelis, especially troubling in the case of soldiers occupying a hostile population. The danger lay, therefore, in a double reversal of roles, whereby Jews were transformed from victims into occupiers, and the Palestinians were perceived not as an occupied people but as potential murderers.[84]

Israeli national identity is grounded in two events, the Holocaust and the conflict with the Arabs. While the former is in the past, it retains a strong presence in personal and collective memory and anxieties. And while the circumstances of the latter have greatly changed over the decades, it remains a central preoccupation, both as memory and as reality, and maintains a hold over people's perceptions of the future. These two components of Israeli identity are so strongly bound to each other historically and ideologically that by now it has become very difficult to speak or write on one without constantly referring to the other. It is for this reason that attempts to seek shelter from overexposure to Holocaust rhetoric in Israel are so closely related, though in different ways, to the Arab-Israeli conflict. Thus, for instance, Israelis will justify their reluctance to hear any more about the Holocaust by saying that they have more urgent matters on their minds, invariably related to issues of security ranging from military service to the demands of an economy straining under the pressure of enormous army budgets. In a rather different vein, those

---

84. See, for example, Uri Ram, "The Map and the Board: Introductory Comments to the History of Memory and Forgetting," *Teoria ve-Bikoret* (forthcoming, in Hebrew). Ram refers to the influential short article published in the daily *Ha'aretz* by Yehuda Elkana in 1988, "In Favor of Forgetting." See also Moshe Zuckermann, *Shoah in the Sealed Room: The "Holocaust" in the Israeli Press during the Gulf War* (Tel Aviv, 1993, in Hebrew).

scholars engaged in rewriting the history and memory of Israel, a project described by some as an attempt to "slaughter the sacred cows" of traditional national symbolism and myth, often combine an accusatory rhetoric about Zionist policies vis-à-vis the Arabs with a no less accusatory rhetoric concerning the policies of the Yishuv toward the Diaspora during the Holocaust and the reception of the survivors by the Jewish state. Indeed, most "new historians" in Israel, whether their research focuses on the Arab-Israeli conflict or on Israel and the Holocaust, have expressed themselves in various forums on both issues and have drawn a variety of links between them. This should come as little surprise, of course, since these scholars are primarily engaged in delineating the making of Israeli national identity, and such an undertaking must consider the relationship between the trauma of the Holocaust and struggle for Jewish nationhood.[85]

All this is to say that Israeli attitudes toward the Holocaust are complicated by a variety of factors, such as Zionist anti-Diaspora rhetoric, but also frustration over the Yishuv's inability to save the Diaspora, deep feelings of guilt combined with accusations concerning the callous treatment of the survivors, the long-term effects of individual and national trauma along with the political and demographic role of the Holocaust in the creation of the state, and finally the exploitation of the Holocaust for political purposes, including the legitimization of what some consider indefensible policies, and the disconcerting fact that Israel itself has undergone a process of brutalization in its treatment of an increasingly rebellious occu-

---

85. For a comprehensive introduction to the Israeli historians' controversy, see Yechiam Weitz, ed., *From Vision to Revision: A Hundred Years of Historiography of Zionism* (Tel Aviv, 1997, in Hebrew); and my review of this volume in *Sefarim,* 3 June 1998 (in Hebrew). See also Gulie Ne'eman Arad, ed., *Israeli Historiography Revisited,* special issue of *History and Memory* 7 (spring/summer 1995). A scathing critique of the new historians is Efraim Karsh, *Fabricating Israeli History: The "New Historians"* (London, 1997); and my review of this book, "Of Past Wrongs—and Their Redressing," *Times Literary Supplement,* 31 October 1997, 13–14; and a rebuttal by one of those attacked, Benny Morris, "Refabricating 1948," *Journal of Palestine Studies* 27 (winter 1998): 81–95. Another critique is Jacob Katz, "History and Historians, New as Old," *Alpayim* 12 (1996): 9–34 (in Hebrew); see also an unusual, but no less scathing, attack on the current critique of Zionism, made this time from the Left: Yitzhak Laor, "Pam-Pram-Pam-Pam, Post-Zionism," *Ha'aretz,* 15 August 1997 (in Hebrew). A good brief survey can be found in Jonathan Mahler, "Uprooting the Past: Israel's New Historians Take a Hard Look at Their Nation's Origins," *Lingua Franca* 7 (August 1997): 24–32; and Amos Elon, "Israel and the End of Zionism," *New York Review of Books* 43, no. 20 (19 December 1996): 22–30. A more analytical and informed inquiry is Uri Ram, "Memory and Identity: A Sociology of the Historians' Controversy in Israel," *Teoria ve-Bikoret* 8 (summer 1996): 9–32 (in Hebrew). For an illuminating comparison between the German and Israeli historical controversies, see José Brunner, "Pride and Memory: Nationalism, Narcissism, and the Historians' Debates in Germany and Israel," *History and Memory* 9 (fall 1997): 256–300.

pied population. From this perspective, simplistic theses such as that offered by Goldhagen strike the wrong chord among his potential readership, most of whom belong to an academic and intellectual elite involved in a dispute over their nation's history. For the Left, his book can be seen as providing ammunition for those who claim that "the world is against us," that Israel is still facing potential extinction, and that therefore it is justified in pursuing any policies that would ensure its security and must not heed the advice or bow to the pressure of anyone else. But even for the Right, Goldhagen's book may seem a threat, both because it portrays the Jews as helpless victims, and because its focus on the effects of a dehumanizing ideology and the brutalization of armed men confronted with an innocent civilian population provokes comparisons of a disturbing nature.[86]

Consequently, the Israeli public is interested mainly in such studies on Nazism and the Holocaust that touch on topics relevant to contemporary debates, question the consensus, and problematize conventions. A good example is Tom Segev's *The Seventh Million,* a pioneering analysis of changing Israeli attitudes toward the Holocaust since the foundation of the state.[87] Although he came in for a great deal of criticism, Segev succeeded in establishing this very question as a legitimate and important field of inquiry. Other works have reevaluated the absorption of Holocaust survivors into a society that felt great affinity and sympathy for them but at the same time had raised its children on an ideology of "shelilat ha'galut" (negation of the Diaspora).[88] These young Sabras were taught to despise the Jews who "went like sheep to the slaughter" and were determined to correct this "shameful" episode in Jewish history by emulating the mythical Hebrew heroes of antiquity, to the point of describing death in battle for the national cause as the supreme virtue.[89] Also related to this issue

86. For two recent English-language histories of Israeli politics and society that provide some insight into these issues, see Martin Gilbert, *Israel: A History* (London, 1998); and Alan Dowty, *The Jewish State: A Century Later* (Berkeley, 1998); see also my review of these books, "Helmet and Rifle at the Ready," *Times Literary Supplement,* 22 May 1998, 26.

87. Segev, *The Seventh Million.* One aspect of Israel's difficulty in coming to terms with the Holocaust was the rejection of Arendt's book on Eichmann. The first conference on Arendt was held in Israel only in 1997. See also *History and Memory* 8 (fall/winter 1996), special issue, *Hannah Arendt and "Eichmann in Jerusalem".*

88. Irit Keynan, *Holocaust Survivors and the Emissaries from Eretz-Israel: Germany, 1945–1948* (Tel Aviv, 1996, in Hebrew); Hanna Yablonka, *Foreign Brethren: Holocaust Survivors in the State of Israel, 1948–1952* (Jerusalem, 1994, in Hebrew).

89. Yael Zerubavel, *Recovered Roots: Collective Memory and the Making of Israeli National Tradition* (Chicago, 1995); Nachman Ben-Yehudah, *The Masada Myth: Collective Memory and Mythmaking in Israel* (Madison, Wis., 1995); Nurit Gertz, *Captive of a Dream: National Myths in Israeli Culture* (Tel Aviv, 1995, in Hebrew); Oz Almog, *The Sabra—A Profile* (Tel Aviv, 1997, in Hebrew); Anita Shapira, *New Jews, Old Jews* (Tel Aviv, 1997, in Hebrew); Shapira, *Visions in Conflict* (Tel Aviv, 1997, in Hebrew).

was a recent work by Idith Zartal, which unleashed yet another public debate. Zartal argues that the Yishuv's efforts to bring the "she'erit ha'-pleta" (the surviving remnants) of the Holocaust to Palestine involved a great deal of Zionist indoctrination, arm-twisting, and attempts to deny the survivors access to any other path out of the DP (displaced persons) camps. She also insists that these policies were motivated primarily by the desire rapidly to expand the manpower resources of the future state, not least because of the expectation of imminent war.[90] Conversely, the Hebrew translation of Saul Friedländer's *Nazi Germany and the Jews* was welcomed in Israel because it portrays, in a complex manner, the gradual process of disassociation between German Jewry and its gentile environment. Rather than demonizing the Germans and mocking the Jews for having refused to read the handwriting on the wall, Friedländer forcefully demonstrates the "betrayal of the intellectuals" that characterized the German elites, and the bewilderment and confusion that beset German Jewry during the early years of the Third Reich. He thus undermines several conventions that are still particularly strong in Israel and may have also struck a chord with those who are aware of the Israeli intelligentsia's own complex—and not always admirable—relationship with the politically powerful, the military elite, and the Arab minority.[91] Similarly, the

90. Idith Zartal, *From Catastrophe to Power: Jewish Illegal Immigration to Palestine, 1945–1948* (Tel Aviv, 1996, in Hebrew). Original title is *Zehavam shel ha'yehudim,* or "the Jews' gold." For a scathing critique, see Haim Gouri, "On Books and What Is Between Them," *Alpayim* 14 (1997, in Hebrew). For earlier works on Zionist policies toward the Holocaust, see Dalia Ofer, *Escaping the Holocaust: Illegal Immigration to the Land of Israel, 1939–1944* (New York, 1990); Yehuda Bauer, *Jews for Sale? Nazi-Jewish Negotiations, 1933–1945* (New Haven, 1994); and Dina Porat, *The Blue and the Yellow Stars of David: The Zionist Leadership in Palestine and the Holocaust, 1939–1945,* trans. David Ben-Nahum (Cambridge, Mass., 1990).

91. The Hebrew translation of Friedländer, *Nazi Germany and the Jews,* was published in late 1997. See, for example, Ilana Hammermann, "The Shoah and Best-Sellers," *Ha'aretz,* 26 December 1997 (in Hebrew), in which she laments the failure of such important publications as the new Hebrew edition of Emmanuel Ringelblum's journal and the newly published diary of Salek Perehodnik (known in the English translation as Calel Perechodnik) to attract the public's attention, and Goldhagen's immediate popularity, which she estimates is greater even than Friedländer's book. She describes Goldhagen's book as "a pamphlet" that calls upon the reader to "reach out for his sword . . . and take revenge against the monster" but at the same time enables him "to calm himself, since there is no one to slay anymore." To her mind, "this simplistic thesis—which has the added convenience of not awakening any commitment and sensibility in the reader for the social reality in which he lives here and now, neither against racism and the dehumanization of others, nor against repression and political violence in all its forms—this simplistic thesis apparently attracts readers." She further accuses Goldhagen of inventing details of horror that do not exist in his sources, "a consequence of that (certainly unconscious) seductive pull of the dark need in people's souls to peep as closely as possible, with a mixture of horror and pleasure, at the atrocity being perpetrated on others." Instead, she greatly recommends Friedländer's book as portraying "the

recent publication in Hebrew of my own *Hitler's Army* seems to have aroused a fair amount of interest because it tries to reconstruct the manner in which a variety of factors—existing prejudices and pre-army schooling, military indoctrination and punitive discipline, hardship at the front and criminal orders—led to the brutalization of German troops in World War II and distorted their perception of the very reality they had helped to create. Once more, it appears, this study both provided a more complex picture of German society under Nazism than was commonly known in Israel, and was associated with domestic issues regarding the admittedly still very different conduct of Israeli troops in their daily clashes with the Palestinian population.[92]

Seen as controversial in the United States and Germany, and as largely irrelevant in France, within the Israeli context Goldhagen's book thus both stated the obvious and underlined themes that were crucial components of the early Israeli national myth and for this very reason were

---

terrifying proximity that gradually developed in the daily life of German society in the 1930s between a normal and developed human society, in the heart of the 'civilized world,' and the exclusion, the incitement, the persecution, and the murder that were taking place in its midst, and the willingness to accept them and even to become complicit in them through indifference or action." It seems, however, that Friedländer's book will have sold at least as well as Goldhagen's in Israel. See also Oded Heilbrunner, "German Antisemitism and the Question of Its Continuity in German History," *Ha'aretz,* 23 January 1998 (in Hebrew), reviewing both Goldhagen's and Friedländer's books, very much to the detriment of the former, about which he writes that "apart from descriptions of horrors (which no one would deny, despite the author's insistence on presenting his study as innovative), one learns very little from it." He predicts that the controversy will encourage more studies on antisemitism: "Friedländer's book will certainly be cited in many of them; as for Goldhagen's book, I doubt it." For an attack on Heilbrunner's interpretation of the role of antisemitism in Nazism and its historical roots in German history, see Dina Porat, "Where Is 'the Dustbin of History'?" *Ha'aretz,* 6 February 1998.

92. The Hebrew translation of *Hitler's Army* was published in April 1998. See, for example, Ruvik Rosental, "Stupid Soldiers," *Ma'ariv,* 24 April 1998, who writes that the book is part of "a growing and important preoccupation with the Third Reich, the mental make-up of its citizens, as an attempt to understand how the Nazi monster rose from the midst of a complex, wise, and culturally highly endowed people. Moreover, it is of paramount importance to deal with this topic in order to understand the potential of human evil, and under which conditions it is realized, or, if one may put it this way, reaches maximum productivity. . . . What happened in Germany before and after the war demonstrates that the Nazi period revealed a terrible, cruel, and stupid aspect of the German people, and prevented another critical, wise, and humane aspect from being expressed. . . . [A book] about what happened not far from here just half a century ago, by the hands of the people of Beethoven, Goethe, and Kant." Batya Gur, review of *Hitler's Army, Ha'aretz,* 7 May 1998: "This book is an important part of an on-going work on the puzzle—Friedländer's book is yet another part of this puzzle—whose theme is a reconstruction of the precise historical picture of German public opinion in all its sectors, without stereotypes and emotional manipulations in the style of Steven Spielberg and Daniel Goldhagen."

coming under attack from left-leaning academic and intellectual circles. The demonization of the Germans, often seen as representative of most other European gentiles, and especially the Poles—whose obverse side, namely, the state's official recognition of "righteous gentiles," merely highlights the alleged essential characteristics of the majority—has always served as a fundamental legitimization for Israeli policies, indeed for the very existence of the state. One should point out, however, that criticism of the book did not come only from the Left. Indeed, many of those who perceive the "new historians" as anti-Zionists engaged in undermining the legitimacy of the state dismissed the book on scholarly and intellectual grounds. Thus Shlomo Aronson, who has often attacked the "post-Zionist" trend in new Israeli historiography, criticized the book severely in a November 1996 newspaper article. It is also of some interest to cite his comments on the reason for the different reception of the book in other countries:

> Goldhagen's book . . . has given rise to a huge storm, especially in Germany. . . . But in Israel, the book has not drawn much public attention, perhaps because the attitude toward Germany here has changed and become much more moderate than it is in the United States, where many praised the book, and many condemned it. Many will agree with Goldhagen a priori that Nazi Germany carried out what generations of Germans had been born into, had absorbed at home, in school, in church and in bars. That violent antisemitism prepared the path to extermination.[93]

This is a telling statement, since it contains an interesting contradiction. The Israeli public has indeed greatly moderated its attitudes toward Germany. On the one hand, unlike in the 1950s and 1960s, Israelis now make no apologies for driving German cars or traveling on vacation to Austria and the Federal Republic. On the other hand, most Israelis continue to view the Holocaust primarily as a product of antisemitism. Thus, while Israelis might be less anti-German than Americans are, they are more convinced of the overwhelming role that antisemitism played in the Nazi genocide of the Jews. But for most Israelis, acknowledging German or gentile antisemitism, then as now, merely serves the function of legitimizing the existence of their state and their decision to live in it. It thus plays a positive, constructive role in Israeli self-perception and the consolidation of national identity. Conversely, American Jews, proportionately probably Goldhagen's most avid consumers in the United States, perceive antisemitism as remaining a potential threat to their national identity as Americans; and precisely because antisemitism is a contemporary worry, it

---

93. Shlomo Aronson, "Hatred in the Blood," *Ma'ariv,* 22 November 1996.

is easier to accept its centrality for Nazism, and, at the same time, it is quite a relief to see it confined geographically and chronologically to pre-1945 Germany and the Holocaust. Hence the anxieties evoked and reflected by the book (and its author) are much more in line with American than Israeli conditions and sensibilities.[94]

One final point on the Israeli reception. It has been said that Goldhagen's focus on the horrors of the killing had a voyeuristic element that appealed to certain readers. There is no doubt that some elements in his text seem to reflect his own fantasies—themselves most probably the product of (over)exposure to media representations of the Holocaust and other massacres—rather than the information culled from the documentation he cites. Goldhagen wants us to imagine with him the thoughts that went through the minds of a German policeman and the little girl he shot, he wants us to imagine what the shooting actually looked like; in short, he demands that we fantasize atrocity and be morally outraged by the horrors conjured up in our minds. This kind of prose may have appeared innovative, or even morbidly fascinating, to certain American and German readers who were dissatisfied with the drier, more detached depictions and interpretations of conventional Holocaust scholarship. Especially in the United States, this insistence on the most explicit aspects of horror must have, at the same time, been quite familiar to readers exposed to a tremendous number of real and staged representations of violence in the media. But precisely because of their association with the media, that is, with entertainment, Goldhagen's images of horror remained sufficiently distant to prevent alienation through anxiety and disgust. In Israel, however, this type of prose failed to have the same effect on the public, because Israelis are ceaselessly reminded of the horrors of the Holocaust and have never developed a detached attitude to it, even while some do their best to avoid this flood of horrifying images. Long before television came in the late 1960s, young Israelis who had been spared the Holocaust (and we should stress that at the time the population still included a large number of survivors) were exposed to memoir and fiction literature on the Holocaust that provided sufficient graphic horror to last a lifetime.[95] For many Israelis, it seems, Goldhagen's explicit descriptions seemed dangerously close to kitsch. Moreover, as

---

94. See, for example, Yosef Gorny, *The Quest for National Identity: The Place of Israel in Jewish Public Thinking, 1945–1987* (Tel Aviv, 1990, in Hebrew). Interestingly, the English title given in this edition is *The Quest for Collective Identity*. And see the very different approach in *Tikkun,* March/April 1998, special issue, *Israel at Fifty: A Compassionately Critical Analysis.*

95. Omer Bartov, "Kitsch and Sadism in Ka-Tzetnik's Other Planet: Israeli Youth Imagine the Holocaust," *Jewish Social Studies,* spring 1997, 42–76.

always, for Israelis the horrors of the past are intimately linked with those of the present. Daily exposure to the brutalities of the conflict with the Arabs, be they bus bombings by terrorists or beatings and torture by the security forces, means that Goldhagen's type of voyeurism hits too close to home to have the same riveting effect it appears to have had in the United States and Germany. All of this should explain why Goldhagen's book fell flat in the Jewish state.

Conclusion: Prejudiced Behaviorism

Debates over Goldhagen's book were thus clearly framed within the national and historical contexts in which they took place. All four nations examined in this chapter had been preoccupied with certain aspects of Nazism and the Holocaust long before the appearance of *Hitler's Willing Executioners,* and in all cases this involved a wider discussion of national and group identities. Thus the reception of Goldhagen's book serves to illustrate the different ways in which the genocide of the Jews has come to play an important role in self-perception and self-definition, in under-standing the past, facing up to the present, and preparing for the future.

On another level, however, these debates were clearly concerned just as much with the abstract as well as the concrete implications of genocide for our understanding of human nature. This is one reason why Christo-pher Browning's very different interpretation of perpetrator motivation was frequently brought into the debate, quite apart from the more obvious proximity in publication dates, similarity of sources, and Goldhagen's vehement attacks on Browning both in his book and in later disputes. As is well known, in the final chapter of his *Ordinary Men,* Browning cites the theory developed in Stanley Milgram's 1974 book *Obedience to Authority* as an important tool in elucidating the motivation of German policemen who perpetrated murder. Curiously, to the best of my knowledge, not one of the innumerable contributions to this debate in all four countries took the trouble to go back to Milgram's text and analyze it on its own terms rather than merely through the prism provided by Browning. Yet this is a worthwhile exercise. By way of conclusion, I will shed some light on one feature of Milgram's study, which seems to undermine both the objective nature of the experiment it describes and the fundamental assumption made by its author. Without wishing thereby either to wholly reject Browning's thesis or to adopt Goldhagen's ideas, I hope that this brief dis-cussion will demonstrate that we are still very far from having a sufficient explanation for how "ordinary men" are transformed into serial killers. Moreover, I believe that the example of Milgram reminds us once more that none of us comes to this debate as a tabula rasa, and that not even the most careful scholarly assertion can ever be accepted at face value.

Milgram's is a behaviorist interpretation *par excellence,* based on an experiment in which a group of volunteers was ordered to apply ever more powerful electric shocks to a man tied to a chair as part of what was described to them as an experiment in learning under threat of physical punishment. While in reality no electric shock was involved, the actor in the chair convinced most volunteers that he was suffering increasing pain, by physical contortions, pleas, cries, and feigned fainting, unable as he was to release himself from his seat. In a significant majority of cases the volunteers obeyed the instructor's directions to go on applying shocks, even as the dial clearly indicated that they could have lethal consequences.

Milgram interpreted his experiment as proving that "the essence of obedience consists in the fact that a person comes to view himself as the instrument for carrying out another person's wishes, and he therefore no longer regards himself as responsible for his actions. Once this crucial shift of viewpoint has occurred in the person, all of the essential features of obedience follow."[96] Consequently, "obedience is the psychological mechanism that links individual action to political purpose."[97] According to Milgram, "it is the extreme willingness of adults to go to almost any length on the command of an authority that constitutes the chief finding of the study."[98] Milgram assumes—without producing any evidence—that "the Nazi extermination of European Jews is the most extreme instance of abhorrent immoral acts carried out by thousands of people *in the name of obedience*"[99] (my italics). And since he asserts that the participants in his experiment were not "monsters, the sadistic fringe of society," but rather "represented *ordinary people drawn from working, managerial, and professional classes*" (my italics), he concludes "that Arendt's conception of the *banality of evil* comes closer to the truth than one might dare imagine. The ordinary person who shocked the victim did so out of a sense of obligation—a conception of his duties as a subject—and not from any peculiarly aggressive tendencies." Hence, he writes, "the most fundamental lesson of our study" is that "ordinary people, simply doing their jobs, and without any particular hostility on their part, can become agents in a terrible destructive process."[100]

Milgram concedes the limits of his experiment. He notes that "at least

---

96. Milgram, *Obedience to Authority,* xii.
97. Ibid., 1.
98. Ibid., 5.
99. Ibid., 2.
100. Ibid., 5–6.

one essential feature of the situation in Germany was not studied here—namely, the intense devaluation of the victim prior to action against him." He asserts that "in all likelihood, our subjects would have experienced greater ease in shocking the victim had he been convincingly portrayed as a brutal criminal or a pervert." Yet he adds that "many subjects harshly devalue the victim *as a consequence* of acting against him." Moreover, while "many of the people studied in the experiment were in some sense against what they did to the learner, and many protested even while they obeyed," what they lacked was "the capacity for transforming beliefs and values into action. Some were totally convinced of the wrongness of what they were doing but could not bring themselves to make an open break with authority. Some derived satisfaction from their thoughts and felt that—within themselves, at least—they had been on the side of the angels." Nevertheless, Milgram insists that "subjective feelings are largely irrelevant to the moral issue at hand so long as they are not transformed into action. The attitudes of the guards at a concentration camp are of no consequence when in fact they are allowing the slaughter of innocent men to take place before them."[101]

Thus we are left to conclude that most people, if put into a situation similar to that created by Milgram, would act in the same manner. A few unique individuals might resist authority and refuse to obey; others, who had internalized some prejudice against the victim, would cause pain with even less compunction. But generally speaking, the makeup of human psychology and the structure of human society should lead us to expect most people to be the willing executioners of their fellow human beings when told to do so by a recognizable authority. Unlike Goldhagen, Milgram does not believe in choice, since "a person does not get to see the whole situation but only a small part of it, and is thus unable to act without some kind of overall direction. He yields to authority but in doing so is alienated from his own actions."[102] Browning reaches similar conclusions: "Everywhere society conditions people to respect and defer to authority. . . . Everywhere people seek career advancement. . . . bureaucratization and specialization attenuate the sense of personal responsibility. . . . Within virtually every social collective, the peer group exerts tremendous pressures on behavior and sets moral norms. If the men of Reserve Police Battalion 101 could become killers under such circumstances, what group of men cannot?"[103] Conversely, Goldhagen adamantly asserts that "any explanation that fails to acknowledge the actors' capacity to know and to

---

101. Ibid., 9–10.
102. Ibid., 11.
103. Browning, *Ordinary Men,* 189.

judge, namely to understand and to have views about the significance and morality of their actions, that fails to hold the actors' beliefs and values as central, that fails to emphasize the autonomous motivating force of Nazi ideology, particularly its central component of antisemitism, cannot possibly succeed in telling us much about why the perpetrators acted as they did."[104]

There is obviously no simple answer to this central question of human psychology and society. In the present context I will not attempt to articulate my own position, which in any case I have tried to clarify elsewhere. Yet what deserves mention here—and has hitherto escaped notice—is a striking aspect of Milgram's study, namely, that his carefully balanced, apparently objective and scientific conclusions were reached on the basis of an experiment in which his own biases were clearly exhibited and cannot but have influenced his observations. By following Milgram's account of several cases, with special attention to the links he makes between class, "race," and gender, on the one hand, and the subjects' physical features, moral conduct, and most crucially their capacity to withstand malevolent authority, we find that this objective scientist brings to the experiment a baggage of preconceived notions and ideas that belie his assertion that all people are fundamentally the same and would act similarly under identical conditions. It appears, then, that even the most clinical and scientific behaviorist theory is informed precisely by those internalized prejudices whose importance it seeks to diminish.

Let us take a brief look at some of these examples.

1. Mr. Bruno Batta, 37, a welder born in New Haven to Italian parents, has "a rough-hewn face that conveys a conspicuous lack of alertness. His overall appearance is somewhat brutish. An observer described him as a 'crude mesomorph of obviously limited intelligence.' But this is not fully adequate, for he relates to the experimenter with a submissive and deferential sweetness."[105] Mr. Batta, a blue-collar worker of south European, Mediterranean extraction, whose vulgar features and primitive muscularity betray his moral character, acts with "total indifference" to the victim, derives "quiet satisfaction at doing his job properly," and professes that he "got disgusted" when the man he tortured refused to cooperate.

2. A professor, "a somewhat gaunt, ascetic man," who "could be taken for a New England Minister" but in fact "teaches Old Testament liturgy at a major divinity school." This elderly and educated man of religion, obviously of a good north European family, naturally balks after

---

104. Goldhagen, *Hitler's Willing Executioners,* 13.
105. Milgram, *Obedience to Authority,* 45.

administering only 150 volts, asserting ethical reasons, since, he says, "if one has as one's ultimate authority God, then it trivializes human authority."

3.   Jack Washington, drill press operator, 35, "a black subject," born in South Carolina, "is a soft man, a bit heavy and balding, older-looking than his years. His pace is slow and his manner impassive; his speech is tinged with Southern and black accents." An obviously primitive blue-collar worker, this dull-minded and morally insensitive African American from the South casually delivers a lethal charge of 450 volts when instructed to do so and later explains that he was simply "following orders."

4.   Jan Rensaleer, 32, industrial engineer, "sporting blond hair and a mustache . . . self-contained and speaks with a trace of a foreign accent . . . neatly dressed." Having "emigrated from Holland after the Second World War," he "is a member of the Dutch Reform Church . . . mild-mannered and intelligent." Member of the professional middle class, an elegant north European and God-fearing man, Rensaleer has the requisite moral qualities to withstand malevolent authority. He refuses to continue beyond 255 volts and reacts to the standard statement that he has no choice but to continue by emphatically declaring, "I *do* have a choice." Subsequently he accepts responsibility for shocking the victim. Described as being "hard on himself," he remarks that "on the basis of his experience in Nazi-occupied Europe, he would predict a high level of compliance to orders." His own conduct, however, is close to exemplary.[106]

5.   Fred Prozi, about 50, unemployed, "dressed in a jacket but no tie; he has a good-natured, if slightly dissolute, appearance. He employs working-class grammar and strikes one as a rather ordinary fellow." This blue-collar worker, apparently kind but clearly a simple and stupid man, probably of Italian origin, obviously lacks the moral qualities required to withstand authority. Hence he continues giving a lethal electric shock to the victim—who for all intents and purposes appears dead—as long as he is ordered to do so.

6.   Karen Dontz, 40, a "housewife who for the past six years has worked part time as a registered nurse. Her husband is a plumber. She is Catholic and her mother was born in Czechoslovakia. Mrs. Dontz has an unusually casual, slow-paced way of speaking, and her tone expresses constant humility. . . . Throughout the experiment she is nervous." This working-class woman of East European origin betrays the lack of intelligence and nervous disposition typical of her sex and class. She clearly lacks true moral fiber. Consequently she continues administering the lethal 450 volts

---

106. Ibid., 45–52, for description of these experiments.

to a victim who appears to have been perpetually silenced until told to stop. She knows as a nurse that she could have killed the victim but is satisfied that she did what an authority figure told her to perform.

7. Elinor Rosenblum, a housewife, "takes pleasure in describing her background: She graduated from the University of Wisconsin . . . her husband, a film distributor, attended Dartmouth. She does volunteer work with juvenile delinquents . . . has been active on the local Girl Scout organization and the PTA. She is fluent and garrulous and projects herself strongly, with many references to her social achievements. She displays a pleasant though excessively talkative charm." This middle-class, obviously Jewish woman (although Milgram shies away from stating this outright) displays all the stereotypical characteristics of her sex and ethnicity, and all the mannerisms of an outsider newly arrived at a respectable social status. She had the intelligence to climb up the social ladder but still lacks the moral fiber that comes with self-assurance. She is thus hypocritical and self-centered: "Mrs. Rosenblum, even as she administers increasingly more painful shocks to the victim, constantly complains: 'Must I go on? Oh, I'm so worried about him . . . I'm shaking. I'm shaking. Do I have to go up there [on the dial]?'" But she delivers the lethal 450-volt shock three times. Milgram explains that "she was nervous not because the man was being hurt but because *she* was performing the action . . . she asserts her own distress. . . . A self-centered quality permeates her remarks . . . she is not against punishment per se but only against her active infliction of it. If it just 'happens,' it is acceptable." Milgram concludes that "Mrs. Rosenblum is a person whose psychic life lacks integration. She has not been able to find life purposes consistent with her needs for esteem and success. Her goals, thinking, and emotions are fragmented. She carries out her experimental role as teacher showing great outward conviction, while at the same time she displays another side of herself to the experimenter, behaving meekly and submissively. It is not surprising that she failed to mobilize the psychic resources needed to translate her compassion for the learner into the disobedient act. Her feelings, goals, and thoughts were too diverse and unintegrated. All evidence indicates that at the time of her performance she believed the learner was being shocked. But it is not difficult for a woman of hysterical tendencies to adjust her thinking in a manner consistent with a positive self-image. In a questionnaire returned to us a few months later, she states that during the experiment her 'mature and well-educated brain' had not believed the learner was getting shocks. Through a post-facto adjustment of thought, she protects her cherished—if unrealistic—picture of her own nature." Milgram obviously despises this woman.

8. Gretchen Brandt, 35, a "medical technician who works at the

University Medical School. She had emigrated from Germany five years before and speaks with a thick German accent." This cultivated, elegant north European is a model of exemplary conduct: calm and composed, completely sure of herself, combining intelligence with an unwavering moral compass. Milgram's admiration is all the greater because she is a German and a woman from whom he might expect very different behavior, yet she seems both attractive and of the appropriate social and cultural background. After administering 210 volts, "she turns to the experimenter, remarking firmly, 'Well, I'm sorry, I don't think we should continue.'" The experiment is stopped. Milgram comments that she is "firm and resolute throughout. She indicates in the interview that she was in no way tense or nervous, and this corresponds to her controlled appearance throughout." Indeed, "the woman's straightforward, courteous behavior in the experiment, lack of tension, a total control of her own action seems to make disobedience a simple and rational deed. Her behavior is the very embodiment of what I had initially envisioned would be true for almost all subjects." Milgram concludes: "Ironically, Gretchen Brandt grew to adolescence in Hitler's Germany and was for the great part of her youth exposed to Nazi propaganda. When asked about the possible influence of her background, she remarks slowly, 'Perhaps we have seen too much pain.'"[107] One can almost see the scientist falling in love with his subject.

Although Milgram introduces the detailed exposition of his experiment by claiming that people from different professions and classes behaved similarly, his examples do not confirm this assertion, and they reveal his own biases. If we were to sketch a portrait of the typical perpetrator based on the findings of this experiment, he would be working-class, crude, muscular, lacking in education and intelligence, possibly lethargic, badly dressed and speaking ungrammatical English, originating in southern Europe or the American South, probably Black or Italian. Women supporters would belong to the working class, possibly of east European origin, or be hysterical, hypocritical, arriviste Jews. Conversely, those most unlikely to become perpetrators would be middle-class academics, professionals, the clergy or at least men of faith, intelligent, elegant, probably blonds of north European, most likely Protestant background. Those exposed in the past to war, atrocity, and complicity would be unlikely to comply.

The problem is, of course, that the typical supporter of Nazism came from the north German, middle-class, Protestant milieu.[108] We know that the commanders of the Nazi death squads, the elite of the SS and the police, were men with university degrees, often with a Ph.D. in

107. Ibid., 73–85, for description of these experiments.
108. Richard F. Hamilton, *Who Voted for Hitler?* (Princeton, 1982); Michael Kater, *The Nazi Party: A Social Profile of Members and Leaders, 1919–1945* (Oxford, 1983).

law.[109] We know that the medical and legal professions collaborated happily with Nazism and facilitated many of its crimes; that the clergy, Protestant and Catholic, did little to oppose the genocide of the Jews and much to popularize prejudice.[110] We know that the brutalizing effects of World War I played a major role in the success of Nazism.[111] That is, those most unlikely to comply with malevolent authority supported Hitler. We also know that inside Germany it was first and foremost members of the working class who opposed the regime.[112] We know that Nazism's victims came mainly from Eastern Europe and European Jewry, from among the handicapped, the Gypsies, the homosexuals.[113] We know that Italians tried to hinder crimes perpetrated by Germans in Europe, although in Ethiopia their own prejudices facilitated widespread murder.[114] This does not mean that Milgram is necessarily wrong in his

109. Ulrich Herbert, *Best: Biographische Studien über Radikalismus, Weltanschauung und Vernunft, 1903–1989* (Bonn, 1996), parts 1–2; Helmut Krausnick and Hans-Heinrich Wilhelm, *Die Truppe des Weltanschauungskrieges: Die Einsatzgruppen der Sicherheitspolizei und des SD, 1938–1942* (Stuttgart, 1981).

110. On the professions, see n. 15 above, as well as Robert Jay Lifton, *The Nazi Doctors: Medical Killing and the Psychology of Genocide* (New York, 1986). On the churches, see Doris L. Bergen, *Twisted Cross: The German Christian Movement* (Chapel Hill, 1996); Robert P. Ericksen and Susannah Heschel, "The German Churches Face Hitler: Assessment of the Historiography," *Tel Aviver Jahrbuch für deutsche Geschichte* 23 (1994): 433–59; Robert P. Ericksen, *Theologians under Hitler: Gerhard Kittel, Paul Althaus, and Emanuel Hirsch* (New Haven, 1985); Susannah Heschel, "When Jesus Was an Aryan: The Church and Antisemitic Propaganda," and Beth Griech-Polelle, "A Pure Soul Is Good Enough: Bishop von Galen, Resistance to Nazism, and the Catholic Community of Münster," both in Omer Bartov and Phyllis Mack, eds., *In God's Name: Genocide and Religion in the Twentieth Century* (New York, 2000).

111. Klaus Theweleit, *Männerphantasien*, 2 vols. (Basel, 1977); Richard Bessel, *Germany after the First World War* (Oxford, 1993); Jay W. Baird, *To Die for Germany: Heroes in the Nazi Pantheon* (Bloomington, 1990); Peter H. Merkl, *Political Violence under the Swastika: 581 Early Nazis* (Princeton, 1975); Anton Kaes, Martin Jay, and Edward Dimenberg, eds., *The Weimar Republic Source Book* (Berkeley, 1994), esp. chapters 1–6; Bartov, *Murder in Our Midst*, part 1.

112. Tim Mason, *Social Policy in the Third Reich: The Working Class in the "National Community,"* trans. John Broadwin, ed. Jane Caplan (Providence, 1993); Mason, *Nazism, Fascism, and the Working Class,* ed. Jane Caplan (Cambridge, 1995), esp. chapters 2, 4, 7, and 9.

113. Götz Aly, *"Endlösung": Völkerverschiebung und der Mord an den europäischen Juden* (Frankfurt am Main, 1995); Leni Yahil, *The Holocaust: The Fate of European Jewry,* trans. Ina Friedman and Haya Galai (New York, 1990); Michael Burleigh, *Death and Deliverance: "Euthanasia" in Germany, 1900–1945* (Cambridge, 1994); Henry Friedlander, *The Origins of Nazi Genocide: From Euthanasia to the Final Solution* (Chapel Hill, 1995); Michael Zimmermann, *Rassenutopie und Genozid: Die nationalsozialistische "Lösung der Zigeunerfrage"* (Hamburg, 1996); Burkhard Jellonnek, *Homosexuelle unter dem Hakenkreuz: Die Verfolgung von Homosexuellen im Dritten Reich* (Paderborn, 1990).

114. Jonathan Steinberg, *All or Nothing: The Axis and the Holocaust, 1941–43* (London, 1990).

psychological portrait, but rather that he got his history wrong. Had these men and women acted merely out of a sense of obedience to authority, the results of the experiment could not possibly conform to the reality in Nazi Germany. Hence we are left to conclude that the opposite is the case, namely, that middle-class professional Germans supported Hitler for what appeared to them intellectually and morally sound reasons; that Gretchen Brandt, for instance, would have joined the Nazi Women's Organization with the same calm self-assurance that made her refuse to follow an order she did not agree with. It means that, for a while at least, people had a choice, and what they chose indicated their beliefs.

At the same time, Milgram's experiment indicates that what we believe to be an objective reality and sound rational arguments are often so strongly influenced by our biases as to wholly distort our findings. Milgram obviously would never have considered himself a racist, a misogynist, an antisemite, or a social elitist. Yet his descriptions of his subjects' physical, intellectual, and moral qualities are so clearly related to their ethnicity, gender, and social background that one must ask how it is that those who have used the results of his experiment over the years have never noticed his prejudices. One is tempted to argue that a sociopsychological experiment so deeply imbued with bias cannot possibly be taken seriously as anything but a reflection of the prejudices of the experimenter and his time (merely a generation ago). I would not go that far, since some of Milgram's insights seem to me of paramount importance. But I would stress, nevertheless, that what this experiment proves above all is that obedience to authority is not at all merely about a person coming to see himself "as the instrument for carrying out another person's wishes," who "therefore no longer regards himself as responsible for his actions." Rather, I would argue that obedience to authority among those whose collaboration is most necessary, the educated professional elites, men and women of religion and faith, teachers and technicians, generals and professors, comes from accepting the fundamental ideas that guide that authority and wishing to help realize them in practice; and that this becomes possible only if both the authority and those who obey it share the same prejudices, the same view of the world, the same fundamental perception of reality.

What then are we to conclude from this brief analysis of Milgram's experiment, of his social, ethnic, and gender biases? What does this tell us about the relationship between the reception of interpretations of atrocity by different societies in different periods? All we can say at this juncture, I believe, is that while atrocity is the product of numerous factors, some historical, political, and ideological, others psychological and sociological, so too is the interpretation of such events in the past and the present. If we can and must learn from the study of inhumanity, so too can we learn a great deal about our own societies by evaluating the manner in which they react to theories and interpretations of past atrocities. From this perspective, the greatest long-term merit of Goldhagen's study is not to be found in his interpretation of the Holocaust, but rather in the manner with which it was received and what that reception tells us about the world in which we live.

The "Goldhagen Effect": Memory, Repetition, and Responsibility in the New Germany

Atina Grossmann

Background: The Long Prelude

In the inevitably retrospective perspective of a book, the topic "Goldhagen Effect" initially produces the weary sense, both resentful and bemused, that everything that could be said has been said many times over. At the same time, however, those of us—scholars and journalists—who make a habit of observing Germany's tussles with its past remain intrigued by a moving target, swinging between anxious remembrance and resentful denial, that just won't go away and keeps mutating, seemingly with increasing speed and intensity. As soon as "Goldhagen" fades, another debate, another controversy, another scandal, moves in to occupy the political economy of Holocaust memory.[1] The history of the Federal Republic is strewn with what we might term "Holocaust moments," from the first postwar confrontations under Allied occupation (during what Jeffrey Herf has termed the Nuremberg interregnum)[2] to the breaking open of the Adenauer-era consensus in the 1960s, on to the "explosion of memory" in the 1980s and 1990s. Indeed, the entire chronology of postwar

---

1. For a useful English-language compendium of relevant articles (albeit with an introduction that is, to my mind, overly adulatory of Goldhagen), see Robert R. Shandley, ed., *Unwilling Germans? The Goldhagen Debate,* trans. Jeremiah Riemer (Minneapolis, 1998). The German-language documentation is Julius Schoeps, ed., *Ein Volk von Mördern? Die Dokumentation zur Goldhagen Kontroverse um die Rolle der Deutschen im Holocaust* (Hamburg, 1996).

2. See Jeffrey Herf, *Divided Memory: The Nazi Past in the Two Germanys* (Cambridge, Mass., 1997), 201–66.

Germany (especially, but not only, the Federal Republic, which is my focus), loosely clumped by decades, can be read as a continual oscillation between the drive to forget—to draw the proverbial *Schlussstrich* and aim for "normality"—and the injunction to remember, to commemorate, and to work through questions of guilt and responsibility.

In the last several years, we have witnessed a rush of such events. The enthusiastic reception of Goldhagen's *Hitler's Willing Executioners* was more than matched by the astonishing bestseller success of Victor Klemperer's lengthy and meticulous record of the anguished if atypically privileged life of a German Jew during the Third Reich. The diaries were quickly deployed both to reinforce and to refute Goldhagen's claims about the pervasive eliminationist antisemitism of German culture.[3] The seemingly endless, convoluted debates about the construction of Holocaust and war memorials in Berlin, the new capital of united Germany, took on new urgency with the victory in fall 1998 of a new "Red-Green" post-Kohl government.[4] Controversy continues to follow the traveling exhibition "War of Extermination: Crimes of the Wehrmacht, 1941–1944," organized by the Hamburg Institute for Social Research, whose iconoclastic director and patron, Jan Philipp Reemtsma, was an early and energetic supporter of Goldhagen's work.[5] German historians themselves have (very) belat-

3. Victor Klemperer, *Ich will Zeugnis ablegen bis zum letzten: Tagebücher, 1933–1945* (Berlin, 1995). On the German reception, see Hannes Heer, ed., *Im Herzen der Finsternis: Victor Klemperer als Chronist der NS-Zeit* (Berlin, 1997). See the English translation *I Will Bear Witness: A Diary of the Nazi Years, 1933–1941* (New York, 1998); and *I Will Bear Witness, 1941–1945: A Diary of the Nazi Years,* vol. 2 (New York, 2000); see also Omer Bartov's review of volume 1 of the American edition in *The New Republic,* 28 December 1998.

4. See, for example, the cover story "Holocaust Mahnmal in Berlin: Zuviel Erinnerung? Vom Mahnmal zum Wahnmal," *Der Spiegel,* no. 35 (August 1998): 170–81. It is interesting to note that such stories in German journals are almost inevitably accompanied by stock images of the Holocaust (in this case, the selection ramp at Auschwitz). Most recently, SPD (Social Democratic party) cultural official Michael Naumann has unleashed controversy by proposing first to replace the potential Holocaust Memorial in Berlin with a "living memorial" of libraries, museums, and archives, and then to reopen the competition for memorial designs. See *Der Spiegel,* no. 51 (1998). See also Alan Cowell, "Bleak Debate in Berlin on a Holocaust Memorial," *New York Times,* 11 January 1998; and Roger Cohen, "Schröder Backs Design for a Vast Berlin Holocaust Memorial," *New York Times,* 18 January 1999. A documentation of the memorial debate has already been published: Michael S. Cullen, ed., *Das Holocaust-Mahnmal: Dokumentation einer Debatte* (Zurich, 1999).

5. See Hans-Günther Thiele, ed., *Die Wehrmachts ausstellung: Dokumentation einer Kontroverse* (Bremen, 1997). The Institute produces its own journal, *Mittelweg 36, Zeitschrift des Hamburger Instituts für Sozialforschung.* See the English-language catalogue, Hannes Heer, the Hamburg Institute for Social Research, ed., *The German Army and Genocide: Crimes against War Prisoners, Jews, and Other Civilians in the East, 1939–1944,* with a foreword by Michael Geyer and a preface by Omer Bartov (New York, 1999). The American tour of the exhibition "Crimes of the Wehrmacht, 1941–1944," scheduled to open at the Cooper Union in New York in December 1999, was abruptly postponed. See also n. 104 below.

edly entered into the tense debates that have long roiled the ranks of other professions, such as law, medicine, psychiatry, and architecture, interrogating their own guild's implication in National Socialist policies and crimes, especially the connection between current "progressive" social history and the racially inflected social demographic studies of the 1930s and 1940s.[6] The most recent uproar (as of this writing) was ignited by the venerable German author Martin Walser's speech on the occasion of his receipt of the Peace Prize of the German Booksellers' Association in Frankfurt in October 1998. His contention that he had had quite enough of the "Auschwitz moral cudgel" was duly followed by outraged charges from Ignatz Bubis, head of the Central Council of Jewish Communities in Germany, that such utterances were a form of "moral arson."[7] And surely this "debate," too, will have been superseded by the time this essay is published by yet another well-publicized dispute over identity and memory in the new Berlin Republic. Public excitability—always characterized by an ambivalent mixing of denial, defensiveness, obsession, contrition, and the proverbial *Betroffenheit* (being deeply affected)—about the Nazis and their crime is a recurrent, if not constant, feature of German politics and culture, and it shows no sign of abating as the next millennium approaches.

It is also the case that in every decade, starting with the occupiers' denazification and democratization programs, some of the most spectacular interventions, both welcomed and resented by West Germans, have been American products, whether the stage version of *The Diary of Anne Frank* in 1956, William Shirer's 1961 bestselling *The Rise and Fall of the Third Reich*—another book asserting a long genealogy of German evil—or the screening in 1979 of the television series *Holocaust.* The release in 1994 of Steven Spielberg's *Schindler's List* was followed by Goldhagen

---

6. See Peter Schöttler, *Geschichtswissenschaft als Legitimationswissenschaft, 1918–1945* (Frankfurt am Main, 1997). See also the interview with Hans Ulrich Wehler by Dr. Hermann Rudolph, *Tagesspiegel,* 8 December 1998, 25.

7. See, among many sources, "Wir brauchen eine neue Sprache für die Erinnerung," *Frankfurter Allgemeine Zeitung,* 14 December 1998, 39–41; and interviews with Bubis, *Berliner Zeitung,* 21 November 1998, and *Süddeutsche Zeitung,* 21 September 1998. Essentially all the articles and interviews have the same language and quotes. It is worth noting that it was none other than Martin Walser who delivered a controversial (in its insistence on using Klemperer as an example of the positive sides of German-Jewish history) *Laudatio* for Victor Klemperer when he was (very) posthumously awarded the Geschwister Scholl Prize in Frankfurt in March 1996. See also Walser's references to German Jews' efforts to "escape the East European Jewish fate" in his 1998 Frankfurt speech, *Dank: Erfahrungen beim Verfassen einer Sonntagsrede* (Frankfurt am Main, 1998), 45. See Alexandra Przymbel, "Die Tagebücher Victor Klemperers und ihre Wirklung in der deutschen Öffentlichkeit," in Johannes Heil and Rainer Erb, eds., *Geschichtswissenschaft und Öffentlichkeit: Der Streit um Daniel J. Goldhagen* (Frankfurt am Main, 1998), 317–19.

and his book; presently the director, assistant director, and architect of the just-opened Jewish Museum, as well as the architect and chair of the competition committee for the proposed Holocaust Memorial in Berlin, are all American Jews (the first two are also German-born). The frequent overlap between American and Jewish identities is an important subtext to this story.[8]

Certainly in the last twenty years, but in many ways from the very outset, national identity (and political legitimacy) in the Federal Republic was shaped by the confrontation—whether willing or not—with the Holocaust and the persecution of Jews. As Michael Geyer and Miriam Hansen have argued, noting the danger of "cannibalizing the memory of victims for the purpose of reconstructing German history," postwar German identity has depended on, and profited by, this appropriation of the experience of their Jewish victims. Remembrance of the Holocaust has become an integral part of West German national identity. If anything, we have witnessed in the last two decades a kind of "surfeit of memory,"[9] in which official West German identity, arguably, has become as dependent on the Holocaust as Jewish identity.[10] The tortured fate of the "German-Jewish symbiosis" or the debate about German guilt are hardly new topics; they have been on the German political and academic agenda since war's end in 1945. This is hardly a history of silence or amnesia. On the contrary; in every decade, albeit in different ways, remembering Jews has been linked to (and necessary for) the rehabilitation of Germans.[11]

---

8. Michael Blumenthal, director of the Jewish Museum in Berlin; Tom Freudenheim, the assistant director; and Daniel Libeskind, the architect, are all Americans (the first two are also Berlin-born). Peter Eisenman, the designated architect for the planned Berlin memorial, and James Young, chair of the commission vetting plans for the memorial and Professor of Judaic Studies at the University of Massachusetts, are American as well. All also derive authority from their identification as Jews. For a profile of Blumenthal, see Roger Cohen, "An American Jew Tries to Knit Past and Future," *New York Times,* 23 January 1999; and Blumenthal's memoir, *The Invisible Wall: Germans and Jews, a Personal Exploration* (Washington, D.C., 1998). The American Jewish Committee has also now opened an office in Berlin.

9. Charles S. Maier, "A Surfeit of Memory? Reflections on History, Melancholy, Denial," *History and Memory* 5 (fall/winter 1993): 136–52.

10. Michael Geyer and Miriam Hansen, "German-Jewish Memory and National Consciousness," in Geoffrey H. Hartman, ed., *Holocaust Remembrance: The Shapes of Memory* (Cambridge, 1994), 175–90. The story is obviously different in the German Democratic Republic (GDR), although many have remarked on the central role official antifascism played in legitimizing that regime. See especially Herf, *Divided Memory;* also Ulrike Offenberg, *Seid vorsichtig gegen die Machthaber: Die jüdischen Gemeinden in der SBZ und der DDR, 1945 bis 1990* (Berlin, 1998).

11. I am grateful to Molly Nolan for suggesting this formulation. See Wolfgang Benz, "Postwar Society and National Socialism: Remembrance, Amnesia, Rejection," *Tel Aviver Jahrbuch für deutsche Geschichte* 19 (1990): 1–12; and, for another (highly insightful) view,

The "strange affair" between Germans and Jews has been extensively documented and discussed.[12] In many ways, Jews living in Germany (to use the broadest possible formulation) have been the sharpest in their analyses. As Cilly Kugelmann, coeditor of the German-Jewish journal *Babylon,* observed, years before Daniel Goldhagen appeared to play the part, "it seems to belong to the theatrical self-understanding of the Germans' public portrayal of themselves that Jews appear in the role of admonishers and accusers who derive their importance from their experience as victims."[13] The German/Israeli historian Dan Diner also noticed that "the history of the Federal Republic seems to be accompanied by cyclically recurring debates and periodic outbursts in regard to the Nazi past, which are often prompted by questions concerning the interpretation and representation of the Holocaust." Diner's diagnosis of "repetition compulsion" when it comes to Germans discovering the Holocaust will resonate with anyone who pays attention to such matters.[14] In 1986, in the wake of the "Historians' Debate" about the singularity of the Nazis' Holocaust, Saul Friedländer made virtually an identical point:

> Such shock-like confrontations, however, seem to have become, for the majority of the population, a set mechanism, which began with the performance of the Anne Frank story in theaters throughout the *Bundesrepublik* during the late fifties, continued with the trials of the sixties, and found its most dramatic expression in the 'Holocaust' series . . . regularly retrieved,

---

Anson Rabinbach, "The Jewish Question in the German Question," *New German Critique* 44 (spring/summer 1988): 159–92. For a highly critical analysis of West German philosemitism, see Frank Stern, *The Whitewashing of the Yellow Badge: Antisemitism and Philosemitism in Postwar Germany* (Oxford, 1991).

12. See "A Strange Affair," *Newsweek,* 15 June 1998, 36–38. Perhaps the most acerbic critic of postwar German philosemitism and efforts at reconciliation was the late German journalist and historian Eike Geisel. See *Lastenausgleich, Unschuldig: Die Wiedergutwerdung der Deutschen* (Berlin, 1984); *Die Banalität der Guten: Deutsche Seelenwanderungen* (Berlin, 1994); and his posthumously published essay collection, *Triumph des guten Willens: Gute Nazis und selbsternannte Opfer: Die Nationalisierung der Erinnerung,* ed. Klaus Bittermann (Berlin Edition, 1998). For the pre-1989 period, see Anson Rabinbach and Jack Zipes, eds., *Germans and Jews since the Holocaust: The Changing Situation in West Germany* (New York, 1986); and, for the post-1989 period, Sander L. Gilman and Karen Remmler, eds., *Reemerging Jewish Culture in Germany: Life and Literature since 1989* (New York, 1994). Since the 1970s, the journal *New German Critique* has carefully and astutely chronicled the past and present of German-Jewish relations.

13. Cilly Kugelmann, "'Tell Them in America We're Still Alive!': The Jewish Community in the Federal Republic," *New German Critique* 46 (winter 1989): 129–40, special issue on minorities in German culture, 136.

14. Dan Diner, "On Guilt Discourse and Other Narratives: Epistemological Observations regarding the Holocaust, " *History and Memory* 9 (fall 1997): 301–20. Diner also coined the phrase "negative symbiosis" to characterize the "strange affair."

then forgotten once more by the vast majority of Germans. . . . A near automatic process.[15]

In fact, the more one reads backward, the less surprising the "Goldhagen effect" appears. It becomes difficult to distinguish what was indeed new and different, and what was just another version of the same old, same old—some sort of initiation rite that every generation of postwar Germans has to undergo. All the more reason, therefore, even if it seems a bit tedious—the list is long (and incomplete)—to locate the "Goldhagen effect" in the context of the long record of "Holocaust moments" since war's end in 1945. Lively discussion about victims and perpetrators and German guilt was initiated immediately after the war; its classic statement was Karl Jaspers, *Die Schuldfrage* (1946); its most public forum was the Nuremberg trials and the extensive media coverage they received.[16]

The earliest memorials, it must be said, were constructed by the victims themselves. The first commemorative ceremonies took place at Buchenwald even as Jewish victims were still dying in other parts of the camp; Jewish survivors living as displaced persons in occupied Germany built a memorial at the Landsberg DP camp and attempted to establish an official Jewish day of remembrance. Germans also immediately produced their own powerful memorial narratives, in which they were the primary victims, a stance institutionalized early on in the so-called *Volkstrauertag* (national day of war mourning) in West Germany.[17] In the early years of the Federal Republic, the balance weighed heavily on the side of denying and minimizing guilt and responsibility, a mechanism that must, however, be distinguished from "forgetting." Germans never forgot their own suffering, nor even, as is evidenced by their frequent invocations of equivalent victimization, the crimes committed against the Jews. Norbert Frei's *Vergangenheitspolitik* (Politics of the past)—among abundant other sources—painstakingly and devastatingly details the operations of amnesty, integration, and repression of the Nazi past that constituted, as the Jewish critic

---

15. Saul Friedländer, "Some German Struggles with Memory," in Geoffrey Hartman, ed., *Bitburg in Moral and Political Perspective* (Bloomington, 1986), 27, 32.

16. See especially Rabinbach, "The Jewish Question." It is worth noting the extremely important role played by the journal *New German Critique* in presenting these "moments" and the debates accompanying them to an American scholarly audience.

17. On German perceptions of victimization, see, among many articles, Elizabeth Heineman, "The Hour of the Woman: Memories of Germany's 'Crisis Years' and West German National Identity," *American Historical Review* 101, no. 2 (1996): 354–95; Robert Moeller, "War Stories: The Search for a Usable Past in the Federal Republic of Germany," *American Historical Review* 101, no. 4 (1996): 1008–48; and Atina Grossmann, "Trauma, Memory, and Motherhood: Germans and Jewish Displaced Persons in Post-Nazi Germany, 1945–1949," *Archiv für Sozialgeschichte* 38 (1998): 230–54.

Ralph Giordano has put it, the Germans' *zweite Schuld* (second guilt). The other side of amnesty and reconciliation for what remained a remarkably cohesive, if defeated, *Volksgemeinschaft* was what Frei calls the element of *Abgrenzung,* a distancing from the politics of National Socialism in exchange for restoration of the social and political status of the former Nazi elites.[18] In keeping with the pattern of oscillation, every step toward recognition of guilt or confrontation with Nazi crimes was accompanied by even greater conciliation toward fellow Germans who had been harmed, not by Nazism, but by defeat and denazification. At least until the 1960s, every act of compensation and memorialization toward Jewish victims of Nazism was carefully balanced by recognition of German suffering. The most obvious example remains Konrad Adenauer's masterful coupling in the early 1950s of the unfortunately named *Wiedergutmachung* for persecuted (German) Jews with compensation for German expellees from eastern territories—the so-called *Lastenausgleich.*[19]

If the Federal Republic derived some of its initial legitimacy, predominantly internationally, from its commitment to Western democracy and restitution for Jewish victims, much more of its legitimacy, certainly domestically, was based on support for German "victims" and the rollback of Allied efforts at denazification and punishment of Nazi war criminals. A bargain was struck that ultimately proved much more successful than anyone could have then imagined: that democratization and stability should trump justice. Former members of the NSDAP (Nazi party), whether opportunist or committed, minor or relatively major, were rehabilitated and declared fit for civil service and professional positions in the young republic, provided they officially relinquished their former political allegiances.[20] Convicted war criminals saw their sentences commuted or lightened; the role of those who had served in the Wehrmacht was not yet even an issue. As Frei points out, reintegration proceeded with rather breathtaking thoroughness and speed; by spring 1951, only 1,800 Germans who had been convicted by the Western allies were still in custody.[21]

After unification, and with the current intensification of debates about memory and responsibility, scholars are now critically revisiting a point made by political philosopher Hermann Lübbe, who defined the

18. Norbert Frei, *Vergangenheitspolitik: Die Anfänge der Bundesrepublik und die NS-Vergangenheit* (Munich, 1996).

19. See Moeller, "War Stories"; and Rabinbach, "The Jewish Question."

20. Frei, *Vergangenheitspolitik;* Herf, *Divided Memory;* and Ulrich Herbert, *Best: Biographische Studien über Radikalismus, Weltanschauung, und Vernunft, 1903–1989* (Bonn, 1996) have all made this argument.

21. Frei, *Vergangenheitspolitik,* 16–21. The Institute for the Investigation of National Socialist Politics, the forerunner of the Institute für Zeitgeschichte in Munich, had been established in the pre-1949 period, in 1947, under U.S. auspices.

issue in a much-quoted 1983 article: "A certain silence was the social-psy-chological and politically necessary medium for the transformation of our postwar population into the citizenry of the Federal Republic of Germany."[22] The dual phenomenon of failed denazification accompanied and followed by successful democratization and stabilization also allowed, as Anson Rabinbach has explained, "the triumph of a view of Nazism which emphasized its criminal aspects at the expense of its broad popular basis and deep social roots in German history and tradition."[23] This postwar history worked as a significant, if underdiscussed, piece of the German Goldhagen discussion. To the astonished frustration of historians (and presumed relief of his German readers), Daniel Goldhagen steadfastly resisted any consideration of this postwar *völkisch* reconciliation—the second guilt—in his confident pronouncements about the sudden demise of "eliminationist" antisemitism under American auspices.[24] For his part, however, Goldhagen could claim to have broken open the myth (in fact, already substantially frayed) of limited popular support for genocide during the Third Reich.

In the mid-1950s, the stage version of *The Diary of Anne Frank,* scripted by Americans Frances Goodrich and Albert Hackett, was credited with puncturing, at least briefly, the combined sense of victimization and self-satisfaction characteristic of West Germans in the 1950s. The German translation of *The Diary of Anne Frank* (first published in Dutch in 1947) arrived in 1949, just in time to accompany the birth of the Federal Republic, but the sensation did not come until the staging of the American play in 1956. Now much maligned for its attempted universalization of a specifically Jewish tragedy, the performance of *Anne Frank* produced a kind of stunned *Betroffenheit,* making accessible, admittedly in sanitized and dejudaicized form, the voice of the victims. Over two decades later, when *Holocaust* hit the television screens in 1979 (albeit on the marginal third channel), it was another commercial product from the United States that managed to provoke a mass reckoning. Indeed, the very term *Holocaust*—significantly in English—only arrived in Germany via the American television series.[25]

---

22. "Der Nationalsozialismus im Deutschen Nachkriegsbewusstsein," *Historische Zeitschrift* 236 (1983), cited in Rabinbach,"The Jewish Question," 161.

23. Rabinbach, "The Jewish Question," 161–62, 165.

24. See, for example, Y. Michal Bodemann, "Ein exotischer Barbarenstamm, Daniel Goldhagen, Deutschland und die USA," *Berliner Debatte INITIAL: Zeitschrift für sozial-wissenschaftlichen Diskurs* 5 (1996): 120–25 (first published in *TAZ*).

25. Most previous references were to *Endlösung* (Final Solution), the term used by the Nazis. For a cogent defense of both *Holocaust* and the Anne Frank play, see Andreas Huyssen, "The Politics of Identification, 'Holocaust' and West German Drama," *New German Critique* 19 (winter 1980): 117–36. See also Peter Märthesheimer and Ivo Frenzel, eds., *Im Kreuzfeuer: Der Fernsehfilm 'Holocaust': Eine Nation ist betroffen* (Frankfurt, 1979).

Anne Frank notwithstanding, and despite some recent scholarly efforts at nuancing our impressions, the 1950s still appear as a pretty dismal time.[26] Caught in the tight grip of the Cold War, and punctuated by the miserable return of German men from Soviet prisoner of war camps, the 1950s were indeed the decade with the least attention paid to the victims of the Germans and the most energetic remembering of German "victims."[27] Indeed, in some cases memorial sites that had been established by the occupiers were dismantled, others simply neglected, overgrown, and turned to other uses.[28]

The "silent" 1950s, characterized in the West by intense Cold War, an "economic miracle," and the integration of former Nazis, concluded in 1958–59 with outbreaks of antisemitic vandalism and desecration of Jewish cemeteries and synagogues.[29] This wave of right-wing and antisemitic activities seemed to demonstrate the failure, or at least the severe limits, of denazification during an Adenauer era that many—Jürgen Habermas is perhaps the most passionately articulate exponent of this view, and it explains a good deal about his soft spot for Daniel Goldhagen—remember as morally and politically bankrupt. It was in that apparently precarious context that the re-emigré T. W. Adorno asked, in a public lecture to the Society for Christian-Jewish Cooperation (later a radio broadcast), "Was bedeutet: Aufarbeitung der Vergangenheit?" (What does coming to terms with the past mean?). In 1959, "at a turning point between the era of the 'economic miracle' and the social upheavals of the 1960s," he echoed Hannah Arendt's earlier warnings about "willful forgetting," "loss of history," and "eradication of memory."[30] These repeated injunctions not to forget became an integral part of the commemoration process.

In 1961, as the Eichmann trial was unfolding in Jerusalem and the Berlin crisis was threatening an emerging détente with the Soviet Union,

---

26. For a complex portrait of the 1950s, see some of the newer cultural history, for example, Uta G. Poiger, "A New, 'Western' Hero? Reconstructing German Masculinity in the 1950s," *Signs* 24 (autumn 1998): 147–62 (see esp. 158 n. 45); Erica Carter, *How German Is She? Postwar West German Reconstruction and the Consuming Woman* (Ann Arbor, 1997); and Heide Fehrenbach, *Cinema in Democratizing Germany: Reconstructing National Identity after Hitler* (Chapel Hill, 1995).

27. See Robert G. Moeller, "'The Last Soldiers of the Great War' and Tales of Family Reunions in the Federal Republic," *Signs* 24 (autumn 1998): 129–46.

28. Detlef Garbe, "Gedenkstätten: Orte der Erinnerung und die zunehmende Distanz zum Nationalsozialismus," in Hanno Loewy, ed., *Holocaust: Die Grenzen des Verstehens: Eine Debatte über die Besetzung der Geschichte* (Reinbek bei Hamburg, 1992), 260–84.

29. There is an ongoing controversy about the possible role of the GDR and the Stasi in inciting some of these attacks.

30. Jeffrey K. Olick, "What Does It Mean to Normalize the Past? Official Memory in German Politics since 1989," *Social Science History* 22 (winter 1998): 547–71, 548. See also Hannah Arendt, "The Aftermath of Nazi Rule: Report from Germany," *Commentary* 10 (1950).

William L. Shirer's runaway bestseller, *The Rise and Fall of the Third Reich,* arrived in West Germany. A kind of Goldhagen forerunner, Shirer challenged conventional 1950s interpretations of Nazism as an awful train wreck in an otherwise benign history, an evil precipitated by a few demonic individuals. Although he focused less on antisemitism than on a generally illiberal, militarist, and authoritarian political tradition, Shirer, like Goldhagen, asserted that Nazism was inextricably knit into the history of the German people and nation, perceiving a ruthless continuity from 1871 to 1945, "in a straight line and with utter logic."[31] Unlike the divided (between negative scholars and positive lay readers) response to Goldhagen, however, the reactions to Shirer's work were almost uniformly defensive. In the shadow of numerous exposés about the Nazi past of German political leaders, the veteran U.S. foreign correspondent was virulently attacked as a German-hater who had a "simplistic and inadequate" comprehension of German history; Martin Broszat and Konrad Adenauer were among those who weighed in against the book. As with *Hitler's Willing Executioners,* German scholars and journalists worried that the book would unfairly tarnish Germans among the American people, and made insinuations about the influence of American Jews in fanning the flames of anti-Germanism. *Der Spiegel* fulminated then, as it still does today, about "New York" dominance in U.S. media.[32] The volatile triangular relationship of Germans, Jews, and Americans established during the early occupation period continued to shadow virtually every moment of West German confrontation with the Nazi past.[33]

The early 1960s did bring a shift. In 1963, a homegrown record, Melita Maschmann's painfully honest but not exculpatory *Fazit* (Account rendered) of her enthusiastic League of German Girls' (BdM) past became a commercial success, going through four printings in six weeks.[34] A slew of further German and especially German-Jewish reckonings with the

---

31. Gavriel D. Rosenfeld, "The Reception of William L. Shirer's *The Rise and Fall of the Third Reich* in the United States and West Germany, 1960–62," *Journal of Contemporary History* 29 (1994): 95–128, 95. See William L. Shirer, *The Rise and Fall of the Third Reich: A History of Nazi Germany* (New York, 1960).

32. Rosenfeld, 115, 118–19. *Der Spiegel*'s propensity for such code words is readily apparent in its coverage of both the Goldhagen and Walser/Bubis/Dohnanyi controversies. See, for example, Michael Brenner, "Sie sind unser Unglück: Der neue alte Antisemitismusstreit," *Süddeutsche Zeitung,* 21 December 1998; and Josef Joffe, "Erinnerung als Staatsräson," *Süddeutsche Zeitung,* 12/13 December 1998.

33. See Frank Stern, "The Historic Triangle: Occupiers, Germans, and Jews in Postwar Germany," *Tel Aviver Jahrbuch für deutsche Geschichte* 19 (1990): 47–76.

34. Melita Maschmann, *Fazit: Kein Rechtfertigungsversuch* (Stuttgart, 1963). See Alf Lüdtke, "'Coming to Terms with the Past': Illusions of Remembering, Ways of Forgetting Nazism in West Germany," *Journal of Modern History* 65 (September 1993): 542–72.

past—the literary scholar Andreas Huyssen has dubbed them *Bewälti-gungsdramas*—appeared in the early 1960s, most prominently Max Frisch's *Andorra*, Rolf Hochhut's *The Deputy*, and finally Peter Weiss's searing *Die Ermittlung* (The investigation), based on transcripts of the Auschwitz trials conducted in Frankfurt from 1963 to 1966. These literary examinations were rooted in a leftist anticapitalist critique and did not specifically address the murderous antisemitism of the Nazis; in fact, Huyssen notes about Weiss's play, "The very word 'Jew' is absent from the best play about Auschwitz."[35] Still, even if the specifically Jewish voices and faces of the victims remained muted, a memorial culture began to develop in earnest in the 1960s. It was significantly propelled by the Frank-furt Auschwitz trials[36] and then by the '68 student movement, whose forceful challenge to the comforts and conventions of West German soci-ety was heavily dependent on an accusatory confrontation with the older generation's Nazi pasts.[37] At the very moment in November 1965 that Chancellor Ludwig Erhard "declared the postwar period 'finished'" in a speech to the Bundestag and announced that "we cannot accept those who infer from previous cruelty a German hereditary sin and try to preserve this for political purposes," German memory as victimizers rather than as victims was in a sense only beginning to be formed.[38]

Gradually, the victims became somewhat more visible. In 1965, the large plaque naming concentration camps as "Orte des Schreckens"—still, to my mind, one of the most effective memorials in Berlin—was erected at the Wittenberg Platz right in front of that monument to Western con-sumption, the resurrected KaDeWe department store. In the mid-1960s, exhibits and memorials were established at death camp sites in the West: Dachau and Neuengamme in 1965, Bergen-Belsen in 1966. In keeping with the wholly Western orientation of the "Goldhagen effect" in post-unification Germany, this article's catalogue of "Holocaust moments" vir-tually ignores any East German trajectory, but it should be noted that by the 1960s, after the clearly antisemitic "anti-cosmopolitan" campaigns of the 1950s, a modest memorial culture also developed in the GDR. On 9 November 1960, a memorial in Grosse Hamburger Strasse, site of the deportation assembly center for Berlin Jews, was inaugurated, and

---

35. Huyssen, "The Politics of Identification," 133.

36. For an intriguing fictional rendition of their impact, see Bernhard Schlink, *The Reader* (New York, 1997).

37. It is important to note that the New Left's antiauthoritarian revolt against the West German fathers was directed not only against the Nazi past that they denied, but perhaps even more viscerally against the Christian moralism of the 1950s Christian Democracy. See Dagmar Herzog, "'Pleasure, Sex, and Politics Belong Together': Post Holocaust Memory and the Sexual Revolution in West Germany," *Critical Inquiry* 24 (winter 1998): 393–444.

38. Lüdtke, "'Coming to Terms with the Past,'" 570–71.

throughout the decade new synagogues, with tiny, intimidated congregations, opened in Leipzig, Halle, and Magdeburg. This process culminated in the large-scale memorials on the occasion of the fiftieth anniversary of Kristallnacht in November 1988.[39]

The back-and-forth between repentance and resentment escalated in the 1960s. The 1967 Arab-Israeli War, only two years after the establishment of formal diplomatic relations between Israel and the Federal Republic, brought a curious turnaround in popular sentiment. Israeli military prowess was glorified on the Right, while a previously philosemitic Left embraced an anti-imperialism and anti-Americanism, which included, among some segments, an increasingly virulent anti-Zionism. As Lutz Niethammer has sarcastically noted, suddenly those who had dutifully picked oranges on Israeli kibbutzim as part of German-Jewish reconciliation programs (Aktion Sühnezeichen) now flocked to anti-imperialist demonstrations in Al Fatah headdress scarfs.[40] The late 1960s also produced another huge bestseller about the Nazi period. The memoirs of Albert Speer, an unquestionably high-ranking Nazi, managed to acknowledge a vague general guilt while simultaneously denying any specific individual agency and surely derived much of its popularity from that sleight of hand. Goldhagen's totalistic indictment of all Germans as direct perpetrators would slice right into the nagging sense that formulas about collective guilt, such as Adenauer's famous acknowledgment of atrocities committed "in the name of" the German people, or perhaps most cleverly Speer's insistence that he hadn't known but he should have known, were specious and simply inadequate.[41]

---

39. See Olaf Groehler, "Erblasten: Der Umgang mit dem Holocaust in der DDR," in Loewy, *Holocaust: Die Grenzen des Verstehens,*110–27, 121; and *Deutsche Volkszeitung,* 24 August 1945. See also Herf, *Divided Memory;* on the relation between Jews and antifascism in the East, see also Frank Stern, "The Return to the Disowned Home—German Jews and the Other Germany," *New German Critique* 67 (winter 1996): 57–72; Y. Michal Bodemann, "Reconstructions of History: From Jewish Memory to Nationalized Commemoration of Kristallnacht in Germany," in Bodemann, ed., *Jews, Germans, Memory: Reconstructions of Jewish Life in Germany* (Ann Arbor, 1996), esp. 196–205; and Ulrike Offenberg, *Seid vorsichtig gegen die Machthaber.*

40. Lutz Niethammer, "Erinnerungsgebot und Erfahrungsgeschichte. Institutionalisierungen mit Kollektivem Gedächtnis," in Loewy, *Holocaust: Die Grenzen des Verstehens,* 29. It's worth adding in this context that Aktion Sühnezeichen was often gleefully referred to (by its beneficiaries) as Aktion Sühneficken (reconciliation fucking), but that is another article. For further interesting reflections, see Herzog,"'Pleasure, Sex, and Politics Belong Together.'"

41. Albert Speer, *Erinnerungen* (Frankfurt, 1969). For an interesting analysis of Speer's obvious preference for the mild guilt of having been a "bystander," or an unwitting accomplice rather than a willing executioner, see Jan Philipp Reemtsma, "Buchenwald wird von andern geschildert werden; ich will mich an meine Erlebnisse halten: Stenogramme aus der Vorhölle," in Heer, *Im Herzen der Finsternis,* 170–87.

In December 1970, Chancellor Willy Brandt's dramatic genuflection at the Warsaw Ghetto Memorial signaled the onset of a new culture of commemoration and repentance. At the same time, younger leftist academics discovered the tradition of the "other Germany" that had been driven out in the 1930s. They began seriously to read, document, interview, and sometimes study with Jewish exiles, especially those associated with critical theory and the Frankfurt School. Clearly, however, this encounter with the past was mediated by a Marxist analysis of fascism; to the extent that it considered antisemitism, it reflected more a sense of loss for Germany—the forfeiture of the cosmopolitan, liberal humanist intellectual and cultural life associated with German Jews—than an interest in the much larger number of East European Jews who were murdered by the Nazis.

Young German students' contact with émigré intellectuals—many of whom were still deeply committed to the German-Jewish symbiosis even though very few had actually returned—sensitized them to the importance of Jewish identity and antisemitism. Ironically, however, this process mostly bypassed any contact with the majority of the resident Jewish population.[42] The mostly East European Jewish survivors who had come to occupy Germany as displaced persons and now lived in the Federal Republic were little inclined to focus on the past and certainly not interested in educating Germans about a German-Jewish legacy with which they did not identify. As Cilly Kugelmann has put it, they maintained a severe distance from German society, leading to "A sort of double life," where "the economic career took place in Germany, but all other values were located in a utopian no-man's land whose horizon was the coast of Israel or the Manhattan skyline."[43] In all the 1960s and 1970s discussions about Germans and Jews, the actually existing postwar Jewish population remained remarkably invisible. The romance with the tragically lost legacy of German Jewry—a considerable portion of whom survived in exile—facilitated a recognition of Nazi antisemitism and its cost but in no way forced the visceral confrontation with the reality of the genocide that a book like Goldhagen's would demand. Goldhagen's enthusiastic recep-

---

42. See, for example, the essay collection *Mein Judentum,* ed. Hans Jürgen Schultz (Stuttgart, 1978). This is echoed in the 1997 book *Mein Israel,* ed. Micha Brumlik (Frankfurt am Main, 1998).

43. Kugelmann, "'Tell Them in America,'" 137. See her discussion of the disinterest expressed by East European Jews living in Germany in the vaunted German-Jewish legacy, as demonstrated for example in the conflicts about the development of historic sites in Frankfurt. See also Jack Zipes's useful review essay "The Holocaust and the Vicissitudes of Jewish Identity," *New German Critique* 20 (spring/summer 1980): 155–76. The articles in that issue, plus some others, are collected in Rabinbach and Zipes, *Germans and Jews.*

tion among many in that generation also reflected some lingering discomfort about this blind spot.[44]

The 1970s concluded, or, rather, "the explosion into memory" of the 1980s began, in fall 1979 with the dramatic nationwide screening of the American television series *Holocaust*. The 1980s brought in force "a spectacularization of the past," rich in exhibitions, publications, and films.[45] Indeed, those astonished by the enthusiastic public reaction to Goldhagen and his book might well have recalled other moments when it seemed that the West German population was uncovering the true nature of their past for the very first time, whether *Anne Frank* or post-*Holocaust*. This latter "epidemic of remembrance" brought its own set of simultaneously cynical and fascinated critics, many of them members of a Jewish "second generation" that had had its "coming out" in the late 1970s and early 1980s. After the demise of the student Left, in which many had participated without specifically announcing their religious background, Jewish veterans of the '68 movement, uncomfortable with the anti-Americanism, anti-Zionism, and nationalistically tinged Green environmentalism of their old comrades, formed their own *Jüdische Gruppen* in Frankfurt and Berlin. The children of returned exiles and Jews who had survived in Nazi Germany (mostly "partial" Jews or in mixed marriages) or, predominantly, of DPs born during the post-Holocaust Jewish baby boom, they opposed the political and religious conservatism of the established *Gemeinde* and the hypocritical philosemitism of their Christian Democratic allies.[46] Many

---

44. From our vantage point in 1999, it is amazing to remember how many prewar German-Jewish intellectuals were still alive and active in the 1970s. For a sample of these encounters with exiles, see Mathias Greffrath, ed., *Zerstoerung einer Zukunft: Gespräche mit emigrierten Sozialwissenschaftlern* (Reinbek bei Hamburg, 1979); and Henri Hempel, *"Wenn ich schon ein Fremder sein muss . . .": Deutsch-jüdische Emigranten in New York* (Frankfurt am Main, 1984). See also Toni Oelsner's revealing interview with Anson Rabinbach and Wieland Schulz-Keil, "Dreams of a Better Life," *New German Critique* 20 (spring/summer 1980): 31–56.

45. Geyer and Hansen, "German-Jewish Memory," 183.

46. Particularly galling was the continued presence within the CDU (Christian Democratic Union) of notorious ex-Nazis like the "hanging judge" Hans Georg Filbinger, Minister President of Baden-Württemberg, finally forced to resign in 1978. Among numerous books about Jewish identity published in the Federal Republic are Henryk M. Broder and Michel R. Lang, *Fremd im eigenen Land: Juden in der Bundesrepublik* (Frankfurt, 1979); and Lea Fleischmann, *Dies ist nicht mein Land—Eine Jüdin verlässt die Bundesrepublik* (Hamburg, 1980). See also Dan Diner, "Fragments of an Uncompleted Journey: On Jewish Socialization and Political Identity in West Germany," *New German Critique* 20 (spring/summer 1980): 57–70; and the other article in that remarkable "Special Issue II: Germans and Jews," which documents this "coming out" of Jews living in Germany. At the same time, Broder published several provocative pieces in *Die Zeit* and *Der Spiegel* proclaiming, as did Lea Fleischmann, disgust with his former German comrades and his intention to emigrate to Israel. For one response, see Atina Grossmann, "Questions of Jewish Identity: A Letter from

entered academia and the media (and to a lesser degree politics), becoming acerbic and self-conscious analysts of the "theater of memory," "mourning rituals" (*Trauerrituale*), and "mourning culture" (*Trauerkultur*) they both shaped and criticized.[47]

Yet, in a clear example of the continual oscillation in *Vergangenheitsbewältigung* between remembering and repressing, the expansive memory culture of the 1980s—after the television series *Holocaust*—coincided with the fiftieth anniversary of the Nazi "seizure of power" in 1983 and the political *Wende* (turnaround) achieved when a conservative coalition under Helmut Kohl came to power. In the 1980s, then, the controversies followed so quickly that journalists and academics could barely catch their breath between "scandals." In 1984, the CDU chancellor Kohl visited Israel and famously proclaimed "the grace of belated birth"; in 1985, he attended a convention of *Heimatvertriebene* (expellees from the East), preparing the ground for the ceremonies at Bitburg a year later. A certain nostalgic fascination with the Third Reich, exemplified by Joachim Fest's biography of Adolf Hitler and Hans Jürgen Syberberg's *Hitler: A Film From Germany* (1977), culminated in 1984 with Edgar Reitz's deliberately named German television series *Heimat*.[48] Providing the most problematic variant of *Alltagsgeschichte* (history of everyday life), this "German" response to the "kitschy" Americanized *Holocaust* served up in 1979 marginalized the persecution of Jews and the Final Solution while being provocatively honest about the good times National Socialism had brought to the majority of Germans. In October 1985, a planned production in Frankfurt of Rainer Werner Fassbinder's play *Garbage, the City, and Death,* about municipal and housing politics, provoked further controversy. On opening night, 31 October, the stage was stormed by demonstrators from the local Jewish community protesting the play's depiction of a corrupt real estate speculator as the "rich Jew." They were outraged by the thinly disguised reference to Ignatz Bubis, a Holocaust survivor who had become prosperous in postwar Frankfurt and was later to become the widely popular and respected leader of the national council of

New York," in Rabinbach and Zipes, *Germans and Jews,* 171–82 (originally published in *TAZ,* 1981). For an angry defensive response to this Jewish identification by former leftist comrades, see *Aesthetik und Kommunikation* 51 (June 1983), with the cover story "Germans, Leftists, Jews." On the baby boom, see Grossmann, "Trauma, Memory and Motherhood," 215–39.

47. See Bodemann, *Jews, Germans, Memory,* 184 (his German book is titled *Gedächtnistheater*); and Micha Brumlik, "Trauerrituale und politische Kultur nach der Shoah in der Bundesrepublik," in Loewy, *Holocaust: Die Grenzen des Verstehens,* 191–212, 191. For an interesting general collection, see Gilman and Remmler, *Reemerging Jewish Culture.*

48. See special issue of *New German Critique* 36 (fall 1985). On the role of *Heimatfilme* in West German reconstruction, see Fehrenbach, *Cinema in Democratizing Germany.*

Jews in Germany.[49] But the issue was clearly larger; Jews in Germany feared that the play's willingness to break taboos about the presentation of "bad" Jews signaled "das Ende der Schonzeit" (the end of the grace period when no hunting was allowed). Even as commemoration became an indispensable component of West German culture, the urge for "normalization" and resentment at what Martin Walser eventually termed the "moral cudgel" of the genocidal past became ever more forceful. As Frank Stern has pointed out, the Jewish community could still block the production of an offensive play, but not the display of power politics at Bitburg. Tellingly, at the height of Bubis's verbal duels with Walser, he bemoaned his new inability to prevent revivals of the Fassbinder production.[50] Reitz represented a prevalent standpoint—Walser's complaint in 1998 is only one very recent example—in which "ordinary" Germans presented themselves as victimized and marginalized in the face of disproportionate attention devoted to the Jews and their fate.

Ronald Reagan and Helmut Kohl's joint visit to Bitburg cemetery on 5 May 1985 was designed to salve such particularly German wounds. In the event, it served neither to open a genuine discussion of German suffering nor to initiate a necessary reevaluation of the role of the Wehrmacht. The Bitburg handshake became rather the occasion of reinforcing the myth of German military innocence. Raul Hilberg reminded his readers at the time that "the German army played a heavy role in Adolf Hitler's Germany, and it cannot be detached from the Nazi regime, because it was an integral part of it,"[51] but the real controversy would not erupt until over a

49. The play, which had been written a decade earlier, was based on a novel by Gerhard Zwerenz, *Die Erde ist Unbewohnbar wie der Mond.* During the first-night discussions between protesters and audience, Daniel Cohn-Bendit, who opposed banning the play, playfully congratulated Bubis for having adopted the confrontational politics of the Left and gleefully welcomed the protestors, predicting that "this will be the first demonstration in the history of Frankfurt that will not be broken up by the police." See James M. Markham, *New York Times,* 1 November 1985. For a comprehensive documentation of this "scandal/debate," see Heiner Lichtenstein, ed., *Die Fassbinder-Kontroverse oder Das Ende der Schonzeit* (Königstein i. Taunus, 1986). For perspective, see the special issue of *Radical America* 19, no. 5 (1985), especially Seyla Benhabib, "Rainer Werner Fassbinder's 'Trash, the City, and Death': When Allegory Becomes Metaphor," 19–23; and Moishe Postone, "Theses on Fassbinder, Antisemitism, and Germany: A Frankfurt Autumn, 1985," 24–33.

50. See Frank Stern, "'The Jewish Question' in the 'German Question,' 1945–1990: Reflections in Light of November 9, 1989," *New German Critique* 52 (winter 1991): 162. For another expression of Jewish disappointment with the German Left's response to Bitburg, see Moishe Postone, "Bitburg, May 5, 1985 and After: A Letter to the West German Left," *Radical America* 19, no. 5 (1985): 10–17. See also the Bubis interview in *Süddeutsche Zeitung,* 21 September 1998.

51. Raul Hilberg, "Bitburg as Symbol," in Hartman, *Bitburg in Moral and Political Perspective,* 21. For discussion of earlier German research on Wehrmacht complicity, see Omer Bartov, "German Soldiers and the Holocaust," *History and Memory* 9 (fall 1997): 162–88.

decade later with the exhibition organized by the privately financed Hamburg Institute for Social Research. Inevitably, the denials of Bitburg were balanced a few days later, on 8 May 1985, when President Richard von Weizsäcker, in a widely praised speech, both acknowledged "general knowledge" of Nazi persecution of Jews and tried to claim the war's end as a liberation also for Germans.

The predictable seesaw effect continued. One year later, on 25 April 1986, Christian Socialist Union (CSU) politician Alfred Dregger rejected in another Bundestag speech any notion of distinguishing between victims and perpetrators. Another clear expression of this continued wrestling with the past, mischaracterized as a drive for "normalization," came, of course, with the *Historikerstreit*. Sparked by Ernst Nolte's "bizarre and acerbic"[52] article in the *Frankfurter Allgemeine Zeitung,* "The Past That Will Not Go Away"—an unimpeachable title, certainly—the historians' disputes were about the origins and the uniqueness of the Holocaust. But in its focus on the "destruction of European Jewry" rather than on the mechanics of National Socialist rule, it also oddly demonstrated, as Mary Nolan trenchantly noted, that "the centrality of the Holocaust to the *Historikerstreit* serves as a deserved reprimand to left historians who have ignored antisemitism, racism and the Final Solution."[53] In fact, if the Wehrmacht and Hitler Youth generation remained solidly in the saddle among the academic elite, those who had been born in the chaos of war's end or the immediate postwar period—the proverbial '68ers—did move aggressively to map Germany's "topography of terror," to build museums and memorials, to publish documentations and histories, and to construct the awkwardly named "Mahn und Gedenkstätten." They pioneered new approaches to the past, using techniques of *Alltagsgeschichte* and oral history (and feminist history, although women played—and continue to play—a remarkably marginal role in the major Holocaust debates).[54]

---

52. Anson Rabinbach's phrase in *New German Critique,* special issue, 44 (spring/summer 1988). 3. Interestingly, the other salvo in the putative "relativization of the Holocaust" campaign, Andreas Hillgruber's *Zweierlei Untergang: Die Zerschlagung des Deutschen Reiches und das Ende des europäischen Judentums* (Berlin, 1986), was published by Jobst Siedler; often associated with conservative views, he later published Goldhagen.

53. Mary Nolan, "The *Historikerstreit* and Social History," *New German Critique* 44 (spring/summer 1988): 52. For documentation of the historians' debate, see *Historikerstreit: Die Dokumentation der Kontroverse um die Einzigartigkeit der nationalsozialistischen Judenvernichtung* (Munich, 1987); also Peter Baldwin and Dan Diner, eds., *Ist der Nationalsozialismus Geschichte? Zur Historisierung und Historikerstreit* (Frankfurt am Main, 1987). The Germans are exceedingly good about producing complete documentation of all these controversies.

54. For discussion of feminist versions of the *Historikerstreit* about the responsibility of women in Nazism and Nazi atrocities, see Lerke Gravenhorst and Carmen Tatschmurat, eds., *TöchterFragen: NS-Frauen Geschichte* (Freiburg im Breisgau, 1990); Atina Grossmann, "Feminist Debates about Women and National Socialism," *Gender and History* 3 (autumn

Ironically, however, even when the Left did turn its attention to the Holocaust, it focused not on its primary victims, the Jews, but on the "others," the "asocials," Sinti and Roma, homosexuals, the eugenically "unfit," all those who were perceived as forgotten, and marginalized by historiography and public memory.[55]

"Divided memory," or "selective remembrance," persisted.[56] Even very recently, in a *Festschrift* for Saul Friedländer, Norbert Frei, one of the best of the new generation of German historians, identified 1983, the fiftieth anniversary of the seizure of power, and the accompanying professional conferences as the "caesura" for renewed interest in the history of Nazi Germany, rather than what many might consider the moment of popular (re)awakening to the history of antisemitism, the screening of *Holocaust* in 1979.[57] In that sense, it did not seem entirely farfetched—even in the mid-1990s and despite the massive amounts of published research on the Final Solution—that the massacred East European Jewish Holocaust victims could be depicted by Daniel Goldhagen as another "forgotten" group in German scholarship. Goldhagen's single-minded focus on Jews and antisemitism seemed to address a problem that Nolan had identified in 1988: that even the newer focus on the "pathology of modernity," which displaced or complemented "train wreck" or structuralist interpretations,[58] "cannot explain why the Jews were singled out."[59] It was the telltale prevalence of such "blind spots" about the place of murderous antisemitism in the historiography of National Socialism and the Final Solution that gave power to Goldhagen's polemics.

The fiftieth anniversary of Kristallnacht in November 1988, almost ten years after the screening of *Holocaust,* unleashed another "epidemic of remembrance" with television programs, panel discussions, restoration of

---

1991): 350–58; and Gudrun Schwarz, *Die Frau an Seiner Seite: Ehefrauen in der "SS-Sippengemeinschaft"* (Hamburg, 1997), and *Frauen in der SS: Sippenverband und Frauenkorps* (Hamburg, 1997).

55. See Nolan, *"Historikerstreit,"* 51–80, for an incisive critique of *Alltagsgeschichte;* also *Freibeuter* 36 (1988), special issue, "Wie schreibt man Geschichte?" For another critical evaluation in the context of the *Historikerstreit,* from both female and male German scholars (for a change), see Heide Gerstenberger and Dorothea Schmidt, eds., *Normalität oder Normalisierung?* (Münster, 1987).

56. See especially Herf, *Divided Memory;* and Frank Stern, "Antagonistic Memories: The Post-War Survival and Alienation of Jews and Germans," in Luisa Passerini, ed., *Memory and Totalitarianism* (New York, 1992).

57. Norbert Frei, "Farewell to the Era of Contemporaries: National Socialism and Its Historical Examination En Route into History," *History and Memory* 9 (fall 1997): 65–66.

58. Detlev J. K. Peukert, "The Genesis of the 'Final Solution' in the Spirit of Science," in Thomas Childers and Jane Caplan, eds., *Reevaluating the Third Reich* (New York, 1993), 234–52.

59. Nolan, *"Historikerstreit,"* 80.

unused synagogues, and exhibits about "the lives of long gone Jews . . . from Berlin to [the] smallest communities."[60] All this "frenzied activity" produced in Frank Stern's jaundiced reporting a kind of "ghostly revival of Jewish life," but again, it spotlighted the fate of German Jews before slave labor and deportations, and before they joined East European Jews as victims of genocide.[61] It provoked also, of course, Philipp Jenninger's (in)famous, ill-fated address to the Bundestag on 10 November, a kind of perverse counterbalance to Weizsäcker's careful speech in 1985. Jenninger, apparently unwittingly, disturbed the sacral atmosphere of the commemorative moment by speaking in the uncritical voice of the "ordinary German" who welcomed the Nazi regime and benefited from it. The resulting outcry forced not a massive public discussion about the mentality and motivation of "ordinary Germans" during the Holocaust—what Goldhagen would later claim to instigate—but the ignominious resignation of the Bundestag president.[62]

In 1992, the fiftieth anniversary of the Wannsee conference was marked in another of the seemingly never-ending series of commemorative rituals that the sociologist Jeffrey Olick has dubbed "guilt occasions."[63] The villa on the shore of the Wannsee in Berlin, which had been used for everything from an American officer's club to a retreat for high school students, now became a memorial and museum, adding to the eighteen specific memorial sites (and approximately 200 initiatives to create them) counted in 1990.[64] At the same time—in counterpoint to the cataloguing of extermination—a huge exhibition, "Jüdische Lebenswelten" (Jewish lifeworlds), opened in Berlin. It attempted to counter criticism that Germans focused more on the killing of the Jews than on the vibrant social, cultural, and religious life that had existed before the Holocaust, and was in turn promptly criticized for giving insufficient due to the horrors that followed.[65]

Obviously, these commemorative endeavors, whether exhibits, separate monuments, museums, or "lieux des mémoires" (*Gedenkstätten*) at actual sites of persecution, produced mixed results; every visitor to such

---

60. Bodemann, "Reconstructions of History," 184, 182.

61. Frank Stern, "The 'Jewish Question' in the 'German Question,' 1945–1990," *New German Critique* 52 (winter 1989): 162. Ironically, a few years later a wave of immigration from the former Soviet Union would actually populate some of those ghost synagogues!

62. See, among many, Bodemann, "Reconstructions of History," 179–223; and Elisabeth Domansky, "Kristallnacht, the Holocaust, and German Unity: The Meaning of November 9 as an Anniversary in Germany," *History and Memory* 4 (spring/summer 1992): 60–94.

63. Olick, "What Does It Mean to Normalize the Past?" 553.

64. Garbe, "Gedenkstätten," 263.

65. See, for example, Bodemann, "Reconstructions of History."

locales has seen the groups of bored and/or uncomfortable-looking high school students trooping through, and read the *betroffen* (uncomfortably touched) or provocative comments scribbled in the ubiquitous comment books. Moreover, they inevitably spawn conflict and trouble, from right-wing attacks to competition about funding, which, while apparently overly generous, is in reality quite limited. Yet there can be no question that genuine and serious engagement with what was by now a quite long-ago history did indeed occur.

By the early 1990s, a certain sea change had been achieved, and it was clear, as Miriam Hansen and Michael Geyer noted, that "today we can no longer say that the Germans have no memory of the Holocaust or that memory is denied." In contrast to Frank Stern's notion of absolutely "antagonistic memories," they insisted that "Jewish memory cannot be considered separate from the German one."[66] In 1993 came the spectacular success of Steven Spielberg's *Schindler's List.* Spielberg's film, with its much-criticized portrayal of a German whose choices, no matter how ambivalent the motivation, made a difference, and Goldhagen's book about "willing executioners" are often presented as opposite in their presentation of the "ordinary Germans." In fact, both in their own ways undermined the cliché of the "choiceless German." And both were immensely popular among younger Germans uncomfortable with the standard explanation that resistance had been both impossible and futile.[67]

In contrast to the events of 1985, with their emphasis on war's end and its interpretations, the fiftieth-anniversary observances in 1995 did foreground the Holocaust, commencing on 27 January, the date Auschwitz was liberated.[68] As eyewitnesses died off and the actual artifacts—from the crematoria walls to the hair and eyeglasses of victims—faded and crumbled, knotty problems of politics and interpretation took on new forms. Politicians, journalists, and the many professional guardians of memory (historians, architects, museum and exhibit organizers) wrestled with, for example, competing survivors' organizations, the

---

66. Geyer and Hansen, "German-Jewish Memory," 176.

67. For some German reactions to *Schindler's List,* see Initiative Sozialistisches Forum, *Schindlerdeutsche: Ein Kinotraum vom Dritten Reich* (Freiburg, 1994). See also, among many others, Geoff Eley and Atina Grossmann, "Watching *Schindler's List:* Not the Last Word," *New German Critique* 71 (spring/summer 1997): 41–62; Miriam Bratu Hansen, "*Schindler's List* is not *Shoah:* The Second Commandment, Popular Modernism, and Public Memory," *Critical Inquiry* 22 (winter 1996): 292–312; and articles in Yosefa Loshitzky, ed., *Spielberg's Holocaust: Critical Perspectives on "Schindler's List"* (Bloomington, 1998).

68. However (as in Roberto Begnini's strange and popular 1998 film *Life Is Beautiful*), most of those commemorations ignored the fact that Auschwitz—or what little was left after the death marches had departed westward—had in fact been liberated by the Red Army.

proper depiction of hierarchies among inmates, the surrounding communities' reaction to newly publicized death and labor camp locations, clearer data about postwar Soviet internment camps for Germans, sometimes at the site (as in Sachsenhausen) of former Nazi camps, and, finally, the fierce debates about how and where to build memorials.[69] The powerful response to *Schindler's List* and the May 1945 commemorations, followed by the remarkable commercial success of Victor Klemperer's diaries (140,000 copies were sold by 1996)—to offer only a few examples[70]—confirmed that debates about how best to preserve memory had only become more acute after the fall of the Berlin Wall in 1989.

Goldhagen in Germany

Goldhagen's dual arrival in Germany, first in English, then in person and with the German translation, therefore marked, in one sense, just another moment in an escalating postwar German struggle with history and national identity. At the same time, the power of the "Goldhagen effect," while limited to West Germany and clearly linked to ongoing debates about victims and perpetrators (*Täter und Opfer*), was exceptional and surprising. The response to the book in Germany therefore is inseparable from its immediate context, including Goldhagen's own very energetic (and largely successful) efforts to stay on top of the critics, to interpret himself and his reviewers to the public, and to maintain tight control over the discussion. It is worth remembering that while Goldhagen's book had been powerfully marketed in the United States, it reached Germany on the heels of an even more spectacular string of publicity.

From spring 1996 onward, when the first press reports about the American edition appeared, Goldhagen himself (with his publisher) was a shrewd and active player in orchestrating the German response. He produced a special preface to the slightly (but carefully and significantly) revised German edition, made numerous public appearances in print, tele-

---

69. This debate has been sharpest in regard to Sachsenhausen. The iconoclastic architect of the just-opened Berlin Jewish Museum, Daniel Libeskind, once seriously proposed to drown the site of Sachsenhausen concentration camp in a pool of water and erect an abstract memorial—a suggestion that drew apoplectic reactions from the director of the *Gedenkstätte.* Personal communication from Günther Morsch. See also Harold Marcuse, *Dachau* (forthcoming); and Sigrid Jacobeit and Grit Philipp, eds., *Ravensbrück: Beiträge zur Geschichte des Frauen-Konzentrationslagers* (Berlin, 1997).

70. On Klemperer's reception, see Heer, *Im Herzen der Finsternis.* Ruth Klüger's memoir of surviving Auschwitz, *Weiter leben: Eine Jugend* (Göttingen, 1992)—pointedly published only in German even though she is a professor of literature at the University of California—also became a bestseller in Germany. On that problematic reception, see Stephan Brase and Holder Gehle, *Ruth Klüger in Deutschland* (Hamburg/Bonn, 1994).

vision, and person, and even published a little companion volume, *Briefe an Goldhagen* (Letters to Goldhagen), reprinting some of the over 700 letters, both admiring and critical, posted by his German audience.[71] The reception was inseparable also, as it was in the United States, from a greedy media, always ready to uncover scandal and sensation when it comes to Germans and Jews, but also always interested in how Germans handle themselves when handling their past. This attitude is exacerbated by a persistent—and somewhat grandiose—German perception that the eyes of the world, or at least what is perceived as a Jewish-dominated high- and middlebrow American media, are continually upon them.

In retrospect, just as one can loosely periodize "Holocaust moments" in postwar German history, one can discern discrete stages of the Goldhagen discussion. The first period was launched—and the terms of debate set—in the weekly journal of record *Die Zeit* on 12 April 1996, with an article by its literary editor, Volker Ulrich, under the dramatic headline (festooned with a question mark) "A book provokes a new historian's debate, were the Germans all guilty after all?"[72] Numerous highly negative reviews by established German historians followed. The very fact that specialists in the history of National Socialism reacted so sharply is interesting; clearly, they were not nervous about trashing the "young Jewish Assistant Professor at Harvard." Indeed, many of the fiercest German critics probably felt legitimated by their own long record of paying dues in the field. They believed that they could credibly leave behind the self-flagellating poses of some of the German public; that their exemplary research, their conferencing, and their easy contact with Jewish U.S. and Israeli scholars had rendered them exempt from having to watch their words.

---

71. See *Briefe an Goldhagen; eingeleitet und beantwortet von Daniel Jonah Goldhagen* (Berlin, 1997). Some examples of the more qualified and milder language in the German translation, including the title: *Hitler's Willing Executioners* became *Hitlers willige Vollstrecker* (agents) (Berlin, 1996); the "vast" majority of the German *Volk* who supported the mass murder became the "grosse [large] Mehrheit"; the "tiny percentage" of Germans who supported Jews became simply a "few" ("wenige"). See "Riesige Mehrheit: Die deutsche Übersetzung glättet Goldhagens Thesen," *Der Spiegel* 33 (1996): 42. It was also in the foreword to the German edition that Goldhagen elaborated his position, relegated to a footnote in the English version, that after 1945 "German society underwent a gradual change." For further discussion of the German response, see Shandley, *Unwilling Germans?* 17–18. Johannes Heil and Rainer Erb report in "Klage und Analyse im Widerstreit," the introduction to their edited collection *Geschichtswissenschaft und Öffentlichkeit,* that in the summer and fall of 1996, the topic generated over 700 articles and radio and television shows in Germany.

72. The first German review was actually by the American journalist Jacob Heilbrunn in *Der Tagesspiegel* on 31 March 1996. See Angelica Königseder, "Streitkulturen und Gefühlslagen: Die Goldhagen-Debatte und der Streit um die Wehrmachtsausstellung," in Heil and Erb, *Geschichtswissenschaft und Öffentlichkeit,* 296.

Besides, much to their relief, American/Jewish and Israeli colleagues seemed to share their highly negative views.[73]

Norbert Frei, for example, lambasted the American edition in the *Süddeutsche Zeitung* on 13 April 1996. It was, he insisted, of little use empirically and missed what was really scary in the history of German National Socialism, namely, not the lustful enthusiasm of the willing executioners but the moral indifference of the many more who watched and knew, or didn't fully know or want to know. He confidently predicted that, since the book had been so roundly rejected by the experts and offered so little new material, the German translation, when it came— from a somewhat suspect publisher with conservative proclivities—would make no splash.[74] As in the United States, the book was rejected by publishers with pretensions to academic prestige, such as Fischer; unlike in the United States, it was taken on by a smaller publisher. The Siedler Verlag, which had published Andreas Hillgruber's relativizing *Zweierlei Untergang,* a central text in the Historians' Debate, did not expect the huge success that ensued.

Other critics assailed a supposed return to outmoded notions of collective guilt and a German *Sonderweg* or the demonization of the entire *Volk,* recalling the outraged response to Shirer's American bestseller decades earlier.[75] The press was filled with dramatic formulations, usually with a question mark at the end. "Ein Volk von Mördern?" asked the German-Jewish historian Julius Schoeps; "Eine Nation der Killer?" wondered the Social Democratic politician Peter Glotz; "A People of 'Final Solutionists'?" queried Norbert Frei.[76] Rudolf Augstein in *Der Spiegel* proclaimed the book's contribution "gleich null" (equal to zero), a judgment, he noted (with recourse to typical *Spiegel* stereotypes), shared by the "Israeli" historian Raul Hilberg.[77]

73. The critical response at the United States Holocaust Memorial Museum panel discussion (which included Christopher Browning and the Israeli historian Yehudah Bauer) in Washington, D.C., on 6 April 1996 was frequently invoked.

74. See Norbert Frei, "A People of 'Final Solutionists'? Daniel Goldhagen Dresses an Old Thesis in New Robes," in Shandley, *Unwilling Germans?* 35–39, originally in *Süddeutsche Zeitung,* 13–14 April 1996.

75. See, for example, Frank Schirrmacher, "Hitler's Code: Holocaust from Faustian Aspirations?" in Shandley, *Unwilling Germans?* 41–46, originally in *Frankfurter Allgemeine Zeitung,* 15 April 1996.

76. See Peter Glotz, "Eine Nation der Killer?" in Schoeps, *Ein Volk von Mördern?* 125–29; and Frei, "A People of 'Final Solutionists'?"; also *Die Deutschen—Ein Volk von Tätern? Zur historisch-politischen Debatte um das Buch von Daniel Jonah Goldhagen "Hitlers Willige Vollstrecker: Ganz gewöhnliche Deutsche und der Holocaust,"* Friedrich Ebert Stiftung, Reihe Gesprächskreis Geschichte 14 (Bonn, 1996).

77. Rudolf Augstein, "The Sociologist as Hanging Judge," in Shandley, *Unwilling Germans?* 47–50, originally in *Der Spiegel,* 15 April 1996.

In particularly irritating but not unfamiliar style, numerous press reports identified participants in the debate, whether German or American, according to whether or not they were Jewish, verging on (certainly to the practiced cynical eye) a casual and arrogant antisemitism and anti-Americanism. The left liberal *Frankfurter Rundschau* informed its readers that the U.S. publicity campaign for the book was waged mostly by Jewish journalists and columnists. Commentators referred not just to Goldhagen's Harvard position (the name seemed to hold even more magic in Germany than in the United States) and youth, but also to his Jewish backers in the United States, and to the "rich" family that had donated millions for his proposed Harvard chair. Daniel Jonah (the double naming was important) Goldhagen was repeatedly identified as Jewish and the son of a "Rumanian"—not even German-Jewish—survivor, as if that sufficed to explain his vehement analysis and necessarily rendered it suspect.[78] At the same time, even as Goldhagen's assessment of German actions during the Holocaust was attacked, little in the German discussion (as far as I'm aware) focused on Goldhagen's ill-informed treatment of the history of German Jewry and antisemitism; probably, one is tempted to assume, because most German commentators knew just as little or less about that topic.

All these strenuous pre–German publication attempts to wish the book away, or at least thoroughly discredit it, failed miserably. September and October 1996 brought the next and most dramatic round. Publication of the (revised) German translation was accompanied by Goldhagen's "triumphal procession" through several cities—and this is noteworthy—in the "old" western states of the Federal Republic.[79] Goldhagen toured from north to south, appearing in Hamburg, Berlin, Frankfurt, and Munich, but he did not venture east, not even to Leipzig, the traditional publishing capital. This geography was barely remarked upon but certainly not accidental; presumably, tour organizers were both worried

---

78. For an example, see *Frankfurter Rundschau,* 12 April 1996. See also Mary Elise Sarotte, "Der Autor von *Hitlers Willige Vollstrecker* und Seine Vier Mitbewerber," *Die Zeit,* 3 January 1997 (taken off H-german), <german@h-net.msu.edu> This aspect has been harshly and effectively criticized by Andrei S. Markovits in "Discomposure in History's Final Resting Place," in Shandley, *Unwilling Germans?* 119–28 (original: "Störfall im Endlager der Geschichte," *Blätter für deutsche und internationale Politik* 6 [1996]). For discussion of such references to the "influence of the Jews" during the Bitburg uproar, see William Boll, "Bitburg: The American Scene," in Hartman, *Bitburg in Moral and Political Perspective,* 78. The argument over the "objectivity" of scholars on the "victim" side was, of course, an important aspect of the Historians' Debate; see the exchange between Saul Friedländer and Martin Broszat, *New German Critique* 44 (spring/summer 1988): 85–126.

79. Volker Ulrich, in *Die Zeit,* 13 September 1996; in English, "A Triumphal Procession: Goldhagen and the Germans," in Shandley, *Unwilling Germans?* 197–202.

about possible right-wing disruptions and simply wary of a lack of interest among East Germans preoccupied with more immediate issues.[80]

The initial highly critical response turned back on itself and helped to pave the way for seemingly ecstatic public enthusiasm. With a certain glee, the reading German public defied scholars' and journalists' smooth predictions that the book would be a dud, that everyone was sick to death of the subject, that Germans were not going to wade through some long fat book about massacres that their own scholarly experts had declared, as Eberhard Jäckel famously remarked, "simply a bad book."[81] Eighty thousand copies of the German edition sold in the first month, and by the time of the book tour, 3,000 books a day were flying off the shelf. It seemed, as the German-Jewish journalist Josef Joffe put it in the *New York Review of Books,* that "Goldhagen Conquers Germany" (or at least four major cities in West Germany).[82] Goldhagen appeared in the press and on television talk shows; filled venerable sites of German bourgeois culture such as the Hamburger Kammerspiel, the Jüdische Gemeinde in Berlin, the Mozart Saal of the Alte Oper in Frankfurt, and the Munich Philharmonic, with all of its 2,000 seats more than packed. People of mixed generations fought for tickets to the panel discussions as if they were headed to a rock concert.

The press had initially polarized the conflict so starkly, reporting that Goldhagen represented a return to a supposedly discredited collective guilt position and the demonization of the entire *Volk,* that Germans expected some young demon, the vengeful "son of a survivor," to come charging at them, filled with anger, bitterness, and accusations. Instead they encountered a boyish, polite (if utterly impervious to any criticism), and friendly young man: a nice Jewish boy. Looking sincere and wide-eyed, "charming and well coiffed" (*charmant und gut-frisiert*), he was certainly more telegenic than the generally older men (no women, of course) recruited as his disputants for live and televised debate. Rather than defending his more extreme positions, the author of *Hitlers Willige Vollstrecker* (now willing agents, rather than executioners) calmly agreed that certain points should have been phrased more carefully and that his stark portrayal of ordinary Nazi-era Germans as "zealots gripped by a drive to kill Jews was overdrawn."[83]

Goldhagen's debate partners, critics and supporters alike, were both charmed and frustrated by his disarming style; they were trapped by his

---

80. To my knowledge, there has been remarkably little discussion of this silence in the former GDR.

81. Eberhard Jäckel, "Simply a Bad Book," in Shandley, *Unwilling Germans?* 87–91, originally in *Die Zeit,* 17 May 1996.

82. Josef Joffe, *New York Review of Books,* 28 November 1996.

83. See report by Tom Heneghan, <reuters@clari.net>, 5 September 1996.

mild and maddeningly conciliatory demeanor, certainly not the usual tone of German *Podiumsdiskussionen.* In one wickedly witty description of the tour, a journalist observed that Jan Philipp Reemtsma of the Hamburg Institute for Social Research was so taken that he seemed to want to "adopt Goldhagen on the spot."[84] The "young American Jewish assistant professor" knew well how to position himself as an *Opfer* (victim) among his professorial critics. Audiences took the opportunity to express their dissatisfaction with the cool pomposity and close-mindedness of some of the historians' guild's (*Zunft*) most respected senior members.

Wary of an atmosphere in which Goldhagen easily appeared as a Daniel in the lion's den who required protection rather than contradiction, panelists seated "at black-draped tables in a stage setting as somber as a wake, were so polite in expressing their criticisms that the moderator had to urge them to speak out."[85] Interestingly, organizers were also careful to ensure that the debate was rarely just between "German" critics and the young American-Jewish survivor's son. Jewish scholars and critics, such as the historians Dan Diner and Mosche Zimmermann, and the writers and journalists Ralph Giordano and Josef Joffe, were included on podiums. Ironically, the historian most severely attacked for his rejection of the young upstart from Harvard (after all) was the venerable Hans Momm-sen—one of the very few truly passionate (at times choleric) critics—who had worked for a lifetime to study and comprehend the Nazi past. A common sense developed that any book so vehemently rejected by established historians must have something good about it. Some self-critical scholars voiced the suspicion that the dismissive professional reaction, and their quick repudiation of any collective guilt thesis (voiced more confidently in print than on the podium), was itself a matter for critical inquiry.[86]

One key to the book's extraordinary impact, even many critics acknowledged, was Goldhagen's insistence on holding "ordinary Germans" and their eliminationist antisemitism, rather than Nazi policies, responsible for genocide. His relentless focus on the personal cruelty of "Hitler's willing executioners" fed right into an inchoate existing dissatisfaction with structural explanations that had failed to personalize the perpetrators, whether they had acted in the field or as "desk murderers." Far from provoking resentment about being implicated in some *Handlungskollektiv Deutschland,* Goldhagen's stress on free agency and his sharp questions about motivations clearly resonated among listeners accustomed to therapeutic self-reflexivity. Many seemed actually relieved

---

84. Evelyn Roll, *Süddeutsche Zeitung,* 9 September 1996.

85. <reuters@clari.net>, Hamburg, 5 September 1996.

86. See, for example, Ulrich Herbert, "The Right Question," in Shandley, *Unwilling Germans?* 109–16; originally in *Die Zeit,* 14 June 1996.

to have the perpetrators named as "Germans" rather than Nazis. Indeed, that shift may turn out to be what most people take away from the book and the controversy it generated. Unquestionably, Goldhagen touched a sensitive nerve; seeming to posit the opposite of the banality-of-evil thesis, he told a vivid story of blood and guts that made not only antisemitism but personal agency central.

Goldhagen's insistence that "ordinary Germans" could have refused to carry out their brutal tasks had they only wanted to came as a certain relief to two generations of *Nachgeborenen* (the later born). They had listened with resentful skepticism to their parents' and grandparents' protestations that they had been utterly powerless, that to "resist" meant the KZ (concentration camp) or death, that one couldn't understand or judge unless "one was there" and had oneself lived under the terror of Nazi dictatorship. Moreover, the painstaking historical scholarship that had been conducted, both on the complex structures of Nazi rule and on everyday life in the Third Reich, ignored and maligned as it might be by Daniel Goldhagen, had in fact contributed to his success and made it much harder to sustain the old "we didn't know" or "we were helpless" arguments.

Myriad studies in almost two decades of *Alltagsgeschichte* (history of everyday life) had revealed that even if Germans (or, for that matter, Jews) did not know exactly what awaited in the East, there was more than enough discrimination, brutality, and daily terror that unfolded in the course of everyday life (but also some acts of solidarity and humanity) that had been visible for all to see. The conventional formulas, whether the weak "Speer solution" of "I didn't know but I should have," or "I was lucky not to be anywhere where anything bad happened" or "we were victims also," had proven, as we have seen, brilliantly functional for the success of the Federal Republic. Despite all the shrill confrontations between parents and children in the 1960s and 1970s, these postwar mantras that allowed Germans to perform guilt and claim innocence at the same time had never been decisively rejected. But now, with democracy quite safely secured in a unified Germany, they had become increasingly unsatisfying. One sensed in the standing-room-only crowds at the panel discussions in Hamburg, Berlin, Frankfurt, and Munich a kind of relief that Goldhagen, with his easy willingness to judge and condemn, offered an out, albeit a surrogate one, from that burden. Moreover, notwithstanding his depiction of unanimous, vicious antisemitism, Goldhagen's description of the Nazi regime as relatively benign toward Germans rather than (as suggested by the most prominent historians) as cumulatively ever more radical and terrorist actually fit well with family stories about the good times before the war turned bad. As many critics have pointed out, it's hard to remember when reading the book that National Socialist Germany was after all a dictatorship. This too was refreshing.

As it turned out, then, *Alltagsgeschichte,* initially criticized as exculpatory, had worked both ways; ferreting out *Resistenz* and opposition in the most improbable places, it could also be deployed quite differently, to document, for example, routine antisemitism or the vast profits reaped from "Aryanization." The "Goldhagen effect" in Germany was thus part of a larger and new interest, by scholars and the media, in *Täter* (both male and female perpetrators). This attention complemented, if it did not displace, a preceding and often romanticized fascination with *Opfer* (victims), especially Jews, Jewish culture, and, in a different fashion, women. The new and excellent research on perpetrators also denotes a qualitative shift from earlier polarized analytic frameworks. Characterized as intentionalist or functionalist/structuralist, they tended to concentrate either on especially visible and evil individuals or on unspecified and hence agencyless masses, maneuvered by faceless and technocratic bureaucratic machines.[87] In all these cases, while there was much room for shock and sorrow (*Betroffenheit* again), there was little necessity for direct personal connection.

Täterforschung is arguably a more challenging but also a more accessible field of inquiry for Germans. Certainly it hits closer to home, given that most Germans know very little about Jews and Jewish history but do in fact have close connections to someone who served the Nazi regime (whether or not they might be classified as some variety of "perpetrator"). This has certainly been demonstrated by the continuing uproar over the role and responsibility of the some eighteen to twenty million German men who served in the Wehrmacht. To underscore the point: Goldhagen's book did not create this shift; it intensified but also profited from what was already in process.

Goldhagen's audiences seemed eager to escape from the apparent "moral indifference" attributed, rather unjustly, to the structuralist (or "functionalist") interpretations of the Holocaust supplied by historians like Hans Mommsen and Martin Broszat.[88] Indeed, probably the most

---

87. Let us not forget the impact of an early text about an "ordinary German," cast in Goldhagen's terms: Rudolf Franz Ferdinand Höss and Martin Broszat, eds., *Commandant in Auschwitz: Autobiographische Aufzeichnungen von Rudol Höss* (Stuttgart, 1958); the book inspired a film, *Ein Deutsches Leben* (A German life), directed by Theodor Kotulla, Germany, 1977.

88. See, for example, Frank Ebbinghaus in *Die Welt,* 27 April 1996. For an astute deconstruction of the intentionalist/functionalist debate and a powerful argument that historians such as Hans Mommsen and Martin Broszat do not negate agency, see Tim Mason, "Intention and Explanation: A Current Controversy about the Interpretation of National Socialism," in Jane Caplan, ed., *Nazism, Fascism, and the Working Class: Essays by Tim Mason* (Cambridge, 1995), 212–30.

sober and detailed German-language critique, Dieter Pohl's careful review of the extensive and sophisticated scholarship that had already moved well beyond the analysis of political structures or decision-making mechanisms to examine the direct actions of perpetrators, nevertheless rehearsed precisely the sober, objective tone that Goldhagen attacked.[89] Important to Goldhagen's appeal, then, was a conviction among his readers that his treatment somehow honored and made visible the victims in a way that most German studies of the Holocaust had not. That aspect, it often seems, had been reserved for Jewish history or for commemorative rather than historical projects. Goldhagen managed to wrap himself in the imagined voice of the victims (as well as the perpetrators). He gained moral authority via what seemed to his critics a grotesque, lurid, virtually pornographic language of witness, which could proclaim a certain docudrama authenticity.[90] Structuralist history had certainly privileged "objectivity," a stance that had already been thoroughly criticized by Saul Friedländer in his now classic exchange with Martin Broszat during the Historians' Debate.[91] This debate about the validity of history produced by "victims" or their descendants reemerged with Goldhagen's insistent appeals for hearing the voices of the victims (although the reader would be hard put to find those "authentic" voices in his opus).

Goldhagen respected no *Schamgrenze* (shame border). He got down to the nitty-gritty graphics of gushing blood and flying body parts with a gusto from which most historians recoil. He offered a kind of living-color Holocaust, not the gray tones of historical documentation or even of *Schindler's List*. His book was neither solemn nor respectful, and yet it came with the dual imprimatur of "Jewish survivor's son" and Harvard University. That too came as a kind of perverse relief to German audiences resentful of the privileged position "objective" historians had assumed in defining contemporary German national identity (not a problem that American historians usually face). Volker Ulrich, who had initiated the debate with his dramatic first article in *Die Zeit*, wrote another one with the headline "Goldhagen and the Germans: Historians criticize. . . . The public perceives the book as liberating."[92]

This warm welcome for Daniel Goldhagen was also, of course, influenced by the current German political scene in the mid-1990s. The resolute reminder that the Nazi past indeed would not pass provided wel-

---

89. Dieter Pohl, "Die Holocaust Forschung und Goldhagens Thesen," *Viertel-jahresheft für Zeitgeschichte* 45 (January 1997): 12–48.

90. On this point, see the insightful reflections of Michael André Bernstein, "Homage to the Extreme: The Shoah and the Rhetoric of Catastrophe," *Times Literary Supplement*, 6 March 1998, 6–8.

91. Reprinted in *New German Critique* 44 (spring/summer 1988): 85–126.

92. Volker Ulrich, "Goldhagen und die Deutschen," *Die Zeit*, 20 September 1996.

come reinforcement for those who, like Jürgen Habermas, mourned the demise of the old Bundesrepublik (Federal Republic) and mistrusted, indeed feared, the "normalization" of Germany into a unified nation that could now, among other things, in good conscience deport refugees from the war in former Yugoslavia, or mobilize the Bundeswehr for actions beyond shoring up dikes when the Oder River flooded. Not only the author of a book on the Holocaust was honored when, to historians' head-shaking, Daniel Jonah Goldhagen was awarded the *Blätter-Demo-kratiepreis* on 10 March 1997. The award, which had not been granted since 1990, when it was given to the citizens' movement of the former GDR, is intended to celebrate the democratic achievements of the Federal Republic, an institution that, as Karl D. Bredthauer noted on behalf of the editors of the *Blätter,* "is a gift that must still be deserved." Clearly, the reception of Goldhagen's book and Goldhagen himself had been perceived as another test of whether the gift was deserved, whether the Germans were worthy of their democracy.

Honoring Goldhagen, with his argument that Germany's democratization and "de-antisemitization" was a result of Western Allied victory in May 1945, became, for many, a way of honoring and recalling Germany's debt to the West. Habermas's much-criticized *Laudatio* for Goldhagen was most of all, I believe, a *Laudatio* (and a bit of a eulogy) for the no longer quite existing Bundesrepublik he had so cherished. It was also no accident that while the previous awards for the GDR dissidents had been presented in Berlin, this event transpired in Bonn, the soon-to-be-defunct capital of the old Federal Republic. The enthusiasm evoked by Goldhagen in western Germany—and remember, only in western Germany—was also, in many ways, a displaced valorization of the Federal Republic that Goldhagen was willing to exempt from the dark patterns of German history. It signaled an affirmation of the Western orientation of a new, united Federal Republic, in the face of the political, economic, and moral uncertainties of unification.

Habermas's address was filled with qualifiers and defense mechanisms; he knew that many of his friends who remembered his forceful intervention "on the right side" in the Historians' Debate didn't want him to be giving this speech.[93] It is clear, however, that what he was hailing was not so much Goldhagen's work itself as the opportunity it gave Germans to respond to his work. The book (and the reaction to it) worked as a

---

93. See Jürgen Habermas, "Vom öffentlichen Gebrauch der Historie," in *Ein Art Schadensabwicklung: Kleine politische Schriften VI* (Frankfurt, 1987). On Habermas's "constitutional patriotism," see also José Brunner, "Ride and Memory: Nationalism, Narcissism, and the Historians' Debates in Germany and Israel," *History and Memory* 9 (fall 1997): 256–300.

confirmation of the power of the West, or of the Enlightenment in the form of the Western victors, to impose democracy. The project worked, it was still working, and Habermas was relieved, relieved enough to give a *Laudatio* (rumor had it that Goldhagen personally begged him to do it, an offer that Habermas couldn't refuse). In his response, Goldhagen remarked that one of the lessons of his book was that the Federal Republic's success depended on "the emergence of a relatively non-nationalist, internationally responsible nation state." Those, like Habermas, to whom such a nation is dear felt that Goldhagen was an ally, not so much perhaps in their view of German history, but in their view of what present-day Germany should be.[94]

The Personal and the Historical

At this point in my analysis, I veer into personal *Exkurs,* in order to convey the peculiar atmospherics surrounding the "Goldhagen effect." As usual, when it comes to this topic of Germans, Jews, and the shadow of the Holocaust (at least as far as outside critics, such as myself, are concerned), the Germans get it wrong no matter what they do. If they remember too effusively, we accuse them of a self-hating, philosemitic obsession with Jews; if they try to forget, we accuse them of irresponsible and immoral denial, of refusing to face the past.[95] But this time, there seemed to be something particularly and intensely creepy about their typically oscillating response: both the enthusiasm with which so many embraced this relentless depiction of German evil, and the vehemence of those few friends and colleagues who thoroughly denounced the book. The latter made even those who, like myself, strenuously rejected the book nervous; this was Germany, after all, and in the emotionally laden milieu, it became difficult to recall one's own reasoned critique. At the same time, even for those of us who, after all these years, are pretty well inured to the bizarreness of doing German history as a Jew (and American) in Germany, it was indeed creepy to observe the delight with which many recognized the broad antisemitic consensus Goldhagen described. The force of that presentation was only very partially mitigated by his having decreed rather unconvincingly that the consensus was broken by unconditional Allied victory in 1945.

Disconcerting situations developed. One began to hear things one

---

94. For the full texts of Habermas's speech, with comments by Karl D. Bredthauer and Jan Philipp Reemtsma, and reply by Goldhagen, see *Aus der Geschichte lernen/How to Learn from History: Verleihung des Blätter-Demokratiepreises 1997* (Bonn, 1997).

95. For one view on this dilemma, see Atina Grossmann, "Ein Blick aus New York," *Mittelweg* 36 (April/May 1997): 17–21.

hadn't heard in à very long time; musings from friends and colleagues about antisemitic comments they had heard, maybe even believed, while growing up. Friends and colleagues suddenly remembered such attitudes in their own families and at school. A weird outbreak of self-accusation and self-criticism followed, reminiscent of nothing so much as well-intentioned white Americans confessing their own racism: "Yes, I am a racist, we are all racists." This therapeutic mode, after all, leaves suspiciously unclear what is to be done after such an admission and turns as easily into excuses as a program for redress.

Goldhagen had not only touched the historiographic nerve discussed earlier, but poked his finger into still open personal wounds. For many Germans, his unshakable insistence on ruthless antisemitism as the motivation for a Holocaust that still seemed finally unfathomable easily reinforced suspicions about the antisemitism of one's own parents and grandparents, and indeed of one's own upbringing. These suspicions had been nurtured not only by diffuse memories of comments made and overheard, but also by a continuing discomfort and anxiety among and around Jews, even one's best friends. With Goldhagen, I began to surmise, "good Germans" did not have to feel so uncomfortable. He assumed that Germans were antisemitic, and therefore if one said anything stupid or insensitive, it wouldn't be so terrible. This too came as a kind of relief.

For Jews, however, this new, partial openness brought a curious barrage of statements and reminiscences from friends and colleagues about their own embeddedness in a hopelessly racist history. I, for one, didn't really want to hear, mistrusted, and didn't know what to do with such reactions. It was truly surreal to sit with friends and colleagues and experience the apparent pleasure with which they accepted Goldhagen's denunciation of their culture as having been saturated with eliminationist antisemitism. The pro-Goldhagen fervor, then, seemed a particularly egregious example of the *Holocaustfixierung* that Heinrich August Winkler has diagnosed as a form of "negative nationalism."[96] Old clichés took on new life; Germans, one couldn't help thinking, really do take a kind of perverse pride in being the most extreme at either evil or repentance (reminding one of the nursery rhyme—when they're good, they're very, very good, and when they're bad, they're horrid). This kind of grandiosity seemed particularly apparent in some of the more enthralled reactions to Goldhagen.

All in all, the multiple conversations I had about Goldhagen during visits to Germany in 1996 and 1997 put me, for example—a child of Ger-

---

96. Heinrich August Winkler, "Lesearten der Sühne," *Der Spiegel* 35 (24 August 1998): 180–81, part of a cover story on the *Mahnmal* (memorial) debate, titled "Zuviel Erinnerung?" (Too much memory?).

man-Jewish refugees—into a very strange position, and one for which I was no longer prepared. I found myself maneuvered into a past whose complexities were denied by Goldhagen's thesis. It was as if I had become a surrogate part of those fatally naive German Jews who believed in the promise of Weimar democracy and did not recognize that they were flourishing in the midst of a society that wanted nothing more than to exterminate them, who were so dumb and blind as to live for generations among Germans and not sense that they were deeply despised. There was no question, I thought, that the book was also a polemic in the old (and tired but not tired enough) conflict between East European and German Jews. But how to explain that adequately to Germans who seemed a bit overeager to applaud Goldhagen's denunciation of deluded (also venal and opportunistic) German Jewry?

In discussion after discussion with fellow academics in *Kneipen* (pubs) in Berlin, Frankfurt, or Hamburg, I found myself speechless or sputtering, astonished at how quickly we seemed to have left the world of scholarly discourse we shared. I could either accept that I was sitting in the midst of a world still so steeped in such "eliminationist" belief structures that they were instantly recognizable to my interlocutors, or I could protest dumbly—much like one's parents and grandparents had, I imagined—that no, no, things couldn't be that bad, they weren't all antisemites, thereby also participating in a perhaps perilous state of denial. After all, the logic of the book is that there was no place in Germany for Jews, and that those who were there, even happily, comfortably, thankfully so, were dangerously duped. It was a ridiculous—and entirely unreal—position to be in, and one that always made me want to leave the *Kneipe* as fast as possible. At the same time, it became painfully obvious in those *Kneipen Gespräche* (informal conversations) that for all the acclaim accorded Goldhagen's "personalizing" of the perpetrators, even close friends and colleagues were still paralyzed when talking about parents who might really fit his notion of perpetrator. One of the least discussed aspects of the Goldhagen phenomenon has been the enthusiasm with which many postwar Germans embraced his thesis of face-to-face personal responsibility even as they still shied away from any direct personal confrontation with that face of evil—in the form of direct discussion with, much less rejection of, their elders.[97] It is worth noting in this context another underdiscussed aspect of the Goldhagen reception, which could not fail to impress me:

---

97. There have of course been numerous attempts by children of *Täter* to write about themselves and their families. See, for example, Niklas Frank, *Der Vater: Eine Abrechnung* (Munich, n.d.); Peter Sichrovsky, *Schuldig geboren: Kinder aus Nazifamilien* (Berlin, 1987); and Dörte von Westernhagen, *Die Kinder der Täter: Das Dritte Reich und die Generation danach* (Munich, 1987).

namely, that, as in the Historians' Debate, no women scholars participated in the public discussions, certainly no one identified with the thriving field of German women's and gender history.[98]

Second Thoughts

Inevitably, this intense phase of publicity and discussion faded, morphing into more or less sober reassessments of the encounter between Goldhagen and the Germans. Sensing that the period of wild adulation had passed, *Der Spiegel*—which can always be counted on to print something offensive to Jews—now tried to keep the sensationalist aspects alive, by reporting breathlessly on Norman Finkelstein's controversial *New Left Review* indictment of *Hitler's Willing Executioners* as a "fraud." Finkelstein, another American-Jewish "son of survivors," carefully dissected the book's sloppy sources and illogical argumentation, but he also, and much more problematically, positioned it as part of a growing Holocaust literature carrying a political agenda committed to justifying the existence of the state of Israel. For the German press, the bitter fight between Goldhagen and Finkelstein was especially titillating because both openly identified—and used as part of their public legitimation—their Holocaust lineage. The *Spiegel* cover story, headlined "Goldhagen—ein Quellenstricker?" (a trickster with his sources), was accompanied by the inescapable photos of Jews about to be massacred and featured side-by-side photos of the two "young" Jewish men.[99]

On the whole, however, a moderate tone prevailed during the final, third stage of the Goldhagen phenomenon. Most journalists and scholars settled into a quiet accommodation: generally critical (fortified by the

---

98. Shandley briefly notes this in his introduction to *Unwilling Germans?* 21.

99. See "Goldhagen—ein Quellenstricker?" *Der Spiegel* 33 (1997): 156–58, and the long, vitriolic exchange between Goldhagen and Finkelstein in the *Frankfurter Rundschau.* A revised version of Finkelstein's review was later published together with a tightly argued and highly detailed critique of Goldhagen's sources by the Canadian historian Ruth Bettina Birn. See Norman G. Finkelstein and Ruth Bettina Birn, *A Nation on Trial: The Goldhagen Thesis and Historical Truth* (New York, 1998). In the acknowledgments to that volume, Finkelstein dedicated his blistering attack on Goldhagen "to the memory of his beloved parents, both survivors of the Warsaw Ghetto and Nazi concentration camps: only a rational apprehension of what happened can give point to their martyrdom." The book itself became the object of extensive controversy; Goldhagen threatened Birn with a lawsuit for libel. On Goldhagen's attacks against Birn, see "Der Schutz des allmächtigen Autors," *Frankfurter Allgemeine Zeitung,* 4 November 1951, 41; and "Holocaust als Andachtsbild: Interview mit NS-Expertin Ruth Bettina Birn über Daniel Goldhagens Attacken auf Kritiker," *Der Spiegel,* no. 46 (10 November 1997): 266–67. On Birn, see also the useful review by István Deák, "Holocaust Views: The Goldhagen Controversy in Retrospect," *Central European History* 30 (1997): 295–307.

mostly negative reviews by their American—and Jewish—colleagues) but also somehow chastened. They were careful to acknowledge Goldhagen's contributions to research on the police and the death marches (this position had already been staked out by Hans-Ulrich Wehler in the original *Zeit* series).[100] They conceded that there were things to be learned from Goldhagen's book, problematic as it was; that he raised legitimate and important questions, about motivation, agency, and personal responsibility. Goldhagen was credited, rather overgenerously, with directing attention away from the structuralist (and potentially amoral) interpretations favored by a past generation of liberal historians.

The "debate" dwindled amidst a proud and relieved sense that Germans had proven once again that they could discuss their past—even under such fierce attack—in a civil and reasonable manner. Once again, the eternally-under-suspicion postwar Germans had been tested and had passed. On the one hand, confronting the Holocaust had become a rite of passage that every generation had to undergo for itself and in its own way. On the other hand, this *Vergangenheitsbewältigung* had become a defining and constitutive part of (West) German civic identity. It should also be said, of course, that Goldhagen had made it bafflingly easy for his readers to accept his devastating accusations. Before 1945, he averred, Germans were like some awful exotic tribe ("Die Gedankenwelt vieler Deutschen damals unterscheidet sich völlig von den unseren"); after 1945, under the benign tutelage of their American occupiers, they became "like us." This exculpatory verdict facilitated his patronizing and conciliatory *Fazit,* formulated in an interview with Rudolf Augstein, that "young Germans should no longer have to feel tormented by their past" (*sollten sich nicht von der Vergangenheit gequält fühlen müssen*).[101] When Germans voice such sentiments, they are not infrequently castigated for wanting to forget and whitewash their history; no wonder that Goldhagen's judgment about "the grace of belated birth" should be so popular.

All in all, then, the book and the discussions surrounding it worked in many ways as yet another test (*Reifeprüfung,* in the words of SPD historian Michael Schneider) for the Federal Republic. The "concerned" German public could congratulate itself for accepting Goldhagen. To have done anything other or less would have been much more embarrassing than the headshaking of those who—like myself—tend to pronounce about the guilt complexes and strange fixations about Jews of their German friends and colleagues. Writing in the Social Democratic journal

---

100. Hans-Ulrich Wehler, "Wie ein Stachel im Fleisch," *Die Zeit,* no. 22 (31 May 1996); the English version is "Like a Thorn in the Flesh," in Shandley, *Unwilling Germans?* 93–104.

101. "Spiegel-Gespäch: Was dachten die Mörder?" dialogue between Rudolf Augstein and Daniel Goldhagen, *Der Spiegel* 33 (1996): 50–55, esp. 55.

Archiv für Sozialgeschichte, Schneider worried that the Goldhagen debate served mainly as a displacement of other urgent questions that should agitate the new Germany, such as European unity, the insecure future of the welfare state, migration from non-Western countries, immigration and citizenship, and the continuing difficult relations between East and West Germany. If Schneider observed avoidance of the present, others, like Habermas, would presumably argue that the past of "willing executioners" addressed by Goldhagen is absolutely implicated—if not explicitly enough—in these contemporary anxieties and debates. Indeed, new controversy is currently brewing about the "left nationalism" of intellectuals who advocate precisely such shifts.[102]

Sequels

As I write, the Goldhagen furor serves as little more than an additional backdrop to a new and ongoing set of "Holocaust moments." Most important, perhaps, has been the intense response to the Hamburg Institute for Social Research–sponsored exhibit "Crimes of the Wehrmacht, 1941 to 1944." There is no doubt that the Goldhagen discussion provided crucial support for an exhibit indicting "ordinary" German soldiers, but the latter has instigated what I believe will be ultimately a much more difficult and significant process. The role of the Wehrmacht in war and extermination is a topic that no German can easily ignore. Between eighteen and twenty million German men had sworn loyalty to the Führer, certainly many more than in the *Ordnungspolizei,* and many more than even the highest estimates of direct involvement in genocide (Goldhagen counted at least 100,000 "executioners"). The Wehrmacht exhibit hits hard at a core postwar narrative, the legend of the clean army, and forces a confrontation that Germans cannot divert by saying, "But my family were not Nazis."

The exhibit and the vehement attacks on it, especially in Bavaria, stronghold of the Christian Socialist Union (CSU), led to a rather astonishing debate in the Bundestag, remarkable not only for the intensity of discussion but its immensely personal tone. Delegates referred to their own wartime experience in the Wehrmacht, or that of their fathers, and/or

---

102. Michael Schneider, "Die 'Goldhagen-Debatte': Ein Historikerstreit in der Medi-engesellschaft," *Archiv für Sozialgeschichte* 37 (1997): 460–81. Schneider used the term *Reifeprüfung.* On the new left-wing nationalism, polemically termed "National Bolshevism," see, for example, "Aus deutschen Landen frisch nach rechts: Horst Mahler, einst bei SDS und RAF, demonstriert gegen den Doppelpass und will eine nationale Sammlungsbewegung gründen," *TAZ,* 2 February 1999; or "Der Nationalbolschewist: Wäre Rudi Dutschke heute ein völkischer Nationalist?" *TAZ,* 24 December 1998.

to their various Jewish grandparents, or in-laws. They revealed once again how very much alive this history is in Germany, not only in the hyperactive culture of commemoration, but also very directly in the personal biographies of current political decision makers. On this subject, it seems, everyone is *betroffen* (touched), widely and intimately.[103]

By now, over 630,000 people—more than have bought Goldhagen's bestseller—have viewed the exhibit, which was inaugurated in Hamburg in March 1995. When the latest venue opened in Kiel in December 1998, some 1,000 visitors crowded in daily, hotly arguing over the images and artifacts displayed.[104] This absolute presence of the past, easily teased out by public events, and sometimes overlooked in all our fretting about amnesia and the passing of the generation of eyewitnesses, has a great deal to do, I think, with the visceral German response to Daniel Goldhagen and his book.

The politics of memory took another turn (another *Wende*) in fall 1998 when the long reign of Christian Democratic chancellor Helmut Kohl was replaced by a "Red-Green" (Social Democratic and Green Party) coalition headed by Gerhard Schröder. Debates about citizenship, immigration, and memorialization of the Holocaust—never really separable—gained force as the "Left" took over planning for the "Berlin Republic." The ever-present discussion about how contemporary Germany should cope with its history was inflamed anew by a speech given in the Frankfurt Paulskirche (a site associated with 1848 revolution and the

---

103. For minutes of the debate, see Thiele, *Die Wehrmachtsausstellung,* 170–219. See also Ulla Roberts, *Spuren der NS-Zeit im Leben der Kinder und Enkel: Drei Generationen im Gespräch* (Munich, 1998); and Alan Cowell, "The Past Erupts in Munich as War Guilt Is Put on Display," *New York Times,* 3 March 1997. On anxieties about right-wing extremism in the present German Army, see Alan Cowell, "Pro-Nazi Incidents in German Army Raise Alarm," *New York Times,* 5 November 1997.

104. See *TAZ,* 9 January 1999, 24. For critical reflections on the mass response to the exhibit in Germany and Austria, see articles in Hamburger Institut für Sozialforschung, *Besucher einer Ausstellung: Die Ausstellung 'Vernichtungskrieg: Verbreachender Wehrmacht 1941 bis 1944' in Interview und Gespräch* (Hamburg, 1998); and *Newsletter des Fritz Bauer Instituts* 14 (April 1998). Since this article was written, there have been some dramatic developments in regard to the "Wehrmachts Ausstellung." After some 900,000 people had viewed the exhibit in thirty-four cities in Germany and Austria, and just as it was about to embark on a U.S. tour, scheduled to open in New York City on 3 December 1999, the Hamburg Institute for Social Research declared a moratorium on the exhibit and withdrew it from public view, pending scholarly review and rethinking. A storm of controversy had erupted in the German press and academia about the labeling of several photographs of massacres (in particular about the role in those cases of NKVD Soviet secret police and German forces) and the general argument of the exhibit regarding the Wehrmacht's central role in a war of extermination on the Eastern Front. A symposium, "Military War Crimes: History and Memory," originally intended to accompany the New York showing, was held on 3–6 December 1999; a documentation of that conference is forthcoming from the New Press (New York).

embattled tradition of German liberalism) on 11 October by the seventy-one-year-old writer Martin Walser. A Wehrmacht veteran with a Nazi family pedigree, Walser chose the occasion of being awarded the prestigious annual Freedom Prize of the German Booksellers' Association to voice his resentment at the continual invocation of "Auschwitz" as a "moral cudgel" (or club, *Moralkeule*) or "dutiful practice" (*Pflichtübing*). Remembrance and repentance had become, he implied, an irritating, routinized ritual that victimized Germans: "everyone knows our historical burden, the eternal shame, no day on which it is not held up to us."[105]

Ignatz Bubis, head of the Central Council of Jewish Communities in Germany, immediately lambasted the initially well-received speech as "moral arson" (*geistige Brandstiftung*).[106] He had heard in Walser's rebellion against the "instrumentalization of our shame [*Schande*] for contemporary purposes," and his warning that "no one can demand from another what he would like to have, but the other does not want to give,"[107] an assault on the long overdue and ever more aggressive, putatively extortionist efforts of Jewish claimants and their lawyers to gain compensation for bank accounts, insurance policies, real estate, and art works confiscated—to their great profit—by Germans and others over a half century ago, as well as on the multiplying general claims for compensation and recognition from forced laborers and other victims of National Socialism.

Klaus von Dohnanyi, former mayor of Hamburg and scion of a well-known Resistance family, further incited the public conversation with the rather astonishing demand that the Polish-born Jewish Holocaust survivor Bubis (now, in Dohnanyi's words, "a German citizen of Jewish faith obviously free of this central German legacy: namely, the Holocaust") account for what he might have done (or not done) had he lived as a German in Nazi Germany.[108] Walser, with his insistence that everyone is "alone with his conscience," and then Dohnanyi, both highly respected public personalities, had self-consciously pushed the limits of acceptable

---

105. Walser, *Dank,* 44–48.

106. See "Das geteilte Gedächtnis: Ignatz Bubis greift Martin Walser an," *Frankfurter Allgemeine Zeitung,* 10 November 1998; and interview with Bubis in *Der Spiegel,* 30 November 1998. It is worth noting that Helmut Schmidt had already complained in 1981 "that German sovereignty should no longer be held hostage to Auschwitz." See Olick, "What Does It Mean to Normalize the Past?" 549–50.

107. Walser, *Dank,* 48.

108. Much of this bitter exchange played out on the pages of the *Frankfurter Allgemeine Zeitung* in November and December 1998. See especially Klaus von Dohnanyi, "Schuld oder Schulden? Ignatz Bubis' unerhörtes Interview," and "Dokumentation: Jeder prüfe sein Gewissen: Eine Antwort auf Ignatz Bubis und Jan Philipp Reemtsma," *Frankfurter Allgemeine Zeitung,* 30 November 1998.

rhetoric. Implicitly included in their severe critiques of Germany's *Betroffenheitskultur* was the overwrought response to Goldhagen's accusatory book. Their contention that memory could no longer be prescribed certainly took on the air of taboo breaking; after all, the entire established culture of official commemoration and remorse, starting with the Allied denazification program so lauded by Goldhagen, has been precisely about such prescriptions. Increasingly, there are those (among the many who didn't sit applauding in the audience during Goldhagen's "triumphal" tour) willing to contest the continuous ritualization of remorse and the insistence on memory. Walser claims to have received at least 1,000 letters of support, and German politicians, journalists, and intellectuals continue to provide a seemingly endless series of faux pas referring to Jews and the Nazi past. It is no surprise, therefore, that Ignatz Bubis, now advanced from "corrupt speculator" of the 1970s to moral conscience of the nation, warns so darkly about a new nationalism and xenophobia, not only among neo-Nazi hooligans, but within German elites, which are, as he carefully puts it, "not free of antisemitic elements."[109]

Almost a decade after unification, the "antagonistic memories" of Germans and Jews seem more fraught than ever. Both Germans and Jews remain caught in the continuing traps and obligations of what Saul Friedländer has termed "the impossibility of remembering and the impossibility of forgetting."[110] As with the Historians' Debate, the angry arguments among Bubis, Walser, Dohnanyi, and also Rudolf Augstein take place among older men with direct experience of Nazism and the war. But they resonate more broadly. The signs are contradictory and confusing. Some Germans, mostly members of the generations young enough to have been socialized post-1989, and those old enough to remember the war, now openly rebel at still being forced to bend before the "Auschwitz club" and at attacks on the integrity of the Wehrmacht.[111] We read daily reports about the ominous growth of extreme right-wing and neo-Nazi groups, encouraged by the Christian Democratic campaign against a liberalization of Germany's restrictive citizenship and immigration policies. At the same time, an ever larger group of younger Europeanized Germans (not only

---

109. See *TAZ,* 21 November 1998, 28; also interview with Ignatz Bubis, *Süddeutsche Zeitung,* 21 September 1998, by Josef Joffe and Mechthild Küpper. Bubis has openly expressed his disappointment that in contrast to 1985, he is now no longer able to block the performance of Fassbinder's play *Garbage, the City, and Death;* see interview, *Berliner Zeitung,* 21 November 1998. See also Roger Cohen, "Anniversary Sets Germans to Quarreling on Holocaust," *New York Times,* 10 November 1998 (on ceremonies marking the sixtieth anniversary of Kristallnacht). See comments on Walser and Bubis in n. 7 above.

110. Friedländer, "Some German Struggles with Memory," 27.

111. See the bizarre conversation between the two Wehrmacht veterans Martin Walser and Rudolf Augstein in "Erinnerung kann man nicht befehlen," *Der Spiegel* 45 (1998).

Wessies, I suspect) has matured. They are less shameful but also less defensive. They seem able to unburden themselves from the "moral cudgel" while still recognizing that Auschwitz is an absolutely central and impossible-to-extinguish element of their history and national identity. Moreover, "Shoah business"[112] continues to provide—in ever increasing amounts—a good and interesting living for many historians, writers, and cultural bureaucrats. (Certainly, it is not without extreme irony, for example, that the Jewish Museum, just inaugurated in Berlin, is the world's largest.)

All these developments are difficult to evaluate, especially in the context of anxieties and hopes for the forthcoming "Berlin Republic." But perhaps the most remarkable aspect of all the "debates" documented here has been their tenacity; within all the oscillation about whether and how to remember, the discussion has hardly ever let up. Indeed, it has become only more intense in the last decade. This is the metaphenomenon that we still need to analyze more intently. The desire to become "normal" by escaping the past has been a fundamental factor in German consciousness ever since the end of the war; as early as June 1945, there were calls in the press for a *Schlussstrich* (concluding line) to discussions about Nazism.[113] These pressures, however, have unquestionably been consistently accompanied by the drive to preserve a sense of "abnormality," marked most concretely, until 1990, by the division of Germany and the presence of the Wall—a sign perhaps more powerful than all the rituals of commemoration combined. And surely, while the desire to become "normal" or "ordinary" may seem dubious (especially given the characterization of the genocidal perpetrators as "ordinary" men or Germans), it is certainly understandable over a half century later.

The challenge post-1989 as Germany prepares for the "Berlin Republic" is the reconciliation of "normalization" as a European nation in a global political economy with the preservation of memory—both of the victims and of the role of "the Germans." The question remains whether it will be possible, as many Germans, including apparently both Walser and Bubis, believe it can and should be—and the intense response to Goldhagen underscores this need—to generate "a new language for memory."[114] Will it be possible, in the next decades, to incorporate into a sense

---

112. To my knowledge, this provocative term was first coined by the Jewish-German journalist Henryk Broder, an expert, merciless, and never-to-be-satisfied critic of German efforts at *Vergangenheitsbewältigung* and German/Jewish relations in general.

113. See Grossmann, "Trauma, Memory, and Motherhood."

114. See "Wir brauchen eine neue Sprache der Erinnerung: Das Treffen von Ignatz Bubis und Martin Walser," and the front-page article "Bubis und Walser haben miteinander gesprochen," *Frankfurter Allgemeine Zeitung,* 14 December 1998; also *TAZ,* 21 November 1998; and *Berliner Zeitung,* 21 November 1998.

of normality a sense of responsibility and ownership for the devastation that Germany produced in the years 1933 to 1945? Will it be possible to reconcile in some new concept of German citizenship both the specific memory of extermination committed by German Nazis with the always present collective memory of German suffering during the Second World War; to incorporate both the already built *Neue Wache* with its national memorial to all the victims of the war, and some still-to-be-determined collective memorial (or memorials) to the specifically Jewish or non-"Aryan" victims of the Holocaust?[115] At this moment, the Bundestag is set to debate—as has already been extensively debated in the press and local politics—intensely practical, as well as moral and political, questions about the financing, placement, and scope of memorialization. It is in that ever-current and ever-changing context that the excited response—now almost forgotten in the rush of new scandals, debates, and controversies—to Daniel Goldhagen and his work must be situated and pondered.[116]

---

115. I refer here, of course, to the debate about the relationship between a still-to-be-determined memorial (*Mahnmal*) in Berlin and other sites of memory, such as the concentration camp sites themselves or various museums and archives, as well as the most recent plan, floated by Michael Naumann, the Social Democratic cultural official, and Michael Blumenthal, the Berlin-born American director of the new Jewish Museum, to combine the Eisenman Memorial with a "living memorial" of museum, library, and research center. For the newest documentation of the memorial discussions, see Cullen, *Das Holocaust-Mahnmal.* Surely it will not be long before we have a published edition of the Bubis/Dohnanyi/Walser arguments.

116. The Bundestag did eventually vote in June 1999 to support, in principle, the construction of the so-called Eisenman II memorial in Berlin, incorporating a monument and an "information center," but many practical matters of design, organization, and funding remain unresolved.

Austrian Non-Reception of a Reluctant Goldhagen

Pieter Judson

German translations of *Hitler's Willing Executioners* appeared in Austria in September of 1996 to a strangely distanced reception. The book did not unleash in Austria the kind of public discussion it called forth in neighboring Germany. The book did not even sell particularly well. Most Austrian reviewers treated it with an exaggerated deference, praising the work for what they called its original focus on the participation of ordinary Germans in the Holocaust. Some went so far as to remind their readers that what Goldhagen had written about the Germans could be said of "Austrian citizens of the German Reich" or "citizens of Greater Germany" (Grossdeutschland) as well.[1] While Austrian reviewers acknowledged that the book's more controversial conclusions had drawn strong criticism in American and German scholarly circles, they seemed to have missed the more interesting phenomenon altogether, namely, the degree of Goldhagen's personal popularity in Germany. Instead, reviewers tended to describe the Goldhagen phenomenon purely as an academic controversy over narrow issues of interpretation.

The bloodless reception in Hitler's homeland of a book that characterized ordinary German attitudes toward Jews as eliminationist and documented the active complicity of ordinary Germans in the Holocaust might seem surprising. After all, public opinion polls of the past decade have consistently registered lingering Austrian bitterness over the Waldheim controversy and a defensive anger directed toward "world Jewry." Did no Austrians reject Goldhagen's accusations as constituting yet

I would like to thank Matti Bunzl, Heidemarie Uhl, and Douglas McKeown for their insightful comments on earlier drafts of this essay.

1. Hans Rauscher, "Ganz gewöhnliche Deutsche," *Kurier,* 17 August 1996, 3; Arbeitskreis Goldhagen, *Goldhagen und Österreich: Ganz gewöhnliche ÖsterreicherInnen und ein Holocaust-Buch* (Vienna, 1998), 8.

another smear campaign? More to the point, given the reasons for the book's popularity in Germany, did not those Austrians seeking to undo the myth of Austrian victim status find it a useful confirmation of their arguments? Or did this nonreaction simply confirm the popular view among American, European, and some Austrian observers that Austrians stubbornly deny their perpetrator past? This latter was, for example, the conclusion reached by the Arbeitskreis Goldhagen, a group of left-wing university students who published the volume *Goldhagen und Österreich* in the summer of 1998.[2]

Whatever else it implied, I do not believe that the bland reception Goldhagen received at the hands of the Austrians simply reflected an ongoing denial of Austrians' historic participation in the Holocaust. The question of how to treat Austria's Nazi and antisemitic pasts is in fact central to public discourse in today's Austria. The question underlies several current controversies, both within the academic community and generally in the public sphere. It permeates almost every new attempt by each of the political parties to reposition itself with particular voting groups. In a sense, the question cannot be escaped. We might find fault with the ways in which the question is debated, with its particular manipulations at the hands of historians, politicians, and journalists, but the general consensus that Austria was Hitler's first victim no longer holds sway.

There is, therefore, some point in seeking to understand why Austrians did not react to *Hitler's Willing Executioners.* In a society where claims and counterclaims about the Holocaust, about Austrians' relationship to the Third Reich, and about the nature of Austrian identity are today more bound together than ever before, it may be useful to investigate the reasons why, in this case, the proverbial dog did not bark. In what follows I will argue that two contingencies—(1) the particular demands of Austrian politics in the fall of 1996, and (2) the nature of Goldhagen's argumentation itself—ensured that *Hitler's Willing Executioners* made few waves in Austria, even as it became a topic of almost obsessional proportion in neighboring Germany.

Austrian History, Austrian Identity

The new Austrian identity pieced together after the collapse of the Third Reich built on several political elements of the imperial and republican pasts, while strongly rejecting the German ethnic basis for national identity that had defined its predecessor. The first Austrian Republic had defined itself literally as the republic of *German* Austrians (the term *Aus-*

---

2. *Goldhagen und Österreich,* 7.

tria had theretofore included people of several national and ethnic identifications). Most citizens of the new state viewed potential *Anschluss* with Germany as their economic and cultural salvation, at least until 1933. After Austria achieved full independence in 1955, however, political leaders of Austria's two major parties, the Socialist Democrats (SPÖ) and the Catholic Peoples' Party (ÖVP) tended to define Austria's unique mission, and thus its identity in a Cold War world, according to its geographic situation between east and west, and its political neutrality.

This new identity ignored the paramount issue of Austria's interwar history, namely, *Anschluss* with Germany. It therefore fostered a kind of amnesia toward Austria's recent past, since it required a thorough denial of the powerful German nationalist traditions of the preceding fifty years. Austrian leaders were aided, of course, by the Allied declaration of November 1943 that proclaimed Austria Hitler's first victim, and by the Allied tendency to equate Prussian German traditions with the cultural origins of Nazism. This official rejection of the recent past for a completely new identity meant that in the public sphere, at least, the recent past would remain largely unexamined.

Amnesia about its recent past, however, did not require a denial of all Austrian history. On the contrary, evocations of Austria's imperial past have recently become a critical ingredient in the global popularization of Vienna as a center for tourism and high culture. It was also a critical ingredient in Austria's chosen identity as mediator between west and east, or between the developed and third worlds. Until the fall of neighboring communist regimes in 1989, Austrians often drew on a nostalgic vision of their imperial multinational, Catholic internationalist past to differentiate themselves from Germans and to construct a relevant mediating role for themselves in the Cold War era. The visible presence of Slovene, Czech, and Hungarian flags waving at Empress Zita's funeral in 1989, for example, was but a small reminder of Austria's historic relationship to those "nations," a relationship the latter now view far more positively than they did before fifty years of Soviet hegemony.[3]

---

3. In 1989 it was decided that a state funeral would be held in Vienna for the recently deceased Empress Zita, wife of the last Habsburg emperor Charles. Imperial tradition dictated the route to be taken by the cortege through the streets of the inner city to the Capuziner Crypt, final resting place of the Habsburgs. More than one commentator noted that the imperial cortege would have to circle the Albertinaplatz, site of Alfred Hrdlicka's recently erected monument to the victims of fascism. Should the coffin of the Empress (a reminder of a glorious tradition) be confronted with this brutal monument to Austria's recent past? Some wondered whether the route might not be changed to avoid the monument's brutal evocation of Jews forced to clean Vienna's streets during the *Anschluss*. The funeral, after all, was an attempt to recreate an imperial past that would evoke contemporary Austria's

When Austrians evoke the imperial past, it is, of course, an extremely selective process. Along with historicist architectural reminders of Vienna's centrality in East Central Europe, the city also houses visible monuments to more unsettling by-products of that very same age. Several monuments, for example, recall the rise of political, cultural, and religious antisemitism in Vienna. Even the most innocent of tourists can't fail to notice the ongoing popularity of Karl Lueger, Vienna's greatest mayor (1897–1911) and founder of the populist antisemitic Christian Social movement in Austria. Several monuments, a church, and a segment of the Ringstrasse testify to Lueger's gargantuan importance in Vienna's construction of its past and present identity. Today's ÖVP situates itself consciously as the postwar legatee of Lueger's Christian Social party.

Historians, both Austrian and American, have themselves given Lueger the necessary alibi to remain a respected and beloved figure in Austrian mythology, for his political use of antisemitism was above all considered opportunist and not ideological, situational and not racialist. Lueger's was the cultural antisemitism of the ordinary person, not at all the virulently racist, ideological ravings of an Adolf Hitler or a Georg von Schönerer. This distinction parallels another important element in post-1945 Austrian public culture that makes it difficult to square today's Austrian identity with the histories of individual Austrians. Immediately after the war, politicians on all sides strongly condemned antisemitism but carefully defined it as the ideologically racialist view held by the Nazis. Their narrow focus on Nazi antisemitism enabled cultural, private, or religious antisemitic prejudice in Austria to survive largely unexamined. The latter forms of antisemitic prejudice became unlinked from the public, ideological Nazi racism and continued to exist barely under cover, as documented by several public opinion surveys in the postwar period. This distinction had several critical repercussions, as Richard Mitten has pointed out: "[It] minimize[d] the significance of non-racial anti-Jewish hostilities, which no longer counted as antisemitic . . . [T]he identification of antisemitism with Nazism *tout court* implied that legitimate anti-Nazi credentials, which the founders of the Second Republic undoubtedly possessed, made one into an opponent of antisemitic prejudice."[4]

---

importance as a mediator between east and west. It would also remind the world of contemporary Vienna's touristic value, explicitly celebrating the city's role as the center of a multiethnic, culturally vibrant Empire. The Hrdlicka monument, however, evoked a past of civil war and fascist cruelty. It is not that anyone would deny the existence of this other past, but rather that this past has no role in the definition of the present. In the end, of course, imperial tradition prevailed, and Empress Zita passed by the Hrdlicka monument.

4. Richard Mitten, *The Politics of Antisemitic Prejudice: The Waldheim Phenomenon in Austria* (Boulder, 1992), 31.

The new post-1945 Austrian identity did, however, take the legacy of the recent interwar period self-consciously into account in one important way. The political leaders of the new Austria were determined to minimize the kind of social and political polarization that had paralyzed the First Republic and produced civil war. In the social partnership system set up in 1957, they devised a way to divide social and economic power proportionately, not only among political parties, but also among the unions, chambers of commerce, and representatives of industry whom the parties directly represent. This system, known as *Proporz,* worked to smooth over all potential conflicts between labor and capital and created an enviable social stability in the Second Republic. While it resembled comparable neocorporatist arrangements in Western Europe, the influence of *Proporz,* as we will see, extended much further into the public sphere than in most other societies.

As the Cold War receded, as traditional taboos faded, and, most importantly, as Austrians themselves began to explore their twentieth-century histories more fully, questions emerged that undermined the traditionally shared assumptions of public life since 1945. The controversy surrounding the 1986 election of Kurt Waldheim to the Austrian presidency was only the most obvious example of ongoing dissonance between public consensus and private memory. The typical answers Waldheim provided to emerging questions about his peace- and wartime records during the *Anschluss* years suddenly no longer sufficed to remove those subjects from public discussion, as they might have in the past. Another such dissonance erupted from public confrontation with the traveling exhibition "Vernichtungskrieg: Verbrechen der Wehrmacht, 1941 bis 1944" in 1995–98. The exhibition documented in photographs the participation of ordinary German soldiers in atrocities on the Eastern Front. It challenged the ways in which thousands of ordinary Austrians had interpreted their personal experiences of war. In doing so it suggested an unsettling newer history that both confirmed individual memory and disputed the traditional public constructions that had up until now been used to interpret those memories. Ruth Beckerman's film *Jenseits des Krieges,* for example, captures this dissonance superbly. Her interviews with Austrian veterans at the exhibition show how similar memories can produce clashing interpretations between those who seek to justify the atrocities and those who can find no justification for them.

Austrian public life in the past decade seems littered with incidents that confront Austrians with events for which they have only recently begun to acknowledge some personal responsibility. These incidents demand more than an admission of complicity, for they challenge the very founding myths of modern Austrian identity. Incidents like the Waldheim affair, confrontations like those surrounding the Wehrmacht exhibition, and, potentially, arguments in the Goldhagen book all point to a chasm between personal, lived memory and public national identity. They also make public a strong undercurrent of continuity between pre- and post-1945 ways of thinking about the world that precisely the public repudiation of Nazi antisemitism after 1945, mentioned above, failed to address. Several scholars have shown convincingly that Austrians often defended Waldheim in 1986 using cultural tropes that strongly evoked antisemitism, *even as Waldheim's defenders publicly repudiated antisemitism.* In the same way, critics of the "Crimes of the Wehrmacht" exhibition imagined an external conspiracy was responsible for denigrating the largely honorable men who had fought to defend their country (Grossdeutschland), while at the same time they deplored the fact that certain atrocities had taken place.[5]

The Austrian System in Trouble

Without a brief explication of Austria's recent political history, incidents like the Waldheim affair, the Wehrmacht exhibition controversy, or even the public response to *Hitler's Willing Executioners* appear to confirm that society's long tradition of hiding behind its status as Hitler's first victim. Yet this interpretation, popular in the West, misses several developments of the past two decades that also help to account for Jörg Haider's meteoric rise. In Austria one cannot speak of a public sphere, or public debate, without invoking the political parties that dominate that sphere so completely. In Austria there is very little public space for any opinion that is not in some way connected to the parties. This is partly a result of *Proporz,* the attempt to avoid the social polarization of the 1930s by giving each of the major parties, the SPÖ and the ÖVP, some official role in almost every public institution, either through appointments or funding. Appointments to university positions largely depend on party relations within those institutions, and institutional research agendas reflect to a large extent party agendas. The extent of government-funded activity in Austrian society (from banks to unions to chambers of commerce to Austria's newspapers) guarantees that particular debates will conform to party political ideological positions. Even Austria's relatively independent newspapers of record, *Standard* and *Die Presse,* are forced to engage in discussions whose parameters are often set by the party press.

In 1996 Austrian society enjoyed relative economic prosperity by gen-

---

5. See the excellent examples cited by Mitten in his *Politics of Antisemitic Prejudice,* chapter 8, "The Campaign against Waldheim and the Emergence of the Feindbild," 198–245.

eral European standards, yet it suffered from an escalating cultural polarization. As the government moved to fulfill the budget-balancing requirements for adopting the euro, anxiety over job security grew. Since 1989 many Austrians feared the dual specter of (1) cheap labor in the formerly communist neighboring states, and (2) a potential influx of southern and eastern European immigrants fleeing war in the former Yugoslavia. Austria alone, it was believed, would have to bear the burden of opportunist immigrants from the East and face the perceived security challenges that would accompany this immigration, while cutting subsidies to state-owned industries and welfare benefits to Austrian citizens. Polls taken in 1995 showed that a third of Austrians believed that guest workers and other foreigners living in Austria already had too many benefits.[6] Enthusiasm for the European Union was also on the wane, particularly given the possibility of its eastward expansion and people's fears that this development would negatively impact Austrian employment.

Since 1986 Austria has been governed by a so-called great coalition of SPÖ and ÖVP, with the socialists as senior partner. During those years, however, the vote totals for both major parties have fallen drastically, particularly in the case of the ÖVP, which by 1992 was garnering only 27 percent of the vote at the federal level. The main beneficiary of this decline was Austria's Freedom Party (FPÖ). The spectacular rise of the FPÖ and its charismatic leader Jörg Haider is the major phenomenon of Austrian politics in the past fifteen years. Originally a minor third party with single-digit popular support at the federal level, the FPÖ traditionally gathered an odd collection of German nationalists, anticlericals, small businessmen excluded from *Proporz,* and economic liberals who opposed the corporatist *Proporz* system. In the 1970s the FPÖ appeared at least superficially to be developing into Austria's counterpart to Germany's Free Democratic Party (FDP). And indeed, from 1983 until 1986, under Norbert Steger and its liberal wing, the party joined the SPÖ in a social-liberal governing coalition. A stunning coup executed by Haider and his nationalist allies in 1986, however, ejected Steger and the liberal wing from prominence and took the FPÖ out of the government and into opposition.

Ideologically the party moved sharply to the right; its program became synonymous with Haider's own positions, themselves a mixture of populist opportunism and German nationalist tradition. And Haider's stunning electoral successes only strengthened his power to dictate policy

6. Tony Judt, "Austria and the Ghost of the New Europe," reprinted in *Contemporary Austrian Studies* 6 (1998): 126–37; Richard Mitten, "Jörg Haider, the Anti-immigrant Petition, and Immigration Policy in Austria," *Patterns of Prejudice* 28 (April 1994): 27–47. Subsequent poll data in 1999 show the number has risen to around half of all Austrians, with even higher numbers among older Austrians.

within the party.[7] The FPÖ took advantage of several realignments among Austrian voters that the two major parties ignored. Its popularity grew despite the fact that in 1993, the remaining social liberals abandoned the FPÖ to form their own party under Heide Schmidt, the progressive Liberales Forum (LiF). By this time, however, Haider had managed to make the FPÖ into a strong, populist, catch-all party of opposition to the status quo in Austria, attracting first the votes of conservatives dissatisfied with the ÖVP and later, increasingly, the votes of workers dissatisfied with the SPÖ.[8]

Far more important to Haider's rise than his German nationalist connections and his implicitly revisionist view of the Third Reich, however, was his strongly xenophobic stance on immigration during a period of economic restructuring and social uncertainty.[9] Linking rising urban crime to the increase in immigrants and a crisis in the welfare system, Haider pushed a referendum to tighten Austria's immigration laws and to force immigrants to work. He vigorously opposed membership in the European Union, and although he lost that particular battle, he soon benefited from the growing perception after Austria's entrance that the drawbacks to the Union in fact outweighed the advantages. In the past four years Haider has even downplayed his explicit German nationalism (much to the disappointment of his original supporters) for an Austrian nationalism grounded in the sacred notion of *Heimat* that conjures German nationalist images less directly but more effectively. The FPÖ juxtaposes the ideal of *Heimat* to the perceived negative results of cultural pluralism, especially the growing threat of urban crime and welfare cheating. A 1998 FPÖ poster in Vienna trumpeted the words "Heimat, Sicherheit, Arbeit," and more explicitly, "Our *Heimat* should remain OUR *Heimat.*"

Haider's successes need further contextualization, however. It is often forgotten that his is only the most successful, but certainly not the only,

---

7. Under Haider the FPÖ raised its federal election vote total in 1986 to 9.7 percent. In the 1990 elections it received 16.6 percent, while in 1994 it gained almost one-quarter of the votes cast. In 1995 the FPÖ vote total fell slightly, to 21.9 percent, but in the 1996 elections to the European Parliament (with no concrete repercussions for Austrian internal policy), the FPÖ gained 27.6 percent. Recently, in the parliamentary elections of October 1999, the FPÖ became Austria's second largest party for the first time. In some of the federal states, the FPÖ regularly receives at least a third of all votes in local elections. In the 1999 elections in Carinthia the FPÖ gained 40 percent, enabling Haider to assume the governorship.

8. In 1983 some 2 percent of Austrian workers voted for the FPÖ, while 70 percent voted for the SPÖ. In the elections to the European Parliament of 1996, however, each of the two parties received about 40 percent of the working-class vote. See Reinhold Gärtner, "Survey of Austrian Politics, 1996," *Contemporary Austrian Studies* 6 (1997): 303.

9. For stunning examples of Haider's statements on the Third Reich, and for his rhetorical uses of the immigration and welfare issues, see Hans-Henning Scharsach, *Haiders Kampf* (Vienna, 1992), particularly chapters 5 and 8.

new party capitalizing on general popular frustration with the Austrian status quo. Austrians on both the left and right of the political spectrum are currently demanding a more democratized, less bureaucratized political culture. To the new parties on the left that entered parliament during this period, the Greens and the LiF, less bureaucracy means more social and cultural pluralism, more *basis Demokratie,* less *Proporz.* For the Haider right, less bureaucracy means less red tape for business, less "welfare corruption," fewer union-boss privileges, as well as an end to *Proporz.*

Up until 1995, Haider's successes in Austrian politics came mainly at the expense of the conservative Catholic ÖVP. Struggling to present a coherent alternative to the socialists, the ÖVP was nonetheless implicated by its presence in the coalition and its historic responsibility for the *Proporz* system. Seeking to reverse his party's freefall, ÖVP leader Wolfgang Schüssel precipitated a crisis in 1995 by calling for new elections. These, he hoped, would be won by an ÖVP that would present a dramatic Thatcherite conservative alternative to socialist policies. Implicitly, however, this strategy relied on the idea of an ÖVP-FPÖ coalition, since by itself the ÖVP was unlikely to gain more than a plurality of votes. In fact, most Austrian voters opposed this option, fearing it would bring economic instability. Schüssel's decision backfired, and while the SPÖ actually increased its vote total to 38 percent, the ÖVP with 28 percent remained only just ahead of the FPÖ with 22 percent.[10] The coalition was renewed, but in the shadow of a fast-growing FPÖ.

The political jockeying among the parties has been played out increasingly in the realm of cultural politics. Haider has all along been a master at exploiting cultural issues and social fears around immigration, antisemitism, and security. Constrained by coalition economic policies that bind it to the SPÖ, the ÖVP too has turned increasingly to the realm of culture and identity to give itself a recognizably differentiated identity. Church, family, and order are its stock-in-trade, along with subtle appeals to a rural nationalism against the cultural immorality of Vienna. Here the powerful influence of parties in the Austrian public sphere is clear. For if the ÖVP had not viewed the election of Kurt Waldheim as a crucial opportunity for it to regain power from the SPÖ in 1986, for example, the public debate, the coded antisemitic attacks on Waldheim's doubters, and the general defensiveness against outsiders attempting to control Austria would have been far less audible. Without the party (and party press) interest in giving it a specific construction, the Waldheim controversy could not have become a major public issue.

---

10. If one adds together the totals for the nongovernmental parties (FPÖ, Greens, LiF), it becomes clear just how much voter attrition has decimated the power bases of the two major parties in the past two decades. Over a third of Austrians now vote for other parties.

Since 1986 and the breakdown of the victim consensus, all the parties appear implicitly to be debating the question of a useful and coherent Austrian national identity. The debate mobilizes three distinct points of view. The ÖVP still defends a modified version of the traditional "victim" thesis against the newer "perpetrator" allegations of the SPÖ, Greens, and LiF. In his ten years in office, SPÖ Chancellor Franz Vranitzky was far more outspoken than any of his predecessors in acknowledging the damaging legacy of Catholic antisemitism to Austria, both past and present. In doing so, he abandoned the original myth that had enabled the SPÖ and ÖVP to find common ground since 1945. During Vranitzky's tenure, and after long debate in 1995, the government finally set up a National Fund for the Victims of National Socialism.[11] Other politicians on the left, notably in the Green and LiF parties, expressed outrage about Austria's hidden perpetrator past. In 1997, after viewing the "Crimes of the Wehrmacht" exhibition, Heide Schmidt, leader of LiF, spoke publicly about her past "blind spot" regarding antisemitism and Austrian participation in the Holocaust.[12] Haider's growing success points to yet another manipulation of the debate. He deals neither in perpetrators nor victims, but rather defends the national honor of patriotic German Austrians who fought in the Wehrmacht and the SS from the accusations of so-called communist sympathizer historians.[13]

The elections to the European Parliament in the fall of 1996 offered activists a particularly fertile context to pursue their cultural agendas. Haider treated this election as the moment of his possible breakthrough ("Wahltag ist Zahltag!" proclaimed a determined Haider on several campaign posters). The ÖVP and FPÖ fought to outflank each other, both for votes on the far right and now, as we will see, for the political center. As in the Waldheim years, history once again became an explicit battleground for struggles over Austrian identity.

The predictable gesturing to victim, perpetrator, or hero status of Greater German Austrians swiftly acquired new significance in the public mind due to a deft coup executed by Haider in the 1996 campaign. The Austrian media rightly treated Haider as the most interesting and perhaps the most important figure on the Austrian political landscape, and in September of 1996, Haider did not disappoint. With an enthusiastic Peter

---

11. This fund is smaller than many critics would have liked, and its use is limited. Several critics on the Left believed that the creation of the fund was far too little, too late, and that Vranitzky has not really earned the reputation he enjoyed as the man who had forced Austrians to face their history more honestly. *Goldhagen und Österreich,* 17–18.

12. Christa Zoechling, "'Mein blinder Fleck': Interview: Heide Schmidt über die Präsidentschaft und ihren Umgang mit der NS-Vergangenheit ihrer Eltern," *Profil* 52/53 (20 December 1997): 25–26.

13. Scharsach, *Haiders Kampf,* 125.

Sichrowsky at his side, Haider announced that the Jewish journalist and expatriate Sichrowsky, of all people, would lead the FPÖ's list in the upcoming elections to the European Parliament. This particular coup scrambled the terrain of Austrian politics further, and it unleashed a storm of controversy within an already divided Austrian Jewish community. Not that this move by Sichrowsky and Haider was entirely unpredictable— Sichrowsky has a record of creating controversy, given his role in the Ignatz Bubis biography and his relatively cordial views toward Waldheim. This alliance, however, immediately provoked the use of terms not frequently seen in the Austrian press, like *Hofjude* and *Alibijude.*

The heightened controversy surrounding the simultaneous opening of the exhibition "Vernichtungskrieg: Verbrechen der Wehrmacht, 1941 bis 1944" in Klagenfurt a week later should be seen in this context. If Haider was going to make a play for the political center, neutralizing accusations of antisemitic crypto-fascism by displaying his Jewish credentials, the ÖVP, not to be outdone, would bid more openly for the crypto-fascist nationalist vote. Thus Bishop Egon Kapellari of Klagenfurt and the ÖVP governor of Carinthia, Christoff Zernatto, publicly declined to patronize or even attend the exhibit. In an interview, the governor rejected the "right-wing extremist clichés" with which Carinthia has been saddled. (In Carinthia, home of Jörg Haider, the FPÖ traditionally garners more of the vote than at the federal level.) The leader of the SPÖ in Carinthia opened the exhibition and claimed that while the majority of Carinthians have nothing to do with right-wing extremism, Nazi chauvinism, and heroizing of the war, still one could not forget that under the Nazi regime Austrians were not simply victims.[14] Interestingly enough, a year before in Vienna the exhibition had been sponsored and praised by politicians from both ÖVP and SPÖ; only when it left for the provinces did it become an object of political controversy.

The decision of the Vienna FPÖ to retain its racist election slogan, "Wien darf nicht Chicago werden," despite the fact that its federal list was now headed by Sichrowsky, a Chicagoan; the studied lack of concern displayed by FPÖ leaders for new evidence that linked the accused desecrators of graves at a Jewish cemetery in Eisenstadt to the FPÖ's *Bundesgeschäftsführer* Karl Schweitzer (and the FPÖ youth organization); and, finally, the academic travails of the ÖVP candidate, the perennial would-be-Ph.D. Karl von Habsburg, all added to a politically polarized environment. Finally, the appearance of a runaway bestseller on Hitler and antisemitism raised the stakes of the debate further, forcing another open discussion of Austrian antisemitism on the public. The bestseller that

---

14. *Profil* 38 (16 September 1996): 34; *Die Presse,* 6 September 1996, 7.

unintentionally helped stoke the flames of Austria's political fires received enormous press coverage. Its author was repeatedly interviewed, and its thesis (particularly its emphasis on a culture of popular and Catholic anti-semitism) was the subject of much public outcry. However, the book that gained so much attention was not Daniel Jonah Goldhagen's *Hitler's Willing Executioners.* It was instead Brigitte Hamann's *Hitlers Wien: Lehrjahre eines Diktators.*

At precisely this moment, late August 1996, the German translation of Goldhagen's book did indeed appear in Austrian bookstores. Its appearance was reported in the media, and the controversy it had unleashed in Germany and the United States duly described. The book was reviewed relatively positively, and editorials appeared on the scholarly aspects of the controversy the book had provoked in Germany and the United States. The book could be found on several journalists' "best pick" lists of the season, but it did not unleash much of a public discussion in Austria, either among historians, in the media, among opportunistic politicians, or generally at large.

Goldhagen and the Austrians

The word *Austria* appears only once in the index of *Hitler's Willing Executioners,* referring to descriptions of how Austrians brutally forced Jews to wash the streets of Vienna after the *Anschluss* in March 1938. "The Austrians' hearty celebrations included immediate symbolic acts of revenge upon the Jews, who in Austria, no less than in Germany, were believed to have exploited and injured the larger society."[15] In subsequent interviews, Goldhagen has stated that he treated the Austrians as part of the greater German people and therefore did not single them out in the book. In a September 1996 interview with Goldhagen, the Austrian newsweekly *Profil* asked him, with little success, to elaborate his views of the Austrians and their particular responsibility for the destruction of the Jews. Goldhagen maintained that because he considered the Austrians to be exactly the same as the Germans, just as enthusiastic and convinced about the destruction of the Jews, there was no need to single them out.

The *Profil* interviewers then asked about the higher percent participa-

---

15. Daniel Jonah Goldhagen, *Hitler's Willing Executioners: Ordinary Germans and the Holocaust* (New York, 1996), 286–87, 605. There are no index entries for Vienna, Karl Lueger, Karl Iro, or Georg von Schönerer, for example, although Mauthausen does appear. The Schönerite Iro, as Hamann pointed out, made the suggestion in a speech to parliament that Hitler may have witnessed that immigrant Gypsies have an identification number tattooed on their forearms. Brigitte Hamann, *Hitlers Wien: Lehrjahre eines Diktators* (Munich, 1996), 191.

tion of Austrians as concentration camp guards than Germans, and whether Goldhagen agreed with the Austrian historians who claimed that antisemitism was particularly deeply ingrained in Austria. Goldhagen couldn't answer this question because, in his words, he treated the Austrians as no different from the Germans and therefore could not say whether they were easier to mobilize for the destruction of the Jews than the Germans. But, the interviewers persisted, if you claim that nineteenth-century antisemitism was the motivating force for the Holocaust, did not Austrian politicians serve as a particularly important and successful example to German antisemites? Did not Hitler emphasize repeatedly that he had learned to hate the Jews in Vienna? And didn't the Austrians develop their own death fantasy for their Jews in the twentieth century, long before they fell under the discriminatory laws of the Third Reich? Goldhagen answered that this distinction between Austria and Germany was hardly relevant, since it was in Germany that Hitler had gained power and not in Austria. However, he repeated that he saw little difference between German and Austrian attitudes toward Jews and speculated that perhaps antisemitism had erupted so powerfully in March 1938 because the Austrians had had to wait longer for the laws.

At the end of the article, the interviewers tried once more to provoke a response on Austria from Goldhagen, this time raising the issue of contemporary antisemitism. Citing an example from school religion classes (children still learn that the Jews nailed Christ to the cross), the interviewers asked just how great a threat contemporary antisemitism poses in a society where a 1987 poll determined that 8 percent called themselves strict antisemites who consider the Jews partially responsible for the Holocaust.[16] Goldhagen's reply inadvertently confirmed the claims of postwar Austrians who rejected Nazi antisemitism but left popular antisemitism untouched. While of course there is antisemitism in contemporary Austria, stated Goldhagen, it has little to do with the antisemitism of the Nazis, and its goal is not the elimination of Jews from society. Here, Goldhagen reverted once again to the example of contemporary Germany in his comments.

In only one instance did Goldhagen seem willing to criticize the Austrians as such, and that was regarding Waldheim. Goldhagen claimed that had Waldheim been running for office in Germany, he would have been forced out of the picture the minute the first accusations were made. This suggested that despite other disclaimers, Goldhagen drew some distinctions between postwar Germany and Austria. At the same time, given the

---

16. Twenty-five percent of respondents in the same poll claimed they would have trouble shaking the hand of a Jew.

current political situation, it seemed an odd example to raise. If one wanted to draw a comparison to Germany, why not bring up Haider? Waldheim's personal popularity was never impressive, his career ended dismally, and he at least claimed to have opposed the Nazis. Haider, on the other hand, is an extremely popular politician with outspoken revisionist views on the *Anschluss* era, the historical role of the SS, and the Holocaust. If the Germans would have abandoned a sullied Waldheim, is it imaginable that a quarter of them could vote for a Haider?

Why did Goldhagen not prepare himself better for an Austrian audience? He might, for example, have dwelt more on the particularities of Austrian or Catholic antisemitism, or he might have tried to demonstrate how in fact those particularities were in his view congruent with Reich antisemitism. The Austrian interviewers certainly encouraged Goldhagen to articulate a critique of Austrians' particular role in the Holocaust, a challenge to which Goldhagen did not rise. But, as I will argue in a moment, any such ruminations would have undermined the central thesis of his book, as well as Goldhagen's oft-asserted claim that post-1945 Germany has developed the democratic and non-antisemitic culture it lacked before 1945.

Austrians and Goldhagen

For some Austrians, independent historians or those on the left, Goldhagen's proved a frustrating approach to their history. While they support writing the social and cultural history of Austrian perpetrators, they argue precisely the opposite of Goldhagen, namely, that the Austrians have their own distinct antisemitic traditions. It was by focusing attention on the crimes of German (not Austrian) Nazis that postwar Austrian society managed to avoid a self-examination. For Austrians on the Catholic Right, Goldhagen's approach subtly reinforces the victim myth they embrace and thus requires no particular response. In his refusal to recognize Austrian antisemitic traditions, in particular his refusal to admit that Christian Social antisemitism may have helped prepare the way for the Holocaust, Goldhagen reinforced the comforting orthodoxy of the Catholic Right. As for the nationalist Right, Goldhagen ironically endorsed its views on two crucial points by arguing that (1) Austrians actually *are* Germans, and (2) given the fundamental break that occurred in 1945, contemporary antisemitism is not related to pre-1945 antisemitism. And if nothing else, Sichrowsky's position heading the FPÖ's election list in 1996 (if not his public statements on the matter) successfully reinforced the FPÖ's tolerance credentials with at least some of the Austrian public.

Despite Goldhagen's fairly tepid remarks on Austrians in the *Profil* interview, some writers attempted by themselves to provoke a debate by encouraging the Austrian public to read the book as if it were about recent Austrian history. In an early *Profil* article from the spring of 1996, before the book had actually appeared in German, Austrian political scientist Walter Manoschek (a curator of the Wehrmacht exhibition) criticized the monocausality of Goldhagen's central thesis on German antisemitism. At the same time, however, Manoschek used the opportunity to stress how much this thesis ought to irritate his fellow Austrians, since in practical terms, the Nazi antisemitic program up until March 1938 had not gone beyond what the Christian Social elites in Austria had long proposed for their society. The antisemitic ground had been well prepared in Austria, according to Manoschek, and the Nazis merely fulfilled an already-pro-grammed development. Writing two years later, in 1998, about the missing Austrian Goldhagen controversy, Manoschek blamed Goldhagen himself for not making an issue of the particularly Austrian roots of Nazi anti-semitism. Goldhagen, he said, was only the latest in a long line of scholars who instead of referring to a semantically and conceptually correct Gross-deutschland (including Austria, the Sudetenland, Alsace, and parts of Slovenia) preferred to speak of "Reich" or "Bundes" Germans. In this case, "language and concepts constitute memory and identity: Germany's de facto monopoly of Nazism and the Shoah harmonizes perfectly with the post-1945 Austrian denial of Nazism." Had he examined Austrian antisemitism, added Manoschek, Goldhagen could also have made his theories on eliminationist antisemitism more convincing.[17]

When the German translation of Goldhagen's book appeared, jour-nalist Hans Rauscher's editorial and review in the *Kurier* added the words *and Austrians* in parentheses after every single mention of the Germans. In addition, the *Kurier* ran a provocative headline, "The Austrians were guilty too," in its encapsulated reporting of the *Profil* interview. The very wording of the headline betrayed the kind of effort it took to get serious consideration for the Austrians from Goldhagen. Rauscher and Manoschek, from quite different political positions, cited specific exam-ples taken from the records of Austrian police battalions involved in the murder of Jews on the Eastern Front to fill the gaps left by Goldhagen, both in his book and in subsequent interviews. To them the problem was not that the Austrian sources and examples of atrocities weren't in the book, but that they were not explicitly identified as such. While Manoschek and Rauscher did criticize the book's central thesis on anti-semitism, both nonetheless appeared very much to want the book to suc-ceed in Austria. Rauscher went so far in one of his articles to point out that

17. *Goldhagen und Österreich*, 8.

the FPÖ chief in the early 1970s, Friedrich Peter, had belonged to one such police battalion, "and he has never said explicitly what he did or did not do in that position," thus directly linking the history in *Hitler's Willing Executioners* to more recent politics.[18] If Goldhagen wouldn't make the connections to Austrian history explicitly himself, there were Austrians ready to do it for him.

The Austrian academic left has little investment in the particulars of the controversy as it played itself out in Germany. Historians on the Left may have taken the lead on research into Austria and Austrians under corporatist Fascism or in the Third Reich, but their scholarship has only recently gained acceptance in academic circles, and not yet in society at large. Austrian historiography in the 1980s was marked less by debate over theoretical approaches such as that of the functionalists or intentionalists. Instead, it was and is marked by explicitly political debates over whether or not to address the question of the Holocaust at all. For Austrians, the term *Historikerstreit* refers to the question of victim versus perpetrator history. Those historians who examine Austrians' roles as perpetrators in the 1940s are criticized in a language that links their work to a kind of "political correctness" of the Left. These scholars are accused, for example, of imposing a moralizing political interpretation on objective facts and thereby ignoring the complexities of the situation ordinary Austrians faced.[19]

The academic left in Austria has indeed set itself to the task of investigating Austria's status in terms of perpetrator rather than victim status as well as stressing a more political understanding of Austrian national identity. This identity is based on the idea of postwar democratic citizenship combined with democratic cultural traditions reaching back from before 1938 and 1918. While alone among the major parties the socialists have recently been most willing to give up Austria's mythical victim status as the foundation for national identity and to address the problem of Catholic antisemitism, they have balanced this sacrifice with a renewed emphasis on an Austrian identity that refers less to history than to institutions. This has led to the paradoxical situation that some of the most vigorous historians of the Left who have done some of the best work to uncover Austria's interwar history nevertheless react viscerally when anyone suggests possible links between Austrian nationality and German nationality. The socialists may have the best research agenda on the 1930s and 1940s, but it is ironically Haider's German nationalist intellectual

---

18. Rauscher, "Ganz gewöhnliche Deutsche."

19. See, for example, Sigrid Löffler, "Der Pseudo Historikerstreit," *Die Presse,* 7 August 1996, 2; and Hubert Braunsperger, "Nunmehr wird Geschichte Zensuriert," *Die Presse,* 17 September 1998, 2.

allies, those who eschew both victim and perpetrator theses, along with some independent intellectuals, who most fully address pre-1945 Austrians' sense of national identity.

The Catholic Right, as mentioned earlier, has no reason to attack Goldhagen. This bloc too stresses a post-1945 citizenship based on democratic and cooperative institutions. But politically, while this bloc deplores the Nazi past (Dolfuss and Schuschnigg were themselves victims of Nazism), it is far less inclined to discuss the specificities of Austrian antisemitism. The ÖVP, or Peoples' Party, is a direct descendant of the Christian Social movement. And while many of its leaders and adherents suffered persecution under Nazi domination, I would argue that the Christian Socials were far more effective in popularizing cultural and rhetorical antisemitism than was any radical German nationalist party in the early part of the twentieth century.

Since Goldhagen neither mentions the tradition of Christian Social antisemitism nor assigns it any particular responsibility either for the eliminationist environment of his theory or as an influence on German antisemites, the book is perfectly acceptable to many politically Catholic Austrians. They can deplore individual Austrian participation in the police battalions, while maintaining the comfortable fiction that Catholic antisemitism, although of course wrong, is not responsible. This explains why a book like Hamann's, which in 600 pages painstakingly retraces Hitler's every step, evaluates every contact of his Vienna years, could provoke far more interest, not simply because it was about Austria, but because it went beyond the limited *völkisch* milieu to discuss openly popular Catholic antisemitism.

Given this political framework for the debate of cultural issues in Austrian public life, the Goldhagen book simply wasn't controversial enough to interest either the Austrian public or its politicians. The Catholic Right saw its positions confirmed in the book, while the nationalist Right saw nothing to be gained by making it an issue. In any case the Sichrowsky incident effectively removed the FPÖ from any discussions around the Holocaust, as the party attempted to reach more centrist voters by projecting a more stable, dependable image. Indeed, Sichrowsky made Haider look, perhaps for a moment, more reasonable (or less dangerous) to moderate voters, and for whatever reason, the elections in October produced a virtual tie for first place among the SPÖ, ÖVP, and FPÖ. Finally, Goldhagen himself would not critique Austria strongly enough to make the book useful to the Left. The 1996 elections to the European Parliament had created a context in which a politics of culture was at the forefront, but a politics of culture that excluded discussion of *Hitler's Willing Executioners.* And while Karl von Habsburg and Peter Sichrowsky sat in the European Parliament, while the ÖVP governor of Salzburg, a trained historian, refused to support the Wehrmacht exhibition when it moved to his province, while Brigitte Hamann's book was on everyone's ten-best-Christmas-books list in 1996, Goldhagen's book went largely undiscussed and unsold.

Postscript

Since the writing of this essay, the particularly Austrian politics of culture remains a critical component of public life there. Very little has changed since 1996. In the summer of 1999 Sichrowsky was reelected to the European Parliament (although Karl von Habsburg, who left the ÖVP to run on a "family values" anti-abortion platform, was defeated).[20] In October Jörg Haider's FPÖ fulfilled almost everyone's long-term prediction, finally becoming Austria's second largest party in parliamentary elections by a margin of some 400 votes. Despite Austria's low unemployment levels and the lowest immigration rate of any European Union state, Austrian voters, particularly those of the working class, feared that immigrants threatened their jobs and their economic future. Only Haider tapped into that fear, while the government parties simply promised more of the same.

The 27 percent or so of Austrians who voted for Haider did not necessarily share his anti-immigrant and occasionally openly racist cultural rhetoric in all its particulars. Nevertheless, this part of his appeal became even more routinized and more acceptable during the 1999 campaign than it had been in 1996. Only the LiF and the Greens, representing a marginalized 10 percent of the electorate on the Left, protested this normalization. Austria's political leaders, President Thomas Klestil (ÖVP), Chancellor Viktor Klima (SPÖ), and Foreign Minister Wolfgang Schüssel (ÖVP), refused to engage Haider, thus remaining silent on the subjects of racism and culture. Despite Klestil's protestations to the contrary, his silence did as much as Haider to earn Austria its diminished reputation in the world press immediately following the elections.

The unwillingness of Austria's leaders to take on Haider's cultural rhetoric this time does suggest one difference separating 1999 from 1996.

---

20. Sichrowsky has reemerged from relative obscurity in 1999 to help Haider fend off accusations of antisemitism and proto-fascism, particularly among American Jewish communities after the election. When Haider traveled to the United States in November of 1999, ostensibly to run in the New York marathon, Sichrowsky accompanied him and was key in arranging meetings with American Jewish groups. While Haider played down his racist rhetoric in the United States, however, his deputies back in Austria threatened to sue the head of Vienna's Jewish community for libel, over exactly the same kinds of statements that American Jews had made.

The ongoing implication of history in contemporary Austrian political rhetoric remains as critical as ever, but increasingly for mobilizing the opposition parties on the Right and Left. It is the FPÖ alone this time, for example, that is protesting plans to bring the Wehrmacht exhibition to Vorarlberg in the fall of 2000.[21] Thus, in 1999 the issue of linking personal identity to Austria's pre-1945 history was debated among the opposition parties, whether Haider, the Greens, or the LiF, but not mentioned by the governing coalition. The coalition parties largely conceded the cultural field, neither adopting comparable appeals nor condemning those made by the opposition. In particular, the ÖVP moved away from its 1996 attempt to compete for the nationalist vote on the Right. And when the SPÖ did invoke the past, it was to emphasize the ongoing importance of Austria's neutrality in determining its current identity, thus reverting to the postwar tradition of defining Austria's identity according to political institutions.

Professional historians, meanwhile, have continued to embrace a research agenda that engages Austrian history in the period 1934–45, yet neither they nor the two main parties have made much progress in popularizing the results of their research. In a post-election comment to *Die Presse,* the respected historian Ernst Hanisch regretted the distance that separates Austria's historical profession from public discussion, commenting that Austria has no historians capable of speaking to a broader audience. "Even today," concluded Hanisch, "there still is no work by a professional historian about National Socialism that is scholarly, yet written in accessible language, and that might kindle a broad and deep debate in Austria." With the failure of the LiF to gain reelection to parliament, with the misplaced efforts of the Greens to reassure the international community of Austria's normalcy, and with the domination of the media by speculation surrounding Haider's next move, Austrian society seems farther away than ever from engaging in that debate.[22]

---

21. "FP-Bösch gegen Wehrmachtsausstellung in Vorarlberg," *Der Standard* (online), 5 November 1999.

22. "Opfer, Täter, Normalbürger, nicht Monster und Dämonen," *Die Presse,* 16 October 1999.

Reflections on the Reception of Goldhagen in the United States

Jane Caplan

An intriguing question, posed by the American historian Mitchell Ash in a public debate in Bremen in January 1997, is why it is so often Americans who have managed to force questions about the Holocaust into broad public recognition in Germany. The case of *Hitler's Willing Executioners* is unusual in that it has straddled the academic and popular camps, but it is not unique as an American import. It is only the latest in a series of public encounters that includes the television series *Holocaust* in the 1970s and the film version of *Schindler's List*. The sequence seems to be that America initiates these cathartic debates, but then Germany experiences them. Of course, this is not to deny that Germany has generated its own widely publicized encounters with its past: the *Holocaust* series fell into the homegrown *Hitler-Welle* ("Hitler wave") of the 1970s, and the 1980s *Historikerstreit*, or "Historians' Debate," about the place of the Third Reich in German history, was an entirely indigenous phenomenon on which foreigners only commented.[1] But the reasons for these repeated American contributions to the German public perception of the Holocaust itself are not hard to find. If Germans are committed to understanding the place of

---

This is a slightly revised version of my essay "Die Goldhagen-Rezeption in den USA," in Johannes Heil and Rainer Erb, eds., *Geschichtswissenschaft und Öffentlichkeit: Der Streit um Daniel J. Goldhagen* (Frankfurt am Main, 1998), 202–17. © 1998 Fischer Taschenbuch Verlag GmbH, Frankfurt am Main.

1. For the *Holocaust* series reception, see the special issues of *New German Critique* 19 and 20 (1980); for visual popularizations more generally, see Saul Friedländer, *Reflections of Nazism: An Essay on Kitsch and Death* (New York, 1984). English-language sources on the *Historikerstreit* include Peter Baldwin, ed., *Reworking the Past: Hitler, the Holocaust, and the Historians' Debate* (Boston, 1990); Geoff Eley, "Nazism, Politics, and the Image of the Past," *Past and Present* 121 (1988): 171–208; Richard Evans, *In Hitler's Shadow: West German Historians and the Attempt to Escape from the Nazi Past* (New York, 1989); and Charles Maier, *The Unmasterable Past: History, Holocaust, and German National Identity* (Cambridge, 1988).

Nazism and its genocidal policies in their history, it is in the United States that Holocaust survivors are most actively dedicated to its memorialization, and that there is in a sense a public culture of survival. The Holocaust is a massively powerful cultural value in the United States: only in Germany and Israel, and for different reasons, do the words of the historian Yehuda Bauer have as much resonance when he writes that in our culture "the Holocaust has no end. We are still living in a world in which the Holocaust happened."[2] Confronting and memorializing this fact remains an American preoccupation, especially now that the inevitable passage of time is sweeping away the survivors and their quintessential work of witness. Academic history alone will not be able to fill the gap left by their vanishing; a broader swathe of cultural projects is mandated. When we add to these needs the marketing power of the U.S. popular culture industry and its global reach, it is not surprising that the United States should be the source of such highly visible cultural exports, or Germany the recipient of them.[3]

How are we to explain the book's initial success in the United States, where within weeks of its publication on 29 March 1996 one reviewer described it as "the focus of animated, almost obsessive discussion, attracting a huge readership"?[4] In the United States as in Germany, the initial academic response to Goldhagen's book was generally negative and indeed dismissive, while press and public reaction was largely enthusiastic.[5] It was deeply antagonizing to many American experts in German history to see a book that they had largely rejected being hailed by other, apparently less qualified critics as a masterpiece of the historian's art, a pathbreaking contribution to the history of German antisemitism and the Holocaust. The rationale and substance of the academic critique of Goldhagen's work were largely comparable in both countries, since they derived from a shared disciplinary and professional expertise against which the book was measured and found wanting. However, I believe that we can understand the popular reactions better if we locate them in the cultural contexts from which they emerged. I will leave others to explore the book's impact on the German public.[6] Here, I would like to suggest

---

2. Yehuda Bauer, "The Significance of the Final Solution," in David Cesarani, ed., *The Final Solution: Origins and Implementation* (London, 1994), 308.

3. For the United States, see the impressive study by Peter Novick, *The Holocaust in American Life* (Boston, 1999).

4. Steven Aschheim, "Reconceiving the Holocaust?" *Tikkun* 11 (July/August 1996): 62.

5. An important exception to the generally approving coverage by nonspecialists was Clive James's critical essay, "Blaming the Germans," *New Yorker,* 22 April 1996, 44–50.

6. See Heil and Erb, *Geschichtswissenschaft und Öffentlichkeit,* especially the essays by Bergmann, Knoch, and Haury. For a range of German and U.S. responses, see Robert R. Shandley, ed., *Unwilling Germans? The Goldhagen Debate* (Minneapolis, 1998).

some tentative explanations for the book's American success that are specific to the American context, and that address both the general circumstances of the book's publication and its own content.

To begin with, when considering the impact of Goldhagen's book we have to remember that tens of thousands of new titles are published every year in the United States, and that there is a continuous fight for space in the bookstores, the press, and other media. The biggest nonfiction sellers in this crowded marketplace are of course usually books that are targeted to carefully identified mass audiences and receive no academic notice whatsoever: popular books on business or management, self-help manuals, guides to personal health, and so on. "Academic" books never break through into this kind of mass market; but a handful of them regularly reach a readership that is much wider than the restricted norms of academic publishing, where sales of a few thousand are counted a success. The fields of history and current affairs are a popular source for such breakthrough bestsellers: one thinks of the publications of Simon Schama or Paul Kennedy, or the more popular histories by Daniel Boorstin, or, to take one of the more recent examples, Dava Sobel's account of the discovery of longitude. Presumably such books are marketed to appeal to the intelligent "general reader," or at least to those who wish to appear so; and they are assisted to success by focused publicity in the "quality" media, both print and broadcast, which these readers also consume. The debate about Goldhagen's book in the United States in the spring and summer of 1996 thus took place in major newspapers like the *New York Times* (which gave it some prominence) and the *Washington Post,* in weekly or monthly reviews such as the *New Republic,* the *Nation,* or *Commentary,* on public radio and television, and through what has now become a familiar public forum in the United States, the author's appearance at a local bookstore to present and discuss her or his work.[7] In America, this last scenario—a function of the proliferation of massive chain bookstores in recent years—

---

7. Examples of press coverage are *New York Times,* 27 March, 1 April, 2 April, 3 April, 25 April 1996; *Washington Post,* 24 March 1996; *Philadelphia Inquirer,* 21 April, 26 April 1996; longer reviews include Omer Bartov, "Ordinary Monsters," *New Republic,* 29 April 1996, 32–38; Thomas M. Disch, "A Nation and People Accursed," *Nation,* 6 May 1996, 50–54; David Schoenbaum, "Ordinary People?" *National Review,* 1 July 1996, 54–55; and Robert Wistrich, "Helping Hitler," *Commentary,* July 1996, 27–31, as well as those by Aschheim and James already cited. Reports on German reactions to the publication of the book followed in due course: see, e.g., Josef Joffe, "Goldhagen in Germany," *New York Review of Books,* 28 November 1996, 18–21 (followed by an exchange of letters between Goldhagen and Joffe in the issue of 6 February 1997, 40); and Amos Elon, "The Antagonist as Liberator," *New York Times Magazine,* 26 January 1997, 40–44. Much of the academic response to the book's U.S. publication took place through the German historians' newsgroup on the Internet in April 1996. A public debate planned for New York in May 1996 was canceled when Goldhagen withdrew.

seems to have substituted for the grand public debates that were staged in Germany during Goldhagen's visit in the autumn of 1996.

In U.S. terms, Goldhagen received an uncommon degree of publicity, and while it would be mistaken to attribute the book's success to this alone, its effects cannot be discounted. And if U.S. cultural consumption is driven by publicity and by market visibility, then controversy is clearly a valuable midwife to commercial success. A similarly notorious beneficiary of this conjunction was the feminist writer Camille Paglia, another academic whose public prominence in the United States has been driven by controversy and press publicity. In the case of Goldhagen's classic *succès d'estime et de scandale,* this visibility was initially orchestrated by some astute prepublication publicity; the media wheels were set in motion as soon as academic historians rose to the challenge and revealed the vast divergence in academic and public reactions. The gap between academic and popular standards of taste is hardly a novelty, not least in the field of Nazi history (and it had evidently not been securely bridged by Christopher Browning's *Ordinary Men* [1992], which received only a fraction of the public attention accorded to *Hitler's Willing Executioners*);[8] but for once these two worlds met head-on, rather than coexisting in mutual indifference to each other. There was a particularly striking demonstration of this according to reports of the public symposium that took place at the Washington Holocaust Museum in April 1996, attended by Goldhagen and some senior specialists (German, American, and Israeli) in the history of German antisemitism and the Holocaust. Whenever Goldhagen spoke, he was greeted by enthusiastic applause from the audience, but when the other historians criticized him, the audience was silent or emitted murmurs of dissent. This was partly because the sound of junior knuckles being rapped by elder statesmen was especially audible and patently offensive to the audience, which rallied to defend the younger man under attack. But they would not have done this, I think, unless they had also had some real sympathy for his views.

The sense of a generational conflict in the reception of the book was not entirely absent in the United States, but it was less prominent than in Germany, where the gap between academics and public was also a gap between the generations.[9] And unlike Germany, where academic reaction was instantaneous and initially furious, it was in fact not the case that U.S. academics universally damned the book or rejected it out of hand. In the earliest reviews, Gordon Craig, doyen of the older generation of American

---

8. Christopher Browning, *Ordinary Men: Reserve Police Battalion 101 and the Final Solution in Poland,* 2d ed. (New York, 1998).

9. Joachim Güntner, "Der Generationsbruch," *Neue Zürcher Zeitung,* 13 January 1997, 19.

historians of Germany, was highly critical but by no means entirely damning in the *New York Review of Books;* neither was Volker Berghahn in his Sunday *New York Times* review.[10] Both men saw a lot to question and criticize, but they also gave a guarded welcome to the book to the extent that it opened up some new questions and reopened older ones that had been neglected in recent historiography on National Socialism. This dual response of acknowledging Goldhagen's tactical shift of focus while at the same time deploring the book's overall strategy is evident in most of the subsequent, far more critical reviews.[11] Without entering into a full review of the historiography, we need to briefly consider the field that Goldhagen's book entered and how he aimed to reorient it.

Generally speaking, academic research on Nazi Germany between the 1960s and 1980s gave substantial priority to reconstructing and analyzing the institutional and social structures of the "Third Reich" and to exploring the precise political functioning and decision-making processes of the Nazi regime (hence the emergence in the 1980s of the "intentionalist-functionalist" debate, and ultimately of the *Historikerstreit,* though these academic rows remained at a somewhat arcane level and never had much public resonance beyond the pages of the West German quality press). By the 1980s, in conformity with a wider shift in historical concerns, a greater interest was emerging, especially among German historians, in the systems and strategies of people's everyday experience, the *Alltagsgeschichte* of life under the Nazis.[12] Insofar as this approach made conspicuous and revalued the normal lives of "ordinary Germans" in Nazi Germany, it occasioned some dismay lest the essential barbarity of Nazism as a political tyranny be marginalized or trivialized by attention to comparatively mundane matters. In the 1980s too, there was a palpable sense that other contexts of explanation for genocide were being offered

10. Gordon Craig, "How Hell Worked," *New York Review of Books,* 18 April 1996; Volker Berghahn, "The Road to Extermination," *New York Times Book Review,* 14 April 1996, 6–7.

11. This convention was later disturbed by the Canadian historian Ruth Bettina Birn's challenging critique of Goldhagen's use of his sources, which was the first to fully take up his demand that critics confront his evidence as well as his arguments: "Revising the Holocaust," *Historical Journal* 40 (1997): 195–215; and see now Norman G. Finkelstein and Ruth Bettina Birn, *A Nation on Trial: The Goldhagen Thesis and Historical Truth* (New York, 1998). However, in Goldhagen's oddly literalist response to Birn's critique, "The Fictions of Ruth Bettina Birn," *German Politics and Society* 25 (fall 1997): 119–65, he purposely elects "not to discuss archival material" on the grounds that Birn's "fictional" representation of his argument vitiates any critique she might offer on this score (156). See also Christopher Browning's afterword in the second edition of his *Ordinary Men,* 191–223.

12. See, for example, Alf Lüdtke, ed., *Alltagsgeschichte: Zur Rekonstruktion historischer Erfahrungen und Lebensweisen* (Frankfurt, 1989); and Detlev Peukert, "Das 'Dritte Reich' aus der 'Alltags'-Perspektive," *Archiv für Sozialgeschichte* 26 (1986): 533–56.

that underplayed the unique status of the Jews in Nazi ideology and the significance of antisemitism. Here I am thinking of work by Götz Aly and others on the economic logic of the Holocaust; or of Detlev Peukert's very influential deployment of the idea of a broader project of biopolitics, a negative eugenics that sought to remake the entire "social body" of the German nation by excising all its vitiating elements.[13] This relocation of antisemitism did not overwhelm all German research on Nazi racism, nor was it in any way intended to diminish the scale or significance of Jewish suffering. Yet perhaps it came too soon after the first serious German historical investigations into the extermination of the Jews to be universally palatable. To some it seemed ironic, or worse, that no sooner had historians begun to pay serious attention to the genocide of Europe's Jewish populations than this Holocaust was forced into the shadow of a larger and not specifically antisemitic program of mass murder.

This is the context in which Goldhagen's study emerged, and it integrates several discernible historiographical approaches. First, the author has repudiated the presiding convention among historians of Germany of focused historical explanation, whether of historical structures or the contingency of unfolding events. He has returned to an older tradition of historiography that advances a long-term, synthetic interpretation of German history, which seeks to explain National Socialism as the culmination of deep-seated flaws in German national culture: specifically, for Goldhagen's purposes, its capacity to generate a cultural belief in what he calls "eliminationist" antisemitism. Second, he has shifted the focus away from the bureaucrats and technicians of genocide, whose agency was the primary target of historians concerned to lay bare the institutional structures and political processes responsible for Nazi policy and practice. Goldhagen focuses instead on the killers at the apparently unmediated moment of individual choice, as they faced and destroyed their victims: as Germans slaughtered Jews. Thus, like Browning before him, Goldhagen attempts to reconstruct and interpret the "everyday" experiences of a particular group of Germans under Nazism, though not of the German working class or women or the Jewish Germans who have been the more usual subjects of this kind of history writing from below. In other words, Goldhagen has soldered an analysis of Germany's alleged cultural peculiarity together with a highly charged evocation of the working life and mentality of mass murderers. Or, to express his project in the telegraphic jargon of the discipline, Goldhagen has produced an *Alltagsgeschichte* of the German *Son-*

---

13. Götz Aly, *Vordenker der Vernichtung: Auschwitz und die deutsche Pläne für eine neue europäische Ordnung* (Hamburg, 1991); Detlev Peukert, *Volksgenossen und Gemeinschaftsfremde: Anpassung, Ausmerz und Aufbegehren unter dem Nationalsozialismus* (Köln, 1982).

derweg: an account of the everyday life of an extraordinary national culture.

Goldhagen's focus on individual motivations and responsibility for acts of barbarous cruelty is the kernel of his account and the element that, as he has repeatedly claimed, distinguishes it from the bulk of previous scholarship. It is important to bear in mind that he has not, by his own account, written a work primarily of historical narrative or explanation: rather, he is a political sociologist interested in testing the explanatory power of a number of hypotheses about the motivation and behavior of participants in the mass killing of Jews.[14] Structurally, therefore, the book consists of a problem, a methodology, and an examination of pertinent evidence; and it is characteristic of the author's project that his text concludes not with the kind of extensive bibliography of archival and written sources that would normally be integral to a work of historical scholarship, but with two methodological appendixes. Methodologically, we are offered an analysis of behavior and motivation that, tendentious as it is about the relationship between ideology and behavior, rests on a concept of the sovereign individual capable of selecting the preferences that his actions then express. The sheer preference to kill assumes a large explanatory place in Goldhagen's argument. And since he pivots this argument on the claim that "there was no *objective* conflict whatsoever"[15] between Germans and Jews, the motivation and will for this had to be entirely manufactured and then sustained, so to speak, in the heads of the killers. Collective practice is then represented as the outcome of these aggregated individual choices in what might be described as a perfect moral market, where, as Goldhagen's rhetoric repeatedly conveys, the choice always lay between two starkly alternative behavioral or emotional preferences—to kill or to spare, to torture or to comfort, to hate and exult or to pity and weep.

My somewhat awkward excursus into the underlying strategy of the book is necessary, I think, to understanding its appeal. For Goldhagen's book offers U.S. readers a package consisting of several culturally familiar and attractive intellectual and emotional elements: (*a*) a synthetic national history that is crudely but seductively sketched; (*b*) a series of detailed short narratives, shocking in their intensity, that are built around specific

---

14. "The book's intent is primarily explanatory and theoretical. Narrative and description, important as they are for specifying the perpetrators' actions and the settings for their actions properly, are here subordinate to the explanatory goals." Daniel Jonah Goldhagen, *Hitler's Willing Executioners: Ordinary Germans and the Holocaust* (New York, 1996), appendix 1, 463.

15. Daniel Goldhagen, "Motives, Causes, and Alibis," *New Republic,* 23 December 1996, 45 (my emphasis).

individuals and understandable episodes; and (*c*) an apparatus of ostensibly sociological analysis that, as David Schoenbaum has suggested, endows the book with "a massive show of social-scientific authority."[16] The result is a kind of collective national psychobiography set in a simplified and readily assimilable historical and moral framework. It presents a devastatingly straightforward and compelling moral tale, in which, as many reviewers have pointed out, depravity confronts innocence in a space of pure containment, uncontaminated by messy historical complexities and ambiguities.

But it is here, in this superficially powerful evocation of moral truth, that one of the book's central weaknesses lies. For it seems to me that Goldhagen's book—whatever its declared objectives as a work of empirical research—works up the history it tells with the unmediated tools of metaphysics, so to speak. This may be capable of producing the metaphysical values that I think suffuse the book, but it does not render anything recognizable at the level of historical explanation. By a metaphysical approach, I mean that Goldhagen ultimately offers readers a representation of "Germans" and "Jews" as two absolutely distinct, essentially opposed, and ultimately abstract principles that have been locked in an eternal struggle whose outcome can only be total victory or total defeat— *Sieg oder Untergang.* To say this is not the same as complaining that his historical analysis of German antisemitism is deficient, though this has in fact been abundantly demonstrated by his critics. Nor is it a claim that he reinstates the canard of an innate German national character: as he has repeatedly pointed out, this was not his argument, even if in many critics' view he has come dangerously close to it. Yet it is surely because the opposition between German and Jew is grasped in an abstract, essentialized form that Goldhagen has such difficulty in constructing a convincing account of the real, textured history of relationships between Jewish and non-Jewish Germans. This is the source of his inability to grasp the fact that, as Aschheim so discerningly puts it, "the whole point about the German-Jewish experience, the source of its enduring fascination and unparalleled creativity, lies in its ambiguous nature, the tension between acceptance and rejection, [the fact that] German-Jewish life was always negotiated in a social field of essentially mixed signals."[17]

This truth may be hard to bear, but ignoring it is worse. In my reading of the book, Goldhagen's artless erection of a rigid and radically ahistorical distinction between German and Jew risks reproducing the antisemitic vision itself. At the very least, it gives the argumentary ground away

---

16. Schoenbaum, "Ordinary People?" 54.
17. Aschheim, "Reconceiving the Holocaust?" 63.

to the extreme antisemites and Nazis who cultivated precisely the same figure of an unbridgeable difference between Germans and Jews and purveyed their apocalyptic nightmare of its historical resolution. The imagery and conclusion offered by Goldhagen disclose a certain fortress mentality, which seems to carry more than a trace of learned bitterness against those Jews who felt that their safety lay in assimilation rather than cultural resistance: those who negotiated the cultural relationship described by Aschheim. Goldhagen's text could almost be read as a displaced polemic against Jewish Germans and their ultimately betrayed strategy of assimilation in the nineteenth century. One could even go on to draw the bitter lesson that eliminationist antisemitism came to an end after 1945 not because of a cultural revolution in the German people, but because the problem—the Jews—had in fact largely been eliminated. To the extent that this is its shocking implication, I find this an ultimately despairing book, the depiction of a catastrophe that comes to seem as inevitable as it was irrational. Although Goldhagen recuperates this comfortless conclusion with his assertion that postwar Germans are no longer uniquely and murderously antisemitic, I do not find this convincing. He wants readers to believe that, following centuries of cultural preparation for exterminationist antisemitism, postwar Germans' "cultural cognitive model" has been effectively reconstituted in a democratic, pluralist mold: they have become, finally, like "us." A mighty change indeed, and one that makes 1945, not 1933, carry the entire weight of historical significance in Germany's past. Yet Goldhagen makes it far from clear by what means or when this process is supposed to have occurred after 1945, and whether its course and results were identical in both East Germany and West Germany before 1989.

Goldhagen has compiled a morally satisfying account of German guilt and redemption, one that may be especially appealing to German readers. But his book also offers his U.S. readers a seductive counterimage of themselves; and this seems to me to constitute a large element in its appeal. It is notorious that Goldhagen recommends his readers to look at the German people before 1945 as an anthropologist would, on the grounds that the Germans were not a "normal society," that they were not like "us," not "rational, sober children of the Enlightenment."[18] The common sense of the Germans in this period of their history, their "cultural cognitive model," was, according to Goldhagen, completely different from "ours." Thus he can assert that "totally normal Germans" could exterminate the Jews, because in Germany to be totally normal *was* to be something quite different from what "we" understand as normal: it was, in Ger-

---

18. Goldhagen, *Hitler's Willing Executioners*, 28.

many, to be a murderous antisemite. This hypothetical construct recurs repeatedly in the book, without any evidence ever being offered for the legitimacy of the comparison.[19] Goldhagen also never positively identifies the "we" against whom the Germans are measured, but it is nevertheless not hard to fill this pronoun with a referent. The pronoun acts as an invitation to his American readers to identify themselves as the heirs of Enlightenment values and to distinguish themselves from the Germans about whom he writes, from their alien values and "radically different"[20] culture. Simultaneously, his book invites readers to identify themselves with the Jews—a double, mutually conditioning move on his part. The book's readers can thus know that they stand on the morally sound side of the partitioned world of guilt and innocence that it presents; they can assure themselves that the United States is not Germany, that Jews can feel secure in the United States, and that the Germans of today are not the Germans of the Holocaust era.[21]

This is a variant on an old, familiar theme: "They," the Germans, are not (or rather until 1945 were not) true children of the Enlightenment, they did not imbibe the Enlightenment values of reason and tolerance that "we" in the West did.[22] Here we have a *reductio ad absurdum* of the *Sonderweg* idea—not to mention a concept of the Enlightenment that is deployed as if Adorno and Horkheimer had never written a word about its ambiguities and repressions, or as if the most recent thirty years of intellectual engagement with these questions had never taken place. Perhaps Goldhagen has deliberately, if silently, elected to resist these critical tendencies by hitching his flag to a conventional but intellectually superficial perspective on Enlightenment rationality. More than this, though, the book's popular reception rests in my view on its character as a massive mechanism of identification, which in the recent cultural climate in the United States has been very difficult to resist. This works both on the individual scale and on the larger scale of U.S. politics.

On the political scale, the loss of familiar collective political identities following the end of the Cold War makes a certain kind of national or group identification even more seductive than it usually is. I think this means that we not only have to understand this book as a contribution to debates about German history and the genocide of the European Jews, but must also put it in the company of earlier publications, such as those by Paul Kennedy or Francis Fukuyama, that addressed broader questions

---

19. Ibid., 15, 27f., 45, for example.
20. Ibid., 15.
21. Ibid., 37.
22. There is even the implication, as Birn has suggested, that the Germans, or at least their actions, lie beyond the realm of the human altogether. "Revising the Holocaust," 213.

about America's status in the history of the world and its role in current international politics.[23]

On the small scale, there is the current cultural power in the United States of what might be termed knowledge-by-identification, in which true knowledge is supposed to be authenticated by its closeness to the subjective experience of the knower. This is a kind of vulgar *Verstehen,* a distorted and reductive form of historicism, with its claim of empathetic knowledge. In "identity politics" the claim works to privilege the stance of the insider, potentially to the exclusion of those who are deemed to be outsiders to the group under discussion. For anyone who does not wish to be pushed into the outer circle of the unknowing, it can be tempting to claim the group identity, whatever it may be, from which a particular authentic knowledge is supposed to flow. As the Israeli historian Gulie Arad has pointed out, this is one of the sources of the proliferation of victim statuses in U.S. popular discourse, which has made itself widely felt in both the cultural and political spheres.[24] In this context, it's worth recalling how the Washington Holocaust Museum makes powerful use of this identification mechanism. At the museum entrance, each visitor is offered a pass bearing the name and photograph of a real Jewish man, woman, or child caught up in the genocidal maelstrom. For the duration of the visit, you are invited to "be" this person; only at the end are you asked to discover your fate—whether you survived, whether you perished.

Goldhagen's repeated "thick" descriptions of the subjective experience of killing are calculated to induce both negative and positive identifications on the part of the reader: a repudiation of the motives and choices that underlay the horrifying acts of the killers, and an empathetic identification with the suffering of their victims. At issue here is not simply the questionable deployment of detailed descriptions of barbaric cruelty, which some critics have deprecated as excessive and poorly judged; nor the legitimacy of Goldhagen's decision to redescribe, in his own language, experiences to which we have more direct and honest access through the testimony of survivors; nor his even more questionable tactic of repeated speculations about the emotional state of the German killers during and

---

23. Paul Kennedy, *The Rise and Fall of the Great Powers: Economic Change and Military Conflict from 1500 to 2000* (New York, 1987), and *Preparing for the Twenty-first Century* (London, 1993); Francis Fukuyama, *The End of History and the Last Man* (New York, 1992).

24. Gulie Ne'eman Arad, "Ein amerikanischer Alptraum," in Julius H. Schoeps, ed., *Ein Volk von Mördern? Die Dokumentation zur Goldhagen-Kontroverse um die Rolle der Deutschen im Holocaust* (Hamburg, 1996), 176–86. For some similar criticisms, see also Norman Finkelstein, "Daniel Jonah Goldhagen's 'Crazy' Thesis: A Critique of *Hitler's Willing Executioners,*" *New Left Review* 224 (July/August 1997): 39–87 (reprinted in Finkelstein and Birn, *A Nation on Trial*).

after the slaughters.[25] It is rather that these moves constitute the text's core strategy, the logic of how it positions its readers.

This essay has tried to suggest, in broad outline, some of the ways in which *Hitler's Willing Executioners* resonates with contemporary American sensibilities. I have not attempted to develop a sustained critique of the book, although I have ventured some criticisms where these are pertinent to exploring the mechanisms of the book's appeal. As a final point, one may cite the unease provoked among many good-willed Americans by the scandal of Holocaust denial, which makes it hard to voice criticism of texts that, like this one, concentrate so fiercely on the empirical detail of genocidal antisemitism. The words of one reviewer captured this sense of embarrassment with fatal accuracy: "There will be those who deny Goldhagen's conclusions, even as there are those who claim to doubt the existence of the Holocaust."[26] While historians should by all means protect the historical record against shameless attempts at falsification, we ought also to ponder the character of a cultural-political climate that can produce such a deeply tendentious equation in its defense.

---

25. For these criticisms, see, e.g., Hans Mommsen, "Die dünne Patina der Zivilisation," *ZEIT Dokument* 1 (1996): 40–46; and Birn, "Revising the Holocaust," 210–12.

26. Disch, "A Nation and People Accursed," 50. For the problem of Holocaust denial in the United States, see Deborah Lipstadt, *Denying the Holocaust: The Growing Assault on Truth and Memory* (New York, 1993).

Contributors

Omer Bartov is John P. Birkelund Distinguished Professor of European History at Brown University. He has written widely on modern German, French, and Jewish history. His books include *The Eastern Front, 1941–45* (1985), *Hitler's Army: Soldiers, Nazis, and War in the Third Reich* (1991), *Murder in Our Midst: The Holocaust, Industrial Killing, and Representation* (1996), *Mirrors of Destruction: War, Genocide, and Modern Identity* (2000), and the edited volume *The Holocaust: Origins, Implementation, Aftermath* (1999).

Jane Caplan is Marjorie Walter Goodhart Professor of European History at Bryn Mawr College, Pennsylvania. Among her publications is *Government without Administration: State and Civil Service in Weimar and Nazi Germany* (1988), and she has edited *Nazism, Fascism, and the Working Class: Essays by Tim Mason* (1995) and *Reevaluating the Third Reich* (1993). She is currently researching the history of individual identity documentation in nineteenth-century Europe, and has coedited a volume of essays, *Documenting Individual Identity: The Development of State Practices since the French Revolution* (forthcoming, 2000).

Geoff Eley is Professor of History and German Studies at the University of Michigan. He is the author of *Reshaping the German Right* (1980), *From Unification to Nazism* (1986), and (with David Blackbourn) *The Peculiarities of German History* (1984). He is the editor of *Society, Culture, and the State in Germany, 1870–1930* (1996) and coeditor of *Culture/Power/History: A Reader in Contemporary Social Theory* (1994) and *Becoming National: A Reader* (1996). His general history of the European Left since the mid-nineteenth century, *Remembering the Future*, will be published in 2001.

Atina Grossmann is Associate Professor of History in the Faculty of Humanities, Cooper Union for Advancement of Science and Art in New York. Her publications include *Reforming Sex: The German Movement for Birth Control and Abortion Reform, 1920–1959* (1995, 1997), *When Biology Became Destiny: Women in Weimar and Nazi Germany* (coeditor, 1984), and numerous articles on gender, population policy, and modernity in interwar Germany, as well as on Germans and Jews in postwar Germany. She is currently working on the study "Victims, Victors, and Survivors: Germans, Allies, and Jews in Occupied Postwar Germany, 1945–1949."

Pieter Judson is Associate Professor of History at Swarthmore College and a senior fellow at the Internationales Forschungszentrum Kulturwissenschaften in Vienna. His 1996 book *Exclusive Revolutionaries: Liberal Politics, Social Experience, and National Identity in the Austrian Empire, 1848–1914* won the Herbert Baxter Adams prize of the American Historical Association and the Austrian Cultural Institute's prize for best book in Austrian Studies. He is the author of *Wien Brennt: Die Revolution von 1848 und ihr liberales Erbe* (1998) and coeditor of the forthcoming *Creating the Other: Origins and Dynamics of Nationalism, Ethnic Enmity, and Racism in Central and Eastern Europe.* He is currently working on a study of tourism and nationalism in the Habsburg Empire.

Index